ADAM, CHRIST AND COVENANT

Covenant theology has played a very important role in the history of Reformed theology and has also often been a source of controversy in that history, especially today. Andrew McGowan's book guides the reader with lucid brevity through the maze of controversy, especially of the past hundred years, setting out fairly and clearly what the issues are and where the differences lie. He then lays out his own proposal, offering a biblical way forward. Finally, he spells out the implications of this in terms of two key contemporary flashpoints of controversy: the role of the law and union with Christ. This book is required reading both for those who wish to know more about controversies concerning covenant theology and for those who already have a view on the subject.
Tony Lane, Professor of Historical Theology, London School of Theology

Covenant theology is a distinctive emphasis of Reformed theology. It has also been something of an Achilles heel, contentious within the Reformed family and puzzling to those on the outside. *Adam, Christ and Covenant*, therefore, will be an indispensable guide for those exploring the developments and debates of covenant theology.

Andrew McGowan offers a masterful survey of the history of covenant theology, especially in the last century, and probes some of the problems with this approach. He then marks out his own position in that history, provocatively suggesting that covenant theology should use the idea of 'covenant' less. His suggestion is that the broader structure of history should be understood in terms of the headship of Adam and Christ rather than covenants. This would preserve the term 'covenant' for the explicit promissory covenants of Scripture and remove a possible obstacle to the wider acceptance of covenant theology.

McGowan shows how significant the covenants are in Scripture and that, at its best, covenant theology has recognized that all human history is arranged around Adam and Christ. Like older covenant theology, his proposal is wonderfully integrative, keeping law in the context of grace and keeping imputation closely related to union with Christ. Anyone who is serious about progressing covenant theology will need to consider this proposal.
John McClean, Vice-Principal and Lecturer in Systematic Theology, Christ College, New South Wales, Australia

The fruit of a lifetime of study, this comprehensive account is an excellent introduction to the history of Federal Vision and to current discussions. Even those of us in other evangelical traditions need to know about this robust and influential theology.
Thomas A. Noble, Research Professor of Theology, Nazarene Theological Seminary, Kansas City; Senior Research Fellow, Nazarene Theological College, Manchester

ADAM, CHRIST AND COVENANT

EXPLORING HEADSHIP THEOLOGY

A. T. B. McGowan

APOLLOS (an imprint of Inter-Varsity Press)
36 Causton Street, London SW1P 4ST, England
Email: ivp@ivpbooks.com
Website: www.ivpbooks.com

© A. T. B. McGowan, 2016

A. T. B. McGowan has asserted his right under the Copyright, Designs and Patents Act, 1988, to be identified as Author of this work.

All rights reserved. No part of this publication may be reproduced, stored in a retrieval system, or transmitted, in any form or by any means, electronic, mechanical, photocopying, recording or otherwise, without the prior permission of the publisher or the Copyright Licensing Agency.

Scripture quotations taken from the HOLY BIBLE, NEW INTERNATIONAL VERSION. Copyright © 1973, 1978, 1984 by International Bible Society. Used by permission of Hodder & Stoughton Publishers, a member of the Hachette UK Group. All rights reserved. 'NIV' is a registered trademark of International Bible Society. UK trademark number 1448790.

Scripture quotations marked ESV are from The Holy Bible, English Standard Version, copyright © 2001 by Crossway Bibles, a division of Good News Publishers. Used by permission. All rights reserved.

First published 2016

British Library Cataloguing-in-Publication Data
A catalogue record for this book is available from the British Library.

ISBN: 978–1–78359–431–3
eBook ISBN: 978–1–78359–489–4

Set in Monotype Garamond 11/13pt
Typeset in Great Britain by CRB Associates, Potterhanworth, Lincolnshire

Inter-Varsity Press publishes Christian books that are true to the Bible and that communicate the gospel, develop discipleship and strengthen the church for its mission in the world.

IVP originated within the Inter-Varsity Fellowship, now the Universities and Colleges Christian Fellowship, a student movement connecting Christian Unions in universities and colleges throughout Great Britain, and a member movement of the International Fellowship of Evangelical Students. Website: www.uccf.org.uk. That historic association is maintained, and all senior IVP staff and committee members subscribe to the UCCF Basis of Faith.

*To William and Jean Watson,
my wife's parents.*

*Over the forty years that June and I have been married,
they have been a constant source of support,
encouragement and practical help.
We are deeply grateful to them.*

CONTENTS

Acknowledgments — xii
Abbreviations — xv

Introduction — 1

PART 1: THE CONTEXT

1. **Covenant theology** — 9
   Introduction — 9
   Exposition — 10
   History — 12
   Scottish covenant theology — 15
   Thomas Boston — 16
   Law and grace — 19
   Conclusion — 21

2. **Karl Barth** — 22
   Introduction — 22
   Barth's use of the covenant concept — 23
   Barth on covenant theology — 30
   Response to Barth on covenant theology — 35
   The Torrance brothers on covenant theology — 40
   Conclusions — 45

3. John Murray   46
Introduction   46
John Murray   46
Murray and the covenants   47
The Adamic administration   56
Conclusion   60

4. Meredith Kline   62
Introduction   62
Meredith Kline   62
The covenants   66
Law and grace   69
Republication   70
Michael Horton   72
Theology of merit   76
Conclusion   78

5. The Federal Vision   79
Introduction   79
Federal Vision: the key themes   80
Different strands   95
Guy P. Waters   100
Critique of the Federal Vision   104
Conclusion   107

PART 2: THE PROPOSAL

6. Headship theology: Adam and Christ   111
Introduction   111
The exegetical evidence   112
Theological interpretation   122
Headship theology   126
Conclusion   128

7. Headship theology: the covenants of promise   129
Introduction   129
The covenant with Noah   130
The covenant with Abraham   133
The covenant with Moses   138
The Abrahamic and Mosaic covenants compared   143
The covenant with David   146

The new covenant with Christ	151
The blood of the covenant	156
Conclusion	160

PART 3: THE IMPLICATIONS

8. The law of God — 165
Introduction — 165
Paul and the law — 166
Adam and the law — 175
Grace and law — 179
Conclusion — 182

9. Union with Christ — 183
Introduction — 183
The *ordo salutis* — 184
Justification in the *ordo salutis* — 189
Union with Christ — 193
Summary and conclusions — 199

Conclusion — 201

Bibliography — 205
Index of authors — 215
Index of Scripture references — 219

ACKNOWLEDGMENTS

This book has been a long time in the making! Covenant theology (sometimes called 'federal theology' from *foedus*, the Latin word for covenant) is a subject to which I have devoted considerable study over many years and has, in fact, been my main academic research interest. My STM dissertation at Union Theological Seminary in New York was entitled 'Were the New England Puritans Federal Calvinists?' My PhD thesis at the University of Aberdeen was entitled 'The Federal Theology of Thomas Boston'. I have also contributed a number of chapters on this subject to various books, as well as writing articles for various historical and theological dictionaries. In addition, I have taught courses or given lectures on covenant theology in Scotland, England, Australia, Indonesia and the USA.

Some of the themes in this book were first tested in papers delivered at conferences, not least at a conference on 'covenant' at Greenville Theological Seminary; at a meeting of the Tyndale Fellowship; and at the Rutherford House Edinburgh Dogmatics Conference. I am grateful for all the invitations to lecture on the subject, give papers at conferences and contribute to various books. Some of these earlier lectures and papers were published. I am grateful for permission to use sections from, or versions of, the following:

- A. T. B. McGowan, 'In Defence of Headship Theology', in Jamie A. Grant and Alistair I. Wilson (eds.), *The God of the Covenant: Biblical, Theological and Contemporary Perspectives* (Leicester: Apollos, 2005), pp. 178–199;

- A. T. B. McGowan, 'The Unity of the Covenant' and 'Scottish Covenant Theology', in J. A. Pipa and C. N. Willborn (eds.), *The Covenant: God's Voluntary Condescension* (Taylors, SC: Presbyterian Press, 2005), pp. 1–13; 61–72;
- A. T. B. McGowan, 'Justification and the *Ordo Salutis*', in Bruce L. McCormack (ed.), *Justification in Perspective: Historical Developments and Contemporary Challenges* (Grand Rapids, MI: Baker, 2006), pp. 147–163;
- A. T. B. McGowan, 'Karl Barth and Covenant Theology', in D. Gibson and D. Strange (eds.), *Engaging with Barth: Contemporary Evangelical Critiques* (Nottingham: Apollos, 2008), pp. 113–135.

I acknowledge with gratitude the help and support of the following in writing this book:

The Church of Scotland, for granting me generous support through its Study Leave Scheme for Ministers, allowing me to spend nine weeks in Cambridge working on this book, in order to bring many years of research and writing together into this volume.

Tyndale House in Cambridge, for providing me with a congenial place to study and a first-class library. The engagement with other scholars was immensely helpful, both academically and spiritually. A long discussion with Brad Green was particularly useful.

My colleagues at Highland Theological College UHI and the students who have attended my Covenant Theology lectures over the years, for helping to clarify and develop my thinking.

My secretary, Mrs Dolina Coventry, for typing up some of my work, even while I was in Cambridge. The technically minded may be interested to know that I read my notes and even sections of the manuscript into an Olympus Digital Voice Recorder and then uploaded the recordings to a shared Dropbox file which my secretary could access. A day or two later, these recordings were emailed back to me as MS Word files! This seems miraculous to a man who typed most of his PhD with two fingers on a manual, portable typewriter! She also helped me to compile the bibliography and indices.

Friends who have read and commented on individual chapters (John Muether) and those who have read and commented on the whole book (John McClean, Malcolm Maclean and Gordon Kennedy). I am deeply grateful to all of them.

My editor at IVP, Philip Duce, for patience and understanding.

Above all, my wife and best friend, June, who has not only supported and encouraged me through forty years of marriage but came with me to Cambridge for the final push towards publication. We had nine very happy weeks together there. I kept my promise to work 9 a.m. – 5 p.m., Monday to Friday, in Tyndale House, so that we could have evenings and weekends together. Spending this time together, without preaching or meetings or any other commitments, was wonderful. We have never had so much time together – and we are still together!

ABBREVIATIONS

ANE	Ancient Near East(ern)
CD	Karl Barth, *Church Dogmatics*, ed. G. W. Bromiley and T. F. Torrance (Edinburgh: T & T Clark, 1956)
EQ	*Evangelical Quarterly*
FV	Federal Vision
LXX	Septuagint
JETS	*Journal of the Evangelical Theological Society*
NPP	New Perspective on Paul
SJT	*Scottish Journal of Theology*
WCF	Westminster Confession of Faith
WTJ	*Westminster Theological Journal*

INTRODUCTION

With the adoption of the Westminster Confession of Faith by the Church of Scotland in 1647, the 'covenant theology' which is at the heart of that confessional statement became the standard theological position held by Reformed theologians, not only in Scotland but throughout the world. Covenant theology had been slowly developing in Europe since the Reformation but this was the most significant codification of the system.

Covenant theology as enshrined in the Westminster Confession of Faith (WCF) teaches that the whole Bible revolves around a 'covenant of works' made with humanity in Adam and a 'covenant of grace' made with the elect in Christ. Many covenant theologians argued that the covenant of grace was founded upon an earlier 'covenant of redemption', by which God the Father and God the Son 'covenanted together' to provide a way of salvation for those whom God had chosen from eternity. Covenant theology brought together two important scriptural themes: first, the teaching in 1 Corinthians 15 and Romans 5 that all human beings are either 'in Adam' or 'in Christ'; and second, the teaching that God's relationship with his chosen people is covenantal in nature.

In the twentieth century, however, covenant theology faced two problems. First, the theological basis of covenant theology was challenged by scholars such as Karl Barth, T. F. Torrance and J. B. Torrance, who argued that it represented a legalistic departure from an earlier pristine theology of grace to be found in the work of John Calvin and John Knox. Second, among those who were committed to covenant theology there emerged significant disagreement as to its nature and structure, not least between John Murray and

Meredith Kline. Murray's position has been taken forward by theologians such as O. Palmer Robertson, while Kline's position has been clarified, developed and taken forward by theologians such as Michael Horton. To add to the mix, others within the Presbyterian tradition have developed a revised version of covenant theology, which has been called the 'Federal Vision'.

The purpose of this book is to review these various challenges and disagreements and to suggest that the strengths of covenant theology can best be retained by separating the two key ideas: first, union with Adam/Christ; and second, God's covenantal dealings with his people. It will be argued that the 'in Adam/in Christ' teaching does not require a covenantal underpinning and would be better called 'headship theology' than 'covenant theology'. It will also be argued that separating these two themes enables us to liberate the word 'covenant' from the strictures of covenant theology, enabling us to see more clearly the relationship between the various covenants mentioned in Scripture and also their historical development. In offering this proposal, we believe that we are following in the footsteps of John Murray, arguing that his partial reconstruction of covenant theology set the trajectory for the present work.

Covenant theology is not a monolithic scheme of thinking which, having appeared in the Reformation and post-Reformation periods, has since remained unchanged. Indeed, it has taken different forms over the centuries and there have been many internal disagreements, as we shall see. Having said that, the fundamental objectives of covenant theology, not least in terms of union with Adam and union with Christ, are clearly taught in Scripture and are vital for a proper understanding of Christianity. We believe that our somewhat revisionist proposal arises naturally out of a study of Scripture and is able to draw together, in a coherent and systematic way, the main themes of Scripture.

One key problem we have identified in some forms of covenant theology is the use made of the law–grace dichotomy. We shall demonstrate this by focusing on two significant Scottish theologians who each taught a covenant theology which can be characterized as a theology of grace, namely, Thomas Boston and John Murray. In doing so, we shall highlight the fact that Thomas Boston, in the eighteenth century, faced opposition from other covenant theologians who put law before grace and became legalistic in their thinking. We shall then demonstrate that a further debate over the place given to law and grace caused a rift within twentieth-century theology, centred on Westminster Theological Seminary. It will be our contention that John Murray's reconstruction of the notion of a covenant of works into what he called the 'Adamic administration' went part of the way towards dealing with an incipient problem within covenant theology but that a further step has to be taken, namely, turning aside from emphasis on the covenants and refocusing attention upon Adam and Christ as the two 'heads' of administration. This then leaves us free to see the covenants of promise as a gracious outworking of God's relationship to his people, rather than as a counterpoint to a covenant of works.

Part 1 of the book consists of the first five chapters. We shall begin in chapter 1 with a summary of the core structure and the main themes of covenant theology, together with its history and development. In chapter 2 we shall consider a serious challenge to covenant theology which has arisen from the wider Reformed tradition. This is an 'external challenge', in that it comes from outside the school of covenant theology. This will involve an analysis of Karl Barth's view of covenant and also the more direct challenges posed to covenant theologians by T. F. Torrance and J. B. Torrance, both of whom shared Barth's fundamental theological commitments. In chapters 3 and 4 we shall turn to an internal disagreement within the school of covenant theology, namely, the differing positions taken by John Murray and Meredith Kline and those who followed them. As we shall see, this is where the issue of the priority of law or grace comes to the fore and is at the root of the disagreement. In chapter 5 we shall provide an analysis and critique of the modern version of covenant theology, called the Federal Vision.

Part 2 consists of the central proposal of the book and is contained in two chapters. In chapter 6 we shall offer a revised way of properly understanding the relationship between Adam and Christ. In chapter 7 we shall show the significance of our proposal for an understanding of the biblical covenants and their internal relationship, not least in their development, culminating in the new covenant.

Part 3 of the book is concerned with the implications of the proposal and comprises the two final chapters. In chapter 8 we shall demonstrate that the view taken on the relationship between the Abrahamic and Mosaic covenants has implications for our understanding of God's law. More specifically, it will enable us to answer questions about Paul's view of the law and his critique of the Jews. In chapter 9 we shall apply the 'headship theology' proposal to some key issues, by showing its implications for a proper understanding of union with Christ, justification and imputation.

So much for the content of the book. Let me now turn to speak of three convictions which underlie the writing of the book: two concerning the nature of Reformed theology and one concerning the method of dialogue within the Reformed community.

The first conviction is that Reformed theology is a 'school' of thought and not a single 'strand' of thought. From the earliest days of Reformed theology there was engagement with and interaction between various strands of thought, all of which together constituted the 'school' of Reformed theology. As I have written elsewhere:

> In the earliest days of the Reformation, scholars throughout Europe were developing Reformed ideas. For example, Martin Bucer in Strasburg, Ulrich Zwingli and Heinrich Bullinger in Zurich, John Calvin and Theodore Beza in Geneva, Caspar Olevianus and Zacharias Ursinus in Heidelberg. This is to say nothing of Peter Martyr Vermigli who was everywhere! Add to this the theologians in Holland, England and Scotland and you have a fascinating 'school' of thought.[1]

These different 'strands' of Reformed theology produced their own confessions and catechisms. These documents present a range of subjects, expressed with significant variety in form and content, while at the same time agreeing on certain key themes.

It is vital that we do not lose this conviction that Reformed theology is a 'school' of theology. Unfortunately, in recent years there have been attempts to narrow the 'school' to a single 'strand' as theologians argue that only their position is 'truly Reformed'. Such an attitude betrays both arrogance and ignorance. It betrays arrogance because it implies that one Reformed theologian (or group of theologians) has the right to tell other Reformed theologians, often from different traditions and even from different countries, that only their approach is acceptable. It betrays ignorance because it demonstrates a lack of knowledge and understanding of the history and development of Reformed theology, with its variety, richness and diversity.

The second conviction is that we must be 'always reforming'.[2] This is a conviction which Reformed theologians often affirm but, in practice, often neglect! One sometimes gets the impression that, for some churches and theologians, theology stopped when the WCF was completed. Any attempt to modify or critique the theology of the Confession is met with firm rebuttal and important doctrinal decisions are made by identifying what the Confession says rather than by asking the question, 'What do the Scriptures say?' Although it would be hotly denied, this approach implies that the Confession is not subject to review or revision and gives the impression that the Westminster Divines made no

---

1. A. T. B. McGowan, 'Crafting an Evangelical, Reformed and Missional Theology for the Twenty-First Century', in S. T. Logan (ed.), *Reformed Means Missional: Following Jesus into the World* (Greensboro, NC: New Growth Press, 2013), p. 242.
2. The importance of this principle is spelled out in A. T. B. McGowan (ed.), *Always Reforming: Explorations in Systematic Theology* (Leicester: Apollos, 2006), pp. 13–18.

mistakes. This resort to what is effectively 'tradition' rather than 'Scripture' would be worrying in any context but is deeply troubling when it takes place within the Reformed churches, whose very existence is based on the priority of Scripture.

This conviction that we must be 'always reforming' has implications for covenant theology. Like other aspects of Reformed theology, covenant theology is not an immutable and static system. It has developed over the years and is still developing, not least because covenant theologians have not always agreed among themselves and because some have devised new formulations to deal with what they perceive to be errors in the writings of others. As we shall see later, John Murray argued, with specific reference to covenant theology, that 'Theology must always be undergoing reformation'.[3]

The third conviction is that we must be respectful in our dealings with other theologians, especially those with whom we disagree. Their arguments must be treated carefully and seriously, even when we may ultimately differ from what is being said. It is a sad reflection on modern Reformed theology that so many of our internal debates are carried out in a hostile and vitriolic manner, rejecting out of hand those who take a different position and making casual (and shocking) use of words like 'heretic' to refer to them. When challenged, those who treat others in this way will often say that they are 'defending the truth', a statement which has so often been used to justify a lack of love towards Christian brothers and sisters. Defending the truth is important but it does not give licence to ignore everything else that Scripture teaches regarding our attitude to others. In our theological dialogue, as in our daily Christian lives, we must remember the words of 1 Peter 3:15–16. Having told his readers to set apart Christ as Lord in their hearts, Peter then says, 'Always be prepared to give an answer to everyone who asks you to give the reason for the hope that you have. But do this with gentleness and respect, keeping a clear conscience, so that those who speak maliciously against your good behaviour in Christ may be ashamed of their slander.'

---

3. J. Murray, *The Covenant of Grace* (London: Tyndale Press, 1954), p. 5.

PART 1:

THE CONTEXT

In this first section of the book we shall provide an outline of covenant theology, as developed in the sixteenth and seventeenth centuries and as 'codified' in the Westminster Confession of Faith, noting that this was once the dominant theological perspective of Christian theologians in the Reformed tradition.

Then we shall consider the main opposition to covenant theology from within the Reformed tradition itself, namely, from Karl Barth and from two of those who followed in his trajectory, T. F. Torrance and J. B. Torrance.

Next, we shall consider the internal debates which have taken place among proponents of Reformed theology who are committed to covenant theology but have offered varying and in some cases revisionist accounts of the system: first, John Murray, then Meredith Kline and finally the school of federal theology.

In this way, we shall provide the general context of current studies in covenant theology, preparing the way for our own proposal in part 2 of the book.

1. COVENANT THEOLOGY

Introduction

The purpose of this chapter is to describe covenant theology and to offer a brief sketch of its historical development. We shall focus particularly on Scottish covenant theology so as to prepare for our later examination of the theology of John Murray, whose significant critique of covenant theology (while holding to its core elements) provides the launching pad for our own proposed challenge to the system.

Covenant theology can be defined as that system of theology in which the relationship between God and humanity is described in covenantal terms. In particular, the focus is on Adam and Christ as the heads of two covenants between God and human beings. In its full-blown form, as we shall see, this involved a complex arrangement of covenants and headship. Covenant theology developed in the post-Reformation period but many theologians in earlier periods had made significant use of the covenant theme, which is so prevalent in Scripture.[1] Others had offered interpretations of Paul's comparison between being in Adam and being in Christ.[2]

---

1. See J. L. Duncan, 'The Covenant Idea in Ante-Nicene Theology', PhD thesis, University of Edinburgh, 1995.
2. See chapter 6 below, with reference to Augustine and Irenaeus.

Exposition

The classic exposition of covenant theology teaches that God entered into a 'covenant of works' with Adam in Genesis 2:16–17, whereby Adam was prohibited from eating from the tree of the knowledge of good and evil. He was told that if he did eat from this tree, he would die, with the corresponding implication that, if he refrained from doing so, he would live. Most covenant theologians asserted that, if Adam had succeeded in obeying God during this period of 'probation' and had not eaten from the forbidden tree, he would have been granted eternal life. This would have involved the permanent conferral of the blessings he already enjoyed in his state of innocence and much more besides.

One vital aspect of covenant theology is that, when God entered into the covenant of works with Adam, he did not do so with Adam as a private individual but as representative of the human race. Thus when Adam disobeyed God and broke the commandment not to eat from the forbidden tree, the judgment which followed fell not only upon Adam but upon all those whom he represented, namely, all humanity (who had not yet been born). This explains why every human being is already corrupted by sin from conception, often called 'original sin'. Correspondingly, if Adam had obeyed God, then the permanent conferral of blessing would also have come to the entire human race.

Despite Adam's disobedience, God did not abandon the human race, each member of which he had created in his own image. Indeed, at the very point of Adam's fall, God made a promise, recorded in Genesis 3:15, that someone would come to destroy Satan, the instigator of Adam's sin. This *protoevangelion* (first promise of the gospel) indicated that God intended to act decisively to overcome the failure of Adam. This action began in Genesis 12 with the call of Abraham, with whom God made a covenant, described in Genesis 15 and 17. Covenant theologians generally view this as the first expression of a 'covenant of grace' which God made with his elect people, with Christ as the 'head' of the covenant. The family of Abraham became, during a period in Egypt, the Hebrew tribes and then ultimately emerged from Egypt as a nation under God. The covenant between God and his chosen people was renewed at Sinai through Moses and the promises made to Abraham were fulfilled as Israel became a nation and was given the 'Promised Land' of Canaan.

The covenant of grace, first intimated to Abraham, involved looking forward to the day when the *protoevangelion* would be fulfilled and Messiah would come. Jeremiah indicated that God would then establish a 'new covenant' in which all the blessings of salvation would come to God's chosen people. Until then, the sacrificial system and a high priest were in place. These sacrifices 'covered' the sins of the people until the day when they could be dealt with permanently. These temple sacrifices themselves could never deal permanently with sin but were types and signs, waiting to be fulfilled when Christ (Messiah) came as the great high priest and, with one sacrifice on the cross at Calvary, paid the penalty for the sins of all God's chosen people in all generations, bringing an end to the law in terms of its sacrificial system. Christ is head of this new covenant, in which the covenant of grace reaches its fulfilment, and all who call upon the name of the Lord will be saved. Christ is able to be the head of the covenant of grace because, although a man, he was born of a virgin and therefore not included under the representative headship of Adam in the covenant of works and hence not tainted with original sin. Also, since he was 'conceived by the Holy Spirit', the Holy Spirit protected him from any effect of Mary's sin.

Covenant theologians developed this concept of Adam and Christ as representative heads of two covenants from 1 Corinthians 15:21–22, 44b–49 and Romans 5:12–21.[3] These verses tell us that we are either 'in Adam' or 'in Christ'. If we are 'in Adam' we shall die and if we are 'in Christ' we shall be made alive. The parallel in these verses between Adam and Christ, in which Paul describes Christ as the 'second man' and the 'last Adam', is used to argue that, just as Adam was the representative head of the covenant of works, so Christ is the representative head of the covenant of grace. Christ takes the place of Adam and fulfils the covenant of works, succeeding where Adam failed and obeying where Adam disobeyed, thus bringing salvation to all those whom he represented, namely, God's elect. Most covenant theologians have also argued that underlying this covenant of grace was a covenant of redemption between God the Father and God the Son, in which the Father promised to forgive sins if the Son would come as representative and substitute, to make atonement for sinners. Christ freely and willingly accepted the terms of the covenant and the incarnation took place.

The whole covenant scheme is set in the context of the post-Reformation Calvinistic theology. Thus it is argued that God, from all eternity, elected a people for himself. Christ died to pay the penalty for the sins of God's elect people, bearing the wrath of God in their place, having qualified himself for this position by his incarnation and by his active obedience. The Holy Spirit then applies the work of Christ to the elect by effectual calling, regeneration,

---

3. Quoted in the chronological order in which they were written, rather than the order in which they are found in the New Testament. We shall explore the exegesis of these passages in chapter 6 below.

justification, sanctification and the other aspects of salvation which are summed up in the doctrines that make up the *ordo salutis*. The sacraments are viewed as signs and seals of the covenant of grace. Thus covenant theology seeks to be an all-embracing system of thought, based on Scripture and encompassing the whole scope of biblical teaching.

History

The scholarly debate concerning the historical development of covenant theology has largely taken place during the past forty years. In the course of this debate, several volumes have sought, inter alia, to chart the history of covenant theology.[4] Although these volumes represent different theological perspectives, both for and against covenant theology, there is now growing agreement on the main line of development.

All Christian theologians must find a place for 'covenant' in their systems since it is such a recurring, even dominant, concept in the Scriptures. It was, however, in the Calvinist strand of Reformation theology that the concept came to be the central means of expressing the relationship between God and humanity. There is, however, disagreement among scholars as to Calvin's own position. Some have argued that there is a radical discontinuity between Calvin and the later covenant theology,[5] whereas others argue that Calvin was one of

---

4. R. T. Kendall, *Calvin and English Calvinism to 1649* (Oxford: OUP, 1979); this was later republished with an additional preface and two appendices, although the body of the text and, indeed, the pagination remained unchanged (Carlisle: Paternoster, 1997); D. A. Weir, *The Origins of the Federal Theology in Sixteenth-Century Reformation Thought* (Oxford: Clarendon, 1990); C. S. McCoy and J. W. Baker, *Fountainhead of Federalism: Heinrich Bullinger and the Covenantal Tradition* (Louisville, KY: Westminster John Knox Press, 1991); D. N. J. Poole, *Stages of Religious Faith in the Classical Reformation Tradition: The Covenant Approach to the Ordo Salutis* (Lampeter: Edwin Mellen Press, 1995).
5. B. Hall, 'Calvin against the Calvinists', in G. E. Duffield (ed.), *John Calvin* (Grand Rapids, MI: Eerdmans, 1966); H. Rolston III, 'Responsible Man in Reformed Theology: Calvin versus the Westminster Confession', *SJT* 23 (1970), pp. 129–156; H. Rolston III, *John Calvin versus the Westminster Confession* (Richmond, VA: John Knox Press, 1972); M. C. Bell, 'Calvin and the Extent of the Atonement', *EQ* 55 (1983), pp. 115–123; M. C. Bell, *Calvin and Scottish Theology: The Doctrine of Assurance* (Edinburgh: Handsel Press, 1985).

the originators of covenant theology.[6] Many who would hesitate to take this latter position would nonetheless argue that covenant theology is a natural and legitimate development from Calvin's own thought.[7] It is certainly clear that the covenant was very important in Calvin's theology.[8] The debate which took place between these three different interpretations, together with the work of those who do not fit neatly into any of these three categories,[9] has been called the 'Calvin versus Calvinism' debate. The recently published work by Andrew A. Woolsey, supporting earlier work by Richard Muller, makes a most persuasive case for the continuity argument.[10]

Covenant theology, as a two-covenant system, began with Zacharias Ursinus (1534–83), Caspar Olevianus (1536–87) and their colleagues in Heidelberg, between 1560 and 1590.[11] There is no unanimous agreement as to the precise origin of the expression '*foedus operum*' (covenant of works), although David Weir's argument that a prelapsarian covenant was first introduced into Reformed theology in 1562 by Ursinus and that Dudley Fenner, in 1585, first called it the *foedus operum* is very persuasive.[12] This is supported by David Poole:

> The centre of covenant thought in the years immediately following 1562 was Heidelberg, the key figures being Ursinus and Olevianus. After that city's return

---

6. P. A. Lillback, *The Binding of God: Calvin's Role in the Development of Covenant Theology* (Grand Rapids, MI: Baker, 2001). Weir does admit one possible reference by Calvin to a prelapsarian covenant: Weir, *Origins of the Federal Theology*, p. 10.
7. P. Helm, *Calvin and the Calvinists* (Edinburgh: Banner of Truth, 1982); P. Helm, 'Calvin and the Covenant: Unity and Discontinuity', *EQ* 55 (1983), pp. 65–81; R. A. Muller, *Christ and the Decree: Christology and Predestination in Reformed Theology from Calvin to Perkins* (Durham, NC: Labyrinth Press, 1986); R. A. Muller, 'Calvin and the "Calvinists": Assessing Continuities and Discontinuities between the Reformation and Orthodoxy', *Calvin Theological Journal* 30 (1995), pp. 345–375; 31 (1996), pp. 125–160; also a number of the essays in C. R. Trueman and R. S. Clark (eds.), *Protestant Scholasticism: Essays in Reassessment* (Carlisle: Paternoster, 1999).
8. See J. Calvin, *The Institutes of the Christian Religion*, tr. F. L.Battles, ed. J. T. McNeill, Library of Christian Classics, vols. 20 and 21 (Philadelphia, PA: Westminster Press, 1977), 2/10 and 2/11.
9. A. N. S. Lane, 'The Quest for the Historical Calvin', *EQ* 55 (1983), pp. 95–113.
10. A. A. Woolsey, *Unity and Continuity in Covenantal Thought* (Grand Rapids, MI: Reformation Heritage Books, 2012).
11. Weir, *Origins of the Federal Theology*, p. 115.
12. Weir, *Origins of the Federal Theology*, pp. 99–114, 133–152.

to Lutheranism in 1576, continental covenant theology came to pivot on Herborn. The seeds of the notion of a first covenant preceding that of grace, had already been sown on the Continent, but it was Dudley Fenner who first introduced the *foedus operum* in his *Sacra Theologia* (Geneva 1585).[13]

Covenant theology was popularized by William Perkins (1558–1602) and was significantly advanced by the later German theologian Johannes Cocceius (1603–69). Covenant theology quickly took root and grew after this point. By the end of the seventeenth century, covenant theology had become the dominant theological position within Reformed theology. In the course of this development, however, covenant theology was expressed in different ways, such that there was no one definitive covenant theology, although most of the key elements were agreed. When covenant theology received confessional status, however, first in a very preliminary form in the Irish Articles of 1615 and then more fully in the Westminster Confession of Faith of 1646 (and its Congregationalist and Baptist variants), this became the definitive version most adopted by Reformed theologians.

The WCF deals with covenant theology in chapter 7, 'On God's Covenant with Man', and, given its influence, is worth quoting in full:

> I. The distance between God and the creature is so great, that although reasonable creatures do owe obedience unto Him as their Creator, yet they could never have any fruition of Him as their blessedness and reward, but by some voluntary condescension on God's part, which He has been pleased to express by way of covenant.
>
> II. The first covenant made with man was a covenant of works, wherein life was promised to Adam; and in him to his posterity, upon condition of perfect and personal obedience.
>
> III. Man, by his fall, having made himself incapable of life by that covenant, the Lord was pleased to make a second, commonly called the covenant of grace; wherein He freely offers unto sinners life and salvation by Jesus Christ; requiring of them faith in Him, that they may be saved, and promising to give unto all those that are ordained unto eternal life His Holy Spirit, to make them willing, and able to believe.
>
> IV. This covenant of grace is frequently set forth in scripture by the name of a testament, in reference to the death of Jesus Christ the Testator, and to the everlasting inheritance, with all things belonging to it, therein bequeathed.

---

13. Poole, *Stages of Religious Faith*, p. 162.

V. This covenant was differently administered in the time of the law, and in the time of the Gospel: under the law it was administered by promises, prophecies, sacrifices, circumcision, the paschal lamb, and other types and ordinances delivered to the people of the Jews, all foresignifying Christ to come; which were, for that time, sufficient and efficacious, through the operation of the Spirit, to instruct and build up the elect in faith in the promised Messiah, by whom they had full remission of sins, and eternal salvation; and is called the Old Testament.

VI. Under the Gospel, when Christ, the substance, was exhibited, the ordinances in which this covenant is dispensed are the preaching of the Word, and the administration of the sacraments of Baptism and the Lord's Supper: which, though fewer in number, and administered with more simplicity, and less outward glory, yet, in them, it is held forth in more fullness, evidence, and spiritual efficacy, to all nations, both Jews and Gentiles; and is called the New Testament. There are not therefore two covenants of grace, differing in substance, but one and the same, under various dispensations.

Most Reformed theologians who stand in the tradition of covenant theology would affirm this statement although, as we shall see in chapters 3–5, significantly different interpretations of the confessional position have been offered, leading to serious disagreements and even calls for theologians to resign from their churches or be removed by disciplinary procedures.

Scottish covenant theology

Covenant theology had been introduced to Scotland by Robert Rollock at the end of the sixteenth century[14] and in the seventeenth century it became the standard form of Reformed theology in Scotland. Scotland ultimately became a major centre for the development and promotion of covenant theology, not least because the theological system became closely allied to political developments, which were also couched in covenantal language.

In 1638, while Charles I was seeking to reimpose Catholicism on the country, the Protestant nobles called upon people to sign what was called the 'National Covenant'. This was a plea for the preservation of the Reformed religion and contained a list of all the Acts of Parliament that established Protestantism as

---

14. *Tractatus De Vocatione Efficaci* (1597). For English translation see W. M. Gunn (ed.), *Select Works of Robert Rollock* (Edinburgh: Wodrow Society, 1849), pp. 1–288.

the religion of Scotland. Then, in 1643, the Solemn League and Covenant was signed, wherein representatives of Scotland, England and Ireland pledged themselves to the preservation of the Reformed faith. Those in Scotland who supported the covenants of 1638 and 1643 were called 'The Covenanters'. The Covenanters were hunted down ruthlessly and many hundreds of them were killed for their beliefs, especially from 1680 to 1688, which was called the 'Killing Time'. Covenant, then, was not simply a theological theme but a concept of significant national importance.

In 1643 the 'Long Parliament' in England set up the Westminster Assembly of Divines, initially to reform the Church of England. This was later expanded to seek the 'covenanted uniformity' of the three kingdoms in matters of religion. Members of both Houses of Parliament, together with the Westminster Divines, subscribed to the Solemn League and Covenant. When their work was completed, the Church of Scotland adopted the WCF in 1647 as its 'Principal Subordinate Standard', Scripture being the primary standard. The other two kingdoms did not follow suit, however, which ensured that covenant theology took root in Scottish soil in a way that it did not elsewhere. There was never the same near-universal commitment to covenant theology in England, although men like William Perkins, William Ames and other Puritan scholars did have significant influence. On the continent, covenant theology was strongest in the Netherlands.

Thomas Boston

In the early eighteenth century, the key figure in covenant theology was Thomas Boston. Indeed, his treatises on the covenants remain standard reading for anyone looking at this area of historical theology. It is instructive to consider Boston's views for three reasons: first, because his exposition of covenant theology post-WCF became the standard view; second, because he was involved in the law/grace dispute which broke out in Scotland among covenant theologians; and third, because when we come to the theology of John Murray, we intend to demonstrate a certain continuity of approach between these two Scottish covenant theologians.

Thomas Boston[15] (1676–1732) was a minister of the Church of Scotland and a gifted theologian. He served for many years in the parish of Ettrick in the

---

15. See A. T. B. McGowan, 'Thomas Boston', in T. A. Hart (ed.), *The Dictionary of Historical Theology* (Carlisle: Paternoster, 2000).

Scottish Borders and became well known through his preaching and his writing. His collected writings were published in twelve volumes in 1853.[16] The most famous of his writings is *The Fourfold State*, which, in its day, was one of the most popular books among devout Christians in Scotland. It has been said that the library of many a crofter and shepherd of the Border hills consisted of a Bible, the Westminster Shorter Catechism, a copy of Bunyan's *Pilgrim's Progress* and Boston's *Fourfold State*.

Thomas Boston was a consistent Calvinist who faithfully held to the WCF and he is recognized for clarifying and expounding the great doctrines of grace. He was one of the finest covenant theologians Scotland has ever produced, not least because of his two treatises, one called 'A View of the Covenant of Works'[17] and the other called 'A View of the Covenant of Grace'.[18] Interestingly, he turned his attention to these subjects as a direct result of the actions of the General Assembly of the Church of Scotland in respect of the Marrow controversy, to which we shall turn shortly.[19]

Following the WCF, Boston taught that God entered into a covenant with Adam in Genesis 2:16–17. He describes this as 'the original transaction between God and our first father Adam in paradise, while yet in the state of primitive integrity'.[20] Adam had the law of God 'engraven on his heart in his creation'[21] but in the making of this covenant of works he was given an additional commandment, namely, that he should not eat from the tree of the knowledge of good and evil. The condition of the covenant was perfect obedience to the whole law of God including this additional commandment.

Crucially, Boston taught that God, when he entered into that covenant with Adam in Genesis 2, was entering into covenant not with Adam as a 'private person' but as federal head of the human race yet unborn. When a Head of State signs a treaty he or she does so in an official capacity and not as a private individual, such that, if he or she ceased to be Head of State, the treaty would still be binding. The Head of State signs as the representative head of the nation

---

16. T. Boston, *The Complete Works of the Late Rev Thomas Boston*, ed. S. McMillan (London: William Tegg & Co., 1853). They have subsequently been republished twice: (Wheaton, IL: Richard Owen Roberts, 1980) and (Lafayette, IN: Sovereign Grace Publishers, 2001).
17. Boston, *Complete Works*, 11:178–339.
18. Boston, *Complete Works*, 8:379–604.
19. Boston, *Complete Works*, 11:176.
20. Boston, *Complete Works*, 11:178.
21. Boston, *Complete Works*, 11:179.

and the whole nation is thereby bound by the treaty. Similarly, Boston argued that Adam was our representative head and so when he broke the covenant (and Boston would argue that Hos. 6:7 refers to this breach) the consequences of the breach came not upon him alone but upon all whom he represented in the covenant. That is why every human being is born with a sinful nature and is an object of God's wrath. We were all represented by Adam and so all of us share in the judgment which resulted from Adam's breach of the covenant. In other words, Adam's sin was imputed to every human being.

Boston goes on to speak about the covenant of grace and how Christ is the federal head of the elect, whereby his righteousness is imputed to us. He begins his famous treatise 'A View of the Covenant of Grace' in this way:

> As man's ruin was originally owing to the breaking of the covenant of works, so his recovery, from the first to the last step thereof, is owing purely to the fulfilling of the covenant of grace; which covenant, being that wherein the whole mystery of our salvation lies, I am to essay the opening of, as the Lord shall be pleased to assist.[22]

Boston structures his exposition of the covenant of grace in six sections. First, he deals with the 'parties in the covenant', being principally the Father, on heaven's side, and Christ, on the human side. He notes that God's elect is the 'party' on whose behalf the covenant is established. Second, he expounds the person and work of Christ, noting that Christ is the 'kinsman redeemer', the 'surety' and the priest of the covenant. Third, he speaks of the conditions of the covenant and the promises contained in the covenant. There are no conditions on the human side except faith in Christ but on Christ's side there are conditions of perfect holiness and righteousness as well as the need to make atonement for sin. The promises of the covenant include the promise of eternal life to God's elect, as they put their faith in Christ. Fourth, he describes what he calls the 'administration' of the covenant, by which he indicates the means through which the covenant is made effective, namely, through Christ who brings us into union with himself. He writes, 'the whole of the covenant is in him: so that he that hath Christ hath the covenant, the whole of the covenant; he that hath not Christ, hath no saving part or lot in it.'[23] In the fifth and sixth parts of his treatise Boston turns to what he calls 'practical improvements', meaning the application of the teaching to the cases of men and women in need of salvation. These sections of the treatise are much more evangelistic in character, as Boston

---

22. Boston, *Complete Works*, 8:379.
23. Boston, *Complete Works*, 8:521.

pleads with people to accept what God has done for them and to seek instatement into the covenant of grace. He writes,

> Thus the covenant is brought to you, and set before you in the gospel; so that ye must needs be either receivers or refusers of it. Refuse it not: that is dangerous beyond expression. Take hold of it; for it is your life. Sinners, ye are under the covenant of works, where there is no life, no salvation for you: but the door of the new covenant is opened unto you: come, enter into it without delay. Flee, and make your escape out of the dominion of the law, the covenant of works, ye were born under, and are living under: and that can in no wise be done, but by your accepting and embracing this covenant offered to you in the gospel; to the instating of you personally in it, to all the purposes of life and salvation.[24]

Boston's teaching on both the covenant of works and the covenant of grace is in agreement with the Westminster Confession of Faith. For Boston, as with the WCF, all human beings are either in Adam, under the covenant of works, or in Christ, under the covenant of grace. If we are in Adam we are subject to death and if we are in Christ we shall be made alive.

As noted earlier, some covenant theologians argued for a covenant of redemption between the Father and the Son as the basis for the covenant of grace but Boston denied the need for a separate covenant of redemption. He argued that it was simply another way of looking at the covenant of grace.[25] This again is consistent with the WCF which does not speak of a covenant of redemption.

Law and grace

As covenant theology developed, tensions began to arise between those whose emphasis was on law and those whose emphasis was on grace. In Scotland, this came to a head at the beginning of the eighteenth century in the Marrow controversy.[26]

---

24. Boston, *Complete Works*, 8:578.
25. Boston, *Complete Works*, 8:396–397, 404–405.
26. For details of the controversy and its implications, see D. Beaton, 'The "Marrow of Modern Divinity" and the Marrow Controversy', *Records of the Scottish Church History Society* 1, part iii (c.1925), pp. 112–134; D. Lachman, *The Marrow Controversy* (Edinburgh: Rutherford House, 1988); W. VanDoodewaard, *The Marrow Controversy*

Boston was a participant in this controversy concerning a book, *The Marrow of Modern Divinity*, which was condemned by the General Assembly of the Church of Scotland in 1720 but which Boston and others regarded as containing a true account of the gospel. The book was published anonymously in 1645 but was probably compiled by Edward Fisher. It was a pastiche of quotations from the works of many Reformed scholars including Calvin, Beza, Sibbes and Rutherford and was one of the books 'approved' by the Westminster Assembly of Divines. A second volume was published later, dealing with the Ten Commandments. It was the first volume which caused the controversy, dealing as it did with covenant theology and related doctrines. The quotations were set in the context of a dialogue between Nomista, a legalist, Antinomista, an antinomian, Neophytus, a young Christian, and Evangelista, a minister of the gospel.[27]

In the course of this controversy it became apparent that there were two parties within the church, both holding to the WCF but with radically opposing views. The one group, led by Principal Hadow of St Andrews, rejected the free offer of the gospel. Hadow took the view that the gospel should be offered only to those who were already showing 'signs of election' and that a universal offer of the gospel was impossible because it would require a universal atonement as its basis. Boston and the other 'Marrowmen', as they were called, resisted this by insisting that the gospel must be preached 'to every creature without exception'. Hadow also argued that repentance was a condition of salvation, whereas Boston argued that repentance flowed from regeneration and justification as a *result*, rather than going before them as a *cause*. Both men held to the WCF as their Principal Subordinate Standard and both held firmly to a Calvinistic soteriology, stemming from the Synod of Dordrecht (1618–19). The dispute also involved disagreements on the doctrine of assurance and various other matters.[28] Ultimately, the 'Marrowmen' were rebuked by the General Assembly of 1722 but permitted to continue to serve in their parishes.

(Footnote 26 cont.) and Seceder Tradition: Atonement, Saving Faith, and the Gospel Offer in Scotland (1718–1799) (Grand Rapids, MI: Reformation Heritage Books, 2011); S. B. Ferguson, *The Whole Christ: Legalism, Antinomianism, and Gospel Assurance – Why the Marrow Controversy Still Matters* (Wheaton, IL: Crossway, 2016); also listen to S. B. Ferguson, 'The Marrow Controversy', three audio lectures (2–9 February 2004), SermonAudio.Com, http://www.sermonaudio.com/main.asp

27. An edition of *The Marrow* with Boston's notes can be found in Boston, *Complete Works*, 7:143–489.

28. For a detailed summary of these arguments, see A. T. B. McGowan, *The Federal Theology of Thomas Boston* (Carlisle: Paternoster, 1997).

The 'Marrowmen' were accused of being antinomian (against the law) but a more accurate judgment would be that they were anti-neonomian (against legalism). In other words, they were protesting against a legalistic strain which had crept into Scottish theology at this time. Some of them, led by Ralph and Ebenezer Erskine, ultimately left the Church of Scotland to found the original Secession Church in 1733. Boston died in 1732 but it is clear that he would not have seceded.[29] He remained a faithful member and minister of the Kirk to the end of his days.

Clearly there were two schools within covenant theology, both claiming allegiance to the WCF and both claiming to be true to the Calvinistic tradition. The key issues in this dispute concerned the relationship between law and grace. These two schools persisted (and persist) within covenant theology. As we shall see when we come to the differences between Murray and Kline and their successors, the priority given to law or grace determines the nature of the subsequent theology.

Conclusion

This description of the nature and historical development of covenant theology, together with an examination of one of its most important Scottish exponents, will help us when we come to consider the work of John Murray. The battle which Boston had with a legalistic strain of covenant theology, not least on the issue of the priority of grace over law, will also contribute to our analysis of recent debates within covenant theology.

---

29. See A. T. B. McGowan, 'Should We Leave Liberal Denominations?', *Reformation and Revival Journal* 13, no. 1 (Winter 2004), pp. 59–74. This is based on a paper given to the Historical Studies Conference in Edinburgh in 1994.

2. KARL BARTH

Introduction

In this chapter we shall consider the views of Karl Barth on covenant and then turn to the work of T. F. Torrance and J. B. Torrance. Covenant theology has been subjected to criticism from a range of perspectives through the centuries but the critique of Barth and his theological successors is undoubtedly the most sustained and the most trenchant, not least because they themselves come from within the Reformed tradition. As we shall see, they view covenant theology as a dangerous innovation which undermines and ultimately destroys a theology of grace. In particular, they argue that covenant theology removes Christ from his central place in God's reconciliation and leads to a skewed understanding of various doctrines, especially the doctrines of predestination, atonement and assurance.

Our intention is to state and assess Barth's use of the covenant concept in his theology. It is, of course, not possible in one chapter to cover all that Barth wrote on the subject of covenant, so closely is the theme interwoven with every aspect of his thinking. That being the case, we shall concentrate on the section in his *Church Dogmatics* (*CD*) 4/1, where Barth expounds his understanding of the covenant concept in theology.[1] After providing an overview of that section

---

1. K. Barth, *Church Dogmatics*, ed. G. W. Bromiley and T. F. Torrance, vol. 4/1 (Edinburgh: T & T Clark, 1956), pp. 3–78.

we shall then focus more specifically on his analysis and critique of covenant theology. Next, we shall provide some assessment of the strengths and weaknesses of Barth's argument. Finally, we shall examine how two of his successors took up this critique and developed it.

Barth's use of the covenant concept

Although Barth does not build his theology on the foundation of a three-covenant system as developed by earlier Reformed theologians, it should not be imagined that thereby he neglects the theme. Quite the reverse is the case because the idea of covenant is very important in Barth's theology. Indeed, he probably speaks more about covenant than any other recent theologian, apart from those in the school of covenant theology. Barth builds the idea of covenant into the central themes of his dogmatic theology. Not only does he relate covenant to the doctrine of election, although in a somewhat different way from others in the Reformed tradition, he also relates it carefully to every aspect of God's gracious action in Christ. Everything is drawn together such that God's grace is the basis for the covenant, election is the outworking of the covenant, creation prepares the ground for the covenant and reconciliation (especially atonement) is the fulfilment of the covenant. As John Webster says, for Barth, 'Creation, covenant and Trinity are indissolubly united in the church's confession.'[2]

In order to understand Barth's use of the covenant concept, we turn now to his extended exposition of the subject in section 57 of his *CD*, entitled 'The Work of God the Reconciler'. It is here, in his exposition of the doctrine of reconciliation, that Barth begins to open up in detail both his general understanding of the theme of covenant and his critique of the older covenant theology. Barth, true to the overall direction of his work, makes it clear that we cannot begin a treatment of reconciliation by speaking about covenant; rather we must begin by speaking about God. Only when we have described God's free act of reconciliation in Christ can we turn to consider the covenantal relationship which God has set in place as part of the outworking of his sovereign and gracious electing action. For that reason, he begins this section with an exposition of the theme 'God with Us'.[3] His intention is to demonstrate that 'the covenant fulfilled in the atonement' is the heart and centre of the church's

---

2. J. Webster, *Barth* (London: Continuum, 2000), p. 98.
3. Barth, *Church Dogmatics*, vol. 4/1, pp. 3–21.

dogmatics.[4] It is difficult to find a better summary of Barth's exposition of this theme 'God with Us' than has been provided by Geoffrey Bromiley:

> What does 'God with us' mean? Barth lists seven successive implications which provide critical clues to the understanding of reconciliation. (1) It means God's being in his act on which our being reposes (6f.). (2) It means God's act aimed at a specific and central goal (7f.). (3) It means an act dealing with man's salvation (8f.). (4) It means an act grounded in God's eternal purpose and taking precedence even to the work of creation (9f.). (5) It means an act on behalf of those who have forfeited their creaturely existence and have no claim to salvation, that is, of undeserving sinners (10–12). (6) It means God's personal identification with us and therefore not just a restoration but rather the very coming of salvation (12–14). (7) It means our being with God ('we with God') as we are lifted up, given a place, awakened to our true being, and made free for God in virtue of his being with us (14–16). Nor is all this a mere idea. It is a history that finds fulfilment in the name of Jesus Christ, not as a sign or symbol, but as an authentic reality.[5]

With that background, Barth turns to the theme of covenant. He begins by saying very clearly that 'reconciliation is the fulfilment of the covenant between God and man'.[6] It is not a coincidence that Barth has no volume devoted to the human condition, the fall and sin. Rather he sets all of these in the context of reconciliation. For him, the covenant between God and humanity is an eternal, gracious, unilateral covenant which has always promised redemption and reconciliation to all who are in Christ. He defines it in this way: 'The fellowship which originally existed between God and man, which was then disturbed and jeopardised, the purpose of which is now fulfilled in Jesus Christ and in the work of reconciliation, we describe as the covenant.'[7]

Barth then goes into a long exegetical section, demonstrating the use of the word 'covenant' in the Scriptures.[8] Despite the fact that there is some uncertainty as to the proper etymology and interpretation of both the Hebrew *bĕrît* and the Greek *diathēkē*, Barth is able to draw certain conclusions from the biblical evidence. His primary conclusion is that the covenant with Israel is

---

4. Barth, *Church Dogmatics*, vol. 4/1, p. 3.
5. G. W. Bromiley, *Introduction to the Theology of Karl Barth* (Edinburgh: T & T Clark, 1979), p. 176.
6. Barth, *Church Dogmatics*, vol. 4/1, p. 22.
7. Barth, *Church Dogmatics*, vol. 4/1, p. 22.
8. Barth, *Church Dogmatics*, vol. 4/1, pp. 22–24.

established by God himself and is therefore a sovereign, gracious covenant. It is also supremely personal, involving the actions of God and of Israel. Recognizing that there are many covenants in the Old Testament (with Noah, Abraham, Moses, David and so on) he rejects the notion that these are all expressions of one underlying or more fundamental covenant. He writes, 'The autonomy and importance which the Old Testament literature gives to each of these many events, quite irrespective of their mutual relationship, seems to make it impossible to try to find some pragmatic, historical connexion.'[9] Nevertheless, there is a unity among them in that they are all expressions of the gracious action of a sovereign, electing God. Barth is also at pains to point out that nothing in our understanding of covenant must lead us to the conclusion that somehow God is under obligation because of the covenant or is restricted in his action. The eternal freedom of the sovereign God is a fundamental thesis which must not be lost in expounding his relationship with his creatures. In other words, the covenant is unilateral in its essence, although bilateral in its outworking. In this context he even quotes Jacques Ellul to the effect that the covenant is 'a contract in which one of the parties makes the arrangements and the other simply agrees'.[10] In using this terminology, Barth specifically rejects the notion of a 'mutually binding contract' but even the use of this language of 'contract' was later rejected by scholars in the Barth tradition. For example, J. B. Torrance preferred to accuse the covenant theologians of thinking contractually and thus failing to see that the covenant was primarily gracious, based on love and not law, as we shall see shortly.

Barth then goes on to make three important points in relation to his understanding of covenant. The first point is that the covenant is with the whole human race. This stands in marked contrast to covenant theology which sees the covenant as made with elect individuals, albeit with a more general reference in respect of the historical nation of Israel. Barth argues for his wider interpretation by beginning with the first covenant mentioned in Scripture, the covenant made with Noah, in which the whole human race is included.[11] He recognizes that the covenant made with Abraham and his descendants in Genesis 12 is restricted to the nation of Israel and thus there are two covenants established in 'concentric circles', the outer one being with Noah and the inner one with Abraham. He does not accept, however, that the covenant with Noah is purely to do with the preservation of the race whereas the covenant with Abraham

---

9. Barth, *Church Dogmatics*, vol. 4/1, p. 24.
10. Barth, *Church Dogmatics*, vol. 4/1, p. 25.
11. Barth, *Church Dogmatics*, vol. 4/1, pp. 26–27.

has to do with grace and salvation. He points out that the Abrahamic covenant had elements of the preservation of Israel in it but, more significantly, he wants to argue that the covenant with Noah was essentially gracious since it involved God's unconditional promise to be faithful to human beings and to refrain from destroying them, despite their sin and disobedience. Hence he can write,

> Therefore the Noachic covenant – in a way which remarkably is much more perceptible than in the case of the covenant or covenants with Israel – is already a covenant of grace in the twofold sense of the concept grace: the free and utterly unmerited self-obligation of God to the human race which had completely fallen away from Him, but which as such is still pledged to Him . . . and as the sign of the longsuffering of God obviously also the promise of the future divine coming which will far transcend the mere preserving of the race.[12]

Barth believes that because this covenant is not an aspect of God's general revelation but represents a specific decision and action of God in relation to fallen humanity, then, even though it is not part of the 'inner circle' of redemptive covenantal agreement, nevertheless it is 'an activity on the basis of which the nations preserved by God cannot be excluded from his redemptive work. In this sense the race, as a whole, is in covenant.'[13]

The second point Barth makes is that the covenant must be understood in terms of the mission of Israel. The intention here is to demonstrate that the covenant is not to be understood as a private arrangement between God and one historical nation. Israel's mission was to be a 'light to the nations' and a 'light to the Gentiles' and so God's redemptive purpose, although initially communicated to and in some senses vested in Israel, was intended for all the nations. Barth exegetes the passages in Isaiah and elsewhere where these and similar expressions occur and also widens the discussion to consider the eschatological significance of the fulfilment of Israel's mission in the coming of Messiah, the declaration of the gospel to the Gentiles and the climax of all of this in the day of Yahweh. That last day, the day of the 'conclusion of the covenant', must not be seen simply as a time of judgment. Rather, 'The last time, the day of Yahweh, will indeed be the day of final judgement – the prophets of a false confidence must make no mistake about that. But as such it will also be the day of Israel's redemption – the day when the covenant which Yahweh has made with it finds its positive fulfilment.'[14]

---

12. Barth, *Church Dogmatics*, vol. 4/1, p. 27.
13. Barth, *Church Dogmatics*, vol. 4/1, p. 27.
14. Barth, *Church Dogmatics*, vol. 4/1, p. 31.

The third point Barth makes is that the covenant made with Israel transposes into the new covenant in Jesus Christ and can only be fully understood in that context. This new covenant was already anticipated in the prophecy of Jeremiah (chs. 31 and 32). In order to stress the unity and continuity of the covenants Barth points out that almost precisely the same formula is found in Jeremiah as is found in the establishment of the covenants with Abraham, Moses and Joshua, namely, 'I will be your God and you will be my people'. This new, eternal covenant would not replace these older covenants but would rather bring them to fulfilment and completion. What then happens to the covenant with Israel? Barth writes,

> What happens to this covenant with the conclusion of a new and eternal covenant is rather . . . that it is upheld, that is, lifted up to its true level, that it is given its proper form, and that far from being destroyed it is maintained and confirmed. There is no question of a dissolution but rather of a revelation of the real purpose and nature of that first covenant.[15]

For Barth, the 'most remarkable thing of all' about this new covenant is that it will become a 'perfect covenant' because sin and God's opposition to sin will finally be a thing of the past:

> This ending and new beginning will be posited in the fact that God not only exercises patience as in the Noachic covenant, but that He remits guilt, that He does not remember sin, and that in this way and on this basis He not only allows an unmerited continuation of life, again as in the Noachic covenant, but reduces to order, and in a sense compulsorily places in the freedom of obedience which we owe Him as His covenant partners.[16]

By moving from the covenant with Noah to the prophecy of Jeremiah 31 and then on to the new covenant in Christ, Barth's whole intention is to demonstrate that the covenant is universal in its design, scope and implications. Thus he can conclude, 'In the light of this passage in Jer. 31 we are indeed enabled and summoned to give to the concept of the covenant the universal meaning which it acquired in the form which it manifestly assumed in Jesus Christ.'[17]

---

15. Barth, *Church Dogmatics*, vol. 4/1, p. 33.
16. Barth, *Church Dogmatics*, vol. 4/1, p. 33.
17. Barth, *Church Dogmatics*, vol. 4/1, p. 34.

Barth is never satisfied with his exposition of a doctrine unless it can be demonstrated to have a Christological focus so, having completed the extended exegetical analysis of the notion of covenant, especially in the Old Testament, he now turns to speak of Christ. Christ is the one who brings the covenant to its place of fulfilment and completion, especially in his atonement. Indeed, Jesus Christ is 'the eschatological realisation of the will of God for Israel and therefore the whole race. And as such He is also the revelation of this divine will and therefore of the covenant.'[18] Again, Barth stresses that this covenant, now brought to fruition in Christ, is for the whole race. God's covenantal purposes for mankind which, from the beginning, have had as their intention the salvation of humanity, are now revealed in Christ. Being both God and man, he is able to reconcile humanity by his atonement. This helps us to understand, says Barth, that 'God does not at first occupy a position of neutrality in relation to man'.[19] Rather, God from all eternity has willed the salvation of humanity and in every situation has 'pledged himself' to humanity. The words 'I will be your God and you shall be my people' are not simply an historical statement made on several occasions but rather a revelation of God's eternal purpose in relation to his creatures. This binding and pledging of himself to humanity is the covenant and is the 'presupposition of the atonement' itself.[20]

In calling this covenant the 'covenant of grace' Barth argues that three things are being affirmed. First, it affirms the freedom of God in establishing and maintaining the covenant. Because of sin, humanity is unable to find reconciliation with God and so it must be provided from outside, from God himself. By our sin we have alienated ourselves from God and caused a breach in the fellowship with God. We have no rights in the situation and can make no demands; we are utterly at his mercy. Only God can act to deal with this situation and there are no factors operating upon him which can force him to take such action. He is entirely free in his self-determination to be our God and in his invitation for us to become his people.

The second implication of speaking about a covenant of grace conditions the first point but only slightly. There are indeed no external factors which limit the sovereign freedom of God to act graciously towards the human race which he has created; his own nature, however, does compel him. In other words, when we speak about a covenant of grace we are actually making an affirmation about the nature of God himself. God does not simply pass on

---

18. Barth, *Church Dogmatics*, vol. 4/1, pp. 34–35.
19. Barth, *Church Dogmatics*, vol. 4/1, p. 37.
20. Barth, *Church Dogmatics*, vol. 4/1, p. 38.

favours or benefits which he might equally well have chosen to deny. Rather the covenant of grace which God makes with all humanity is an expression of his inner nature and true identity. It is himself he gives to humanity and not simply benefits. That is why the fullest explanation of the atonement is that it is the coming of God himself who acts out on this earth the salvation which springs from his essential being. Being and act can never be separated.

The third implication of speaking about the covenant as a covenant of grace is that the obligation on the part of humanity is simply one of gratitude. As we saw earlier, the covenant is unilateral; it represents the free and gracious action of a sovereign God whose heart of love reaches out to the human race which he has created. It is not a covenant to which we as human beings contribute anything. All that is required of us is gratitude.[21] In one of those marvellous passages where Barth the preacher seems to take over, he explains that one of the implications of this is that we must not think of ourselves differently from how God has come to think of us in Christ. Barth writes,

> By deciding for us God has decided concerning us. We are therefore prevented from thinking otherwise about ourselves, from seeing or understanding or explaining man any other way, than as the being engaged and covenanted to God, and therefore simply but strictly engaged and covenanted to thanks. Just as there is no God but the God of the covenant, there is no man but the man of the covenant: the man who as such is destined and called to give thanks.[22]

For many people who find themselves struggling to believe that they have truly been found by God in Christ, this is a marvellous pastoral application of the meaning of the covenant of grace.

At this point Barth adds a word of caution and warning. Nothing that he has said about the covenant of grace can be discovered by natural theology. Only in Christ can we find the revelation of God's saving action. Indeed, 'Apart from and without Jesus Christ we can say nothing at all about God and man and their relationship one with another'.[23] At one level Barth is saying that revelation is vital for us to have any knowledge or understanding of what God has done for us in Christ but at a deeper level he is arguing that the covenant of grace is grounded in the being of God and in his eternal decision to become a man for us. This has huge implications, not least that 'Ontologically, therefore, the

---

21. Barth, *Church Dogmatics*, vol. 4/1, p. 41.
22. Barth, *Church Dogmatics*, vol. 4/1, p. 43.
23. Barth, *Church Dogmatics*, vol. 4/1, p. 45.

covenant of grace is already included and grounded in Jesus Christ, in the human form and human contact which God willed to give His Word from all eternity'.[24] The covenant of grace is revealed only in Christ and especially in his atonement, the culmination of the covenant.

Barth on covenant theology

After this exposition of his general understanding of the theme of covenant, Barth turns more directly to an historical analysis and critique of the older covenant theology, which he calls 'federal theology'.[25] He does not attempt to trace the historical development of federal theology, although he does note some of the key figures in its earliest development and he does recognize that it was the 'ruling orthodoxy' of the Reformed churches in the second half of the seventeenth century.

Barth regards the federal theology as representing a significant improvement on what had gone before, both in medieval Catholicism and in the early Protestant scholastic tradition. In particular, he likes the way in which its proponents did not see the doctrines of the Christian faith as a series of propositional statements to be connected logically and theologically but rather viewed the message of Scripture more dynamically, seeing their task as the presentation and analysis of the history of God's relationship to humanity. In this sense they were following Calvin himself, who also understood theology in this dynamic manner.[26] Unfortunately, from Barth's perspective, there was a fatal flaw in this approach: the federal theologians viewed the atonement as one event in a series of events, rather than as 'the event' which gives meaning to everything else. As Barth says,

> They overlooked the fact that in all the forms of its attestation this single and complete event is a special event which has to be understood in a special way. Because of the difference of the attestation it cannot be broken up into a series of different covenant acts, or acts of redemption, which follow one another step by step, and then reassembled into a single whole. The Federal theologians did not notice that for all the exclusiveness with which they read the Scriptures, in this analysis and synthesis of the occurrence between God and man they were going beyond Scripture and missing its real content.[27]

---

24. Barth, *Church Dogmatics*, vol. 4/1, p. 45.
25. Barth, *Church Dogmatics*, vol. 4/1, pp. 54–66.
26. Barth, *Church Dogmatics*, vol. 4/1, p. 55.
27. Barth, *Church Dogmatics*, vol. 4/1, p. 56.

Barth goes on to speak of some of the earliest occurrences of covenant theology, in Zwingli and in Bullinger, who were using the structure of covenant to undergird their theology of infant baptism. Barth is not convinced that they were successful in this but he does identify in their expression of the covenant a universal significance of which he heartily approves. He goes on to demonstrate that in the more developed forms of federal theology this universalism was lost. In this later federal theology, the covenant of grace applies only to the elect. Instead of seeing a universal atonement as the climax of the covenant, the atonement becomes the means by which God secures the salvation of those elect individuals with whom (and only with whom) he was in covenant. Barth regards this as a 'blind alley' which departed from the earlier 'very remarkable form' of federal theology.[28] As Barth later said, this means that the covenant of grace thus becomes at best 'a secondary and subsequent divine arrangement' rather than 'the beginning of all the ways of God'.[29]

What led to this blind alley? Barth believes that the problems arose principally through the introduction of a two-covenant system, a covenant of works and a covenant of grace, for which he blames Ursinus, although there is increasing evidence to suggest that the idea predates Ursinus.[30] He notes that this gradually became the normative position within Reformed theology, receiving confessional status in the WCF. Barth spells out the developed covenant theology in its two-covenant form, using the writings of Cocceius as his core text. Indeed, he says that Cocceius 'represents the Federal theology in a form which is not only the most perfect, but also the ripest and strongest and most impressive'.[31] Despite this, however, Barth regards him as having made fundamental theological mistakes, especially in his regarding the covenant of grace only in negative terms as an abrogation of the covenant of works.

Barth's most serious criticism of Cocceius, however, is that his understanding of the covenant of grace led to the necessity for an intra-trinitarian covenant which, in later covenant theology, would be called the covenant of redemption. This intra-trinitarian covenant was held to be the basis for the covenant of grace. The Father and the Son covenant together to the effect that if the Son will agree to become incarnate and receive from the Father the punishment for sin on behalf of the elect, then the Father will forgive the sins of the elect and impute to them the righteousness of Christ. Barth's trinitarian theology will not

---

28. Barth, *Church Dogmatics*, vol. 4/1, p. 58.
29. Barth, *Church Dogmatics*, vol. 4/1, p. 66.
30. See D. A. Weir's historical analysis above.
31. Barth, *Church Dogmatics*, vol. 4/1, p. 60.

allow him even to contemplate such a notion. He is quite dismissive of such a theology: 'This is mythology, for which there is no place in a right understanding of the doctrine of the Trinity as the doctrine of the three modes of being of the one God, which is how it was understood and presented in Reformed orthodoxy itself.'[32] Having presented his critique of the older federal theology Barth then completes the picture by speaking of reconciliation as the fulfilment of the covenant.[33]

In order for us to see the full extent of Barth's critique of covenant theology, however, it is necessary for us to move beyond *CD* itself and to consider an earlier work by Barth. In his book *The Theology of the Reformed Confessions*[34] we see a criticism that has only tangentially appeared so far, namely, that covenant theology has an anthropological basis rather than a theological basis.

Barth articulated his opposition to the anthropological approach of covenant theology in the early stages of his theological development, when he gave a series of lectures on the theology of the Reformed confessions. This book, only recently available in English, contains a series of lectures given by Barth in Göttingen in 1923, having taken up his appointment as professor there in 1921. In these lectures we catch a glimpse of the early Barth as he goes back behind the liberal theology in which he was schooled but which he has by this time abandoned, in order to explore his own Reformed tradition. It is interesting to see in these lectures Barth's strong affirmation of the need for confessional orthodoxy and his critique of liberal theology for having abandoned this. The relevance of the book for our present purposes, however, is that already, at this early period, we find Barth spelling out one of his problems with covenant theology, namely, its emphasis on anthropology. For Barth, it is vital to emphasize the priority of theology over anthropology, a theme which will remain central in his later, more mature thought.

We see the first clear exposition of this problem when he deals with the Westminster Confession of Faith. He sets the scene by arguing that the significance of a Reformed confession lies not in itself but rather in that which is beyond itself, that to which it points, namely, to the Word of God. Having established that principle, he is critical of confessions which fail in this regard. It is in this context that he expresses his high regard for the Scots Confession

---

32. Barth, *Church Dogmatics*, vol. 4/1, p. 65.
33. Barth, *Church Dogmatics*, vol. 4/1, pp. 67–78.
34. K. Barth, *The Theology of the Reformed Confessions*, tr. and annotated by D. L. Guder and J. J. Guder, Columbia Series in Reformed Theology (Louisville, KY/London: Westminster John Knox Press, 2002).

of 1560 and also his astonishment that the Scots would exchange it for the WCF![35] Why did he prefer the Scots Confession? Simply because he believed that the WCF, with its emphasis on the application of redemption and the quest for assurance, places the focus too much on anthropology instead of on theology.[36]

Barth makes the same criticism of the Canons of Dort, although not without first praising Dort for its core instincts. He writes, 'There is no way to deny that what is expressed in the canons of Dort is the authentic concern of the Reformation. Their case against the Remonstrants is entirely justified and consistent from the perspective of Luther and Calvin.'[37] It was absolutely necessary to emphasize the freedom of God in his sovereign election. Unfortunately, from Barth's perspective, this fundamentally correct instinct was damaged by their concern with the question as to whether or not particular individuals were elect. He says, 'There is no doubting that they respond with the *Reformation* answer to this question. But in my view, the actual interest in this *question* was the first crack in the wall of the church itself.'[38] Barth goes on to explain what he means:

> They were thinking anthropologically rather than theologically when they made the 'absolute decree' [decretum absolutum], which is a profound statement about God, into a doctrine not just about humanity but about this or that person – even if they did so with logical consistency. The doctrine of a 'limited number' [numerus clausus] of the elect is, in particular, not good doctrine; it ties God down to particular people when the meaning of the entire doctrine is precisely the freedom of God.[39]

Barth goes so far as to call the decisions of the Synod of Dort 'the *mausoleum* of the early Reformed movement'.[40] Despite this, he believes that Dort is still preferable to the WCF, which he compares unfavourably with the Canons of Dort. He writes, 'But I would like to add that the canons of Dort are much superior to the Westminster Confession. Especially the dangerous doctrine of the assurance of election is presented here in a balanced way and does not emerge as the central point and crown of the entire thing, as is the case in the intolerable approach of the English.'[41]

---

35. Barth, *Theology of the Reformed Confessions*, pp. 134–136.
36. Barth, *Theology of the Reformed Confessions*, pp. 150–151.
37. Barth, *Theology of the Reformed Confessions*, p. 215.
38. Barth, *Theology of the Reformed Confessions*, p. 216.
39. Barth, *Theology of the Reformed Confessions*, p. 216.
40. Barth, *Theology of the Reformed Confessions*, p. 212.
41. Barth, *Theology of the Reformed Confessions*, p. 216.

To complete Barth's critique of covenant theology we should make one final point, drawn from his book *Christ and Adam: Man and Humanity in Romans 5*.[42] In this short book Barth deals with the parallel between Christ and Adam in Romans 5, a key text in covenant theology. The point to be noted is that Barth will not allow Adam to have the priority. In most expressions of covenant theology, Adam is dealt with first as the federal head of the race and then later Christ is presented as the federal head of the elect, whom God by this means rescues from eternal punishment. Thus Christ is the second (or last) Adam. Barth writes,

> The relationship between Adam and us reveals not the primary but only the secondary anthropological truth and ordering principle. The primary anthropological truth and ordering principle, which only mirrors itself in that relationship, is made clear only through the relationship between Christ and us. Adam is, as is said in v. 14, *typos tou mellontos*, the type of Him who was to come. Man's essential and original nature is to be found, therefore, not in Adam but in Christ. In Adam we can only find it prefigured. Adam can therefore be interpreted only in the light of Christ, and not the other way round.[43]

In summary, then, Barth's critique of covenant theology consists of seven main points. First, covenant theology divides the single unique 'event' of Christ into a series of covenantal arrangements, thus denying the fundamental significance of 'the event'. Second, in its later forms covenant theology denies the universality of the covenant of grace and becomes particularized in a set of elect individuals. Third, rather than understanding the covenant of grace as the outworking of God's electing purpose for all humanity, covenant theology understands the covenant of grace as a secondary arrangement which is only necessary because of the failure of the original covenant of works. Fourth, covenant theology views the atonement not as the climax of the universal implications of the covenant but as a means of effecting the salvation of the elect. Fifth, covenant theology requires an intra-trinitarian covenant which undermines the doctrine of the Trinity. Sixth, covenant theology has an anthropological rather than a theological approach to salvation. Seventh, in covenant theology Adam is given priority over Christ.

---

42. K. Barth, *Christ and Adam: Man and Humanity in Romans 5* (New York: Collier Books, 1962).
43. Barth, *Christ and Adam*, pp. 39–40.

Karl Barth

Response to Barth on covenant theology

Having presented at some length Barth's understanding of how the concept of covenant ought to function in Reformed dogmatics and having observed his critique of covenant theology, it is necessary now to move towards some assessment of his views. In offering this assessment we begin by commending four aspects of Barth's exposition of the covenant concept, including aspects of his critique of covenant theology which are well founded and which ought to provide a necessary corrective to some forms of that theological system.

Points of agreement

First, as we noted at the beginning of this chapter, Barth does not use the covenant concept as a mere subsection within his general understanding of salvation but rather he integrates the theme theologically into every area of his dogmatics. This is a huge undertaking and emphasizes the seriousness with which he takes the fact that, according to the Scriptures, God's dealings with humanity must be conceived of in covenantal terms. This also means that his view of covenant is internally self-consistent, even if it may be criticized from other theological perspectives. The architectonic structure of his dogmatics is truly impressive and one has to agree that some of his critics lack the deep theological rigour involved in this integrative work, opting instead for a somewhat shallow theological method which does not deeply imbed the covenant concept into the core theological structure of their dogmatics.

Second, Barth is right to affirm that the covenant is unilateral in nature, established by God with a sovereign freedom. The covenant is not a bilateral, conditional covenant. In this context, he is also right to affirm the unity of God's covenantal dealing with humanity, which must not be undermined by polarizing covenants of works and grace.[44]

Third, Barth is right to insist upon the priority of grace over law. This is one point, however, where Barth and J. B. Torrance (as we will see) would have benefited from recognizing the various strands within covenant theology. The differences between these strands on issues of law and grace are quite significant. For example, Torrance says that covenant theology involves giving priority to law over grace and that it is based 'on contract law rather than on the grace and

---

44. See A. T. B. McGowan, 'The Unity of the Covenant', in J. A. Pipa and C. N. Willborn (eds.), *The Covenant: God's Voluntary Condescension* (Taylors, SC: Presbyterian Press, 2005), pp. 1–13.

love of God'[45] but this is not generally true. Some covenant theologians have indeed suggested that law has priority over grace, arguing that grace is entirely a response to the fall. Some of them have insisted that we must not speak about grace until the *protoevangelion* of Genesis 3:15. This was a matter of serious dispute between two recent Reformed theologians, John Murray and Meredith G. Kline. Like Barth and Torrance, although for different reasons, Murray insisted on the priority of grace over law, as Thomas Boston had done before him.[46] Murray was right to do so and so we reject the conclusions of one writer, who compared Murray and Kline and argued that Kline's position was to be preferred.[47] Perhaps the principal lesson to be learned here is that if covenant theologians do make the mistake of arguing that law precedes grace, they are opening the door for a significant critique of their position.

Fourth, Barth was right to insist that there is no intra-trinitarian covenant. This is a weakness in covenant theology which demonstrates a failure properly to integrate its understanding of covenant with its doctrine of the Trinity. In taking this position we are not thereby accepting the Barthian view of atonement, which sees the reconciliation between God and humanity taking place ontologically in the person of Christ, with the emphasis on the incarnation, rather than forensically through penal substitutionary atonement, where the emphasis is placed on the cross. We do believe that on the cross there is an encounter between the Father and the Son, whereby the Son is punished by the Father in our place. We do not believe, however, that this necessitates an intra-trinitarian covenant.

Points of disagreement

Having noted these points of agreement, we must now turn to six points of disagreement.

---

45. See J. B. Torrance, *A Critique of Federal Theology in the Light of the Gospel: Was John Calvin a 'Federal' Theologian?* (Victoria: Burning Bush Society of Victoria, 1997).
46. See A. T. B. McGowan, 'Scottish Covenant Theology', in J. A. Pipa and C. N. Willborn (eds.), *The Covenant: God's Voluntary Condescension* (Taylors, SC: Presbyterian Press, 2005), pp. 61–72; and A. T. B. McGowan, 'In Defence of Headship Theology', in J. A. Grant and A. I. Wilson (eds.), *The God of the Covenant: Biblical, Theological and Contemporary Perspectives* (Leicester: Apollos, 2005), pp. 178–199.
47. J. K. Jeon, *Covenant Theology: John Murray's and Meredith Kline's Response to the Historical Development of Federal Theology in Reformed Thought* (Lanham, MD: University Press of America, 1999).

First, we must take issue with Barth's argument that the federal theologians were wrong to structure the 'event' of redemption as a series of events (or covenants). As we saw, Barth believed that the one 'event' of Christ cannot be divided and there can be no revelation of God except through this 'event'. This betrays Barth's unwillingness, observable throughout his writings, to speak of revelation other than in and through Christ. This is an understandable concern and we share Barth's rejection of natural theology in all its forms[48] but, as the writer to the Hebrews says (1:1–2), this God did speak through prophets and apostles before the final speaking in Jesus Christ. In our view, the federal theologians were simply taking seriously the redemptive history which God reveals to us in the Scriptures and so it is Barth, not the covenant theologians, who has missed 'the real content'[49] of Scripture.

Second, Barth's critique of covenant theology is too tightly focused on one individual (Cocceius) representing one tradition within covenant theology. Covenant theology is not a monolithic structure agreed in all its elements by all its adherents. One of the problems with both Barth and the Torrances (as we will see) is that *some* of their criticisms are legitimate in respect of *some* expressions of covenant theology but are definitely *not* legitimate in respect of every strand of covenant theology. There are many covenant theologians who do not hold to the entirety of the position espoused by Cocceius, Barth's primary source for an understanding of covenant theology. There were (and are) various strands of covenant theology but Barth does not distinguish them. For example, some covenant theologians believed that the Mosaic covenant was a republication of the covenant of works but John Murray did not, for good reasons.

Third, we must disagree with Barth's understanding of Christ the Mediator. Barth argues that even if there had been no fall, Christ would still have come as Mediator. This implies that there is some ontological breach or gulf which has to be bridged between God and humanity, rather than the moral breach of the fall. Even some of those who are generally sympathetic to Barth's overall critique of covenant theology find it difficult to accept his argument at this point because it seems to fly in the face of the teaching of Scripture.[50] For example, J. L. Scott asks, 'is it not going too far to use the word Mediator of the relationship of Christ to unfallen man? Is there any reference in Scripture which clearly

---

48. While recognizing the importance of general revelation, with which natural theology must not be confused.
49. Barth, *Church Dogmatics*, vol. 4/1, p. 56.
50. J. L. Scott, 'The Covenant in the Theology of Karl Barth', *SJT* 17, no. 2 (1964), pp. 182–198.

and unambiguously states that the "eternal purpose" of God for an unfallen world would have been that the Word should become flesh?'[51] After suggesting some passages of Scripture that seem to suggest otherwise, Scott concludes, 'Can we then say with dogmatic assurance that without human sin there would have been no cross, but there would certainly have been Jesus Christ the God-man?'[52] It is our view that, without the fall, human beings do not require a Mediator.

Fourth, we must disagree with Barth's attempt to make the covenant with Noah the primary expression of God's relationship with humanity. In order to widen the covenant beyond simply the scope of Israel and to argue that God's covenant with humanity is a universal covenant, Barth takes the covenant with Noah to be the primary covenant and works out most of his subsequent argument from that basis. In the biblical witness, however, it is the Abrahamic covenant which is quoted again and again through the subsequent generations and which seems to form the basis for a true understanding of the nature of God's dealings with humanity. Barth, however, takes a different approach. As we saw, when he is expounding his understanding of the new covenant, he sets it in the context of the covenant with Noah and not the covenant with Abraham. This flies in the face of the New Testament teaching about the new covenant, which both Paul and the writer to the Hebrews set firmly in the context of the covenants with Abraham and Moses. In other words, Barth's argument that the covenant (and therefore the atonement) is universal, based on an exegesis of the covenant with Noah, is not persuasive. It asks the 'outer circle' (as he calls it) of God's covenantal dealings to do theological work for which it was not intended. Far more persuasive is John Murray's analysis of the relationship between the various biblical covenants, as we shall see in the next chapter.[53]

Fifth, we disagree with Barth's development of a Christological view of predestination. Once again, Barth's intention is to maintain a universal focus for the reconciliation which takes place in Christ. If predestination has to do only with some individuals and not with every human being, then the outworking of God's electing grace will naturally take the form which it does in covenant theology and will result in limited atonement. As most covenant theologians have argued, Christ died only for the elect, since otherwise there would be a double payment for sin by those who go to hell. To avoid this conclusion, Barth must argue that Christ is the one who is predestined and that he is both the

---

51. Scott, 'The Covenant in the Theology of Karl Barth', p. 196.
52. Scott, 'The Covenant in the Theology of Karl Barth', pp. 196–197.
53. J. Murray, *The Covenant of Grace* (London: Tyndale Press, 1954).

electing God and the elect man. We are not suggesting that this is the reason why Barth arrived at his Christological understanding of predestination. We accept that he reached his position out of deep-seated convictions about the nature of God and his grace. It is, however, a crucial element in his opposition to covenant theology and we believe that in this matter he has departed from the teaching of Scripture as well as from Calvin and the Reformed tradition.

Sixth, we would argue that Barth has failed to provide a satisfying account of the relationship between Christ and Adam. This is undoubtedly the most significant of our criticisms because it takes us to the very nub of the conflict between Barth and covenant theology. Covenant theologians argue that the relationship between Adam and Christ as spelled out by Paul in Romans 5:12–21 and in 1 Corinthians 15:12–34 (esp. vv. 21–22) requires us to structure our theology in a particular way. These passages tell us that, through the actions of the one man Adam, all became sinners and, through the actions of the one man Christ, sinners can become righteous. How are we to explain this connection? It is very difficult to read those passages in Paul without concluding that God entered into a relationship with humanity in Adam such that Adam's disobedience brought judgment not only upon himself but upon all those he represented as he stood before God in Genesis 2, namely, all humanity yet unborn. Similarly, it seems clear that God has entered into a new relationship with humanity in Christ such that what was done by Adam was reversed by Christ. Given the weaknesses of an Augustinian account of the transmission of sin, how are we to make sense of the imputation of Adam's sin and the imputation of Christ's righteousness if we do not accept some form of covenant theology? The recapitulation theory of Irenaeus is helpful in some limited ways but it does not properly handle imputation. We are not denying that there are some difficulties in the way these matters have sometimes been handled in covenant theology but our view is that most of these difficulties are removed by talking about headship theology, where the focus is firmly on two men, Adam and Christ, rather than on two covenants. We must also take care to emphasize the importance of union with Christ and not see this as an alternative account to that of headship and imputation.

Barth's natural instinct to give priority to Christ over Adam is understandable. Adam was a 'type' of the one who was to come and therefore in some fundamental sense we must view Adam in the light of Christ. Nevertheless, Christ is also the second (or last) Adam. In his desire to be Christocentric, Barth has failed to take the biblical account of history seriously. Indeed, it can perhaps be argued that one of the overall weaknesses of Barth's theology is a lack of proper 'grounding' in the redemptive–historical context set out for us in Scripture. We do understand also Barth's anxiety about the primacy of grace. As we noted earlier, the traditional account of the relationship between Adam and Christ in covenant theology has sometimes been guilty of giving the priority to law over grace and has sometimes spoken unwisely about 'merit'. We would argue, however, that these are problems which can be (and in the cases of some covenant theologians have been) resolved. These concerns certainly do not justify abandoning any concept of headship theology. In any case, as we have argued, the alternative proposals are deeply unsatisfying.

The Torrance brothers on covenant theology

Given our focus on Scottish covenant theology and given our intention to use John Murray as representing a point of departure from the traditional exposition of covenant theology, it is useful to consider the work of two prominent Scottish theologians who shared Barth's fundamental theological convictions and who were deeply opposed to covenant theology.

The various themes in Barth's theology have been taken up by many scholars but few scholars in the Barthian tradition of theology have done more to advance Barth's critique of covenant theology than T. F. Torrance and his brother J. B. Torrance. Indeed, it might fairly be said that James Torrance in particular had a single-minded passion for this subject and devoted most of his academic career to an assault on covenant theology.[54] He did this not for any abstract academic or intellectual reasons but out of a deep personal conviction that the gospel itself was fundamentally damaged by covenant theology and that this theology must be rejected if we are truly to proclaim Christ.

In the writings of J. B. Torrance there are several recurring themes, some of which are found in Barth but which Torrance spelled out in more detail. First, he argued that by placing the doctrine of election at the beginning of the theological corpus and by defining it as God's choice of certain individuals and rejection of certain other individuals, election becomes the controlling dogma and everything else is worked out from that starting point. Second, he argued

---

54. For a selection of his writings on this subject see J. B. Torrance, 'Covenant or Contract?' *SJT* 23 (1970), pp. 51–76; 'The Contribution of McLeod Campbell to Scottish Theology', *SJT* 26 (1973), pp. 295–311; 'The Covenant Concept in Scottish Theology and Politics and Its Legacy', *SJT* 34 (1981), pp. 225–243; 'Strengths and Weaknesses of the Westminster Theology', in A. I. Heron (ed.), *The Westminster Confession in the Church Today* (Edinburgh: St Andrew Press, 1982), pp. 40–54; 'The Incarnation and Limited Atonement', *EQ* 55 (1983), pp. 83–94.

that by defining election as referring to individuals rather than to Christ, the result is limited atonement and a denial of the universal scope of Christ's atoning death. Third, he argued that the doctrine of assurance is fatally damaged by this view of election because the question becomes 'How do I know that I am elect?' This results in people looking inward to themselves for 'signs of election', instead of looking outward to Christ. Torrance had a deep appreciation for John McLeod Campbell, who rejected the doctrines of election and limited atonement as defined by traditional covenant theology precisely because he discerned a lack of assurance among the members of his congregation and traced this back to these central federal doctrines.[55] Fourth, covenant theology puts nature before grace and justice before love, thus inverting the biblical order. Fifth, covenant theology makes the mistake of confusing covenant and contract, leading to a bilateral covenant whereby grace is obtained when certain conditions have been met, most notably repentance.

Most significantly, however, J. B. Torrance was concerned by covenant theology's understanding of the relationship between law and grace. Among his many criticisms of covenant theology, he argued that it involved giving priority to law over grace. In relationship to the Marrow controversy discussed in the last chapter, in which Boston and Hadow were among the principal combatants, J. B. Torrance saw clearly that Hadow was placing law before grace. Unfortunately, he then applied this criticism to covenant theology as a system. The truth is that many of his criticisms were legitimate in respect of the Hadow school but were *not* legitimate in respect of Boston, nor of covenant theology per se. Torrance argued that federal theology is based 'on contract law rather than on the grace and love of God'[56] but his critique of covenant theology fails to distinguish clearly between different types or strands of federal theology. Undoubtedly there have been covenant theologians who did (and do) put law before grace and speak of the covenant in contractual terms but such views are not of the essence of covenant theology; rather they represent a legalistic deviation from a more authentic covenant theology.

Thomas Boston's covenant theology, for example, is clearly a theology of grace, in which he teaches that even the establishment of the covenant of works was the action of a gracious God in granting to his creatures undeserved favour. Torrance finds himself in the curious position of warmly agreeing with Boston's

---

55. J. B. Torrance wrote an introduction to a new edition of Campbell's famous work in which he spelled out his theological appreciation for the work: J. M. Campbell, *The Nature of the Atonement* (Carberry: Handsel Press, 1996), pp. 1–16.

56. See Torrance, *A Critique of Federal Theology*, p. i.

theology but having to argue that he was trapped in a federal system in which his marvellous insights did not appear in their best light![57]

T. F. Torrance shared his brother's critique of covenant theology and elements of that shared critique can be seen at various points in his writing. It was, however, in one of his last publications that it came most fully to the surface. Having been asked to contribute to a history of New College, Edinburgh, he ended up writing a book on the history of Scottish theology![58] The book consists of a long spelling out of a core thesis, namely, that the gracious and biblical theology of John Calvin, John Knox and the early Reformers was fundamentally damaged by the development of covenant theology, which is not a legitimate development from that early Reformed theology but is, in fact, a serious aberration.

This 'older Scottish tradition', as represented, for example, by the Scots Confession of 1560, was incarnational and inclusivist, like the theology of Athanasius, and held to a universal atonement, like Calvin. Unfortunately there was a return to a scholastic theological model through the creation of federal theology by High Calvinists such as Perkins, Rutherford, Dickson and Durham, a conditionalist, legalistic and contractual theology which emphasized limited atonement and led to every conceivable problem, particularly the lack of assurance among Christians. John McLeod Campbell, recognizing this error, restored the 'older Scottish tradition' and suffered the consequences.

T. F. Torrance, in advocating what he regards as an Athanasian view of the incarnation, urges us to understand properly the relationship between Jesus Christ and the fallen human race. Torrance argues that, because the Son took to himself fallen human flesh, there took place ontologically in Christ a reconciliation between God and humanity. Torrance argues for this position as over against the Western, Latin view which describes the relationship between Christ and humanity in forensic or juridical categories and sees what Christ did in terms of obtaining benefits which are then passed on. This Western view also places the Father and the Son over against one another, since the Son pays the penalty for sin through being punished by the Father in the place of human beings.[59]

---

57. In private conversation with the author during doctoral supervision. The same view was taken by D. J. Bruggink, 'The Theology of Thomas Boston 1676–1732', PhD thesis, University of Edinburgh, 1956; compare also M. C. Bell, *Calvin and Scottish Theology: The Doctrine of Assurance* (Edinburgh: Handsel Press, 1985), p. 161.
58. T. F. Torrance, *Scottish Theology: From John Knox to John McLeod Campbell* (Edinburgh: T & T Clark, 1996).
59. T. F. Torrance, *God and Rationality* (Oxford: OUP, 1971), pp. 63–65.

In Torrance's view, the Western church has failed to recognize the atoning significance of the incarnation.[60]

One of the problems in Torrance's view is that if we follow the logic of his argument in which he argues that all humanity is united to Christ in an incarnational union, it is difficult to avoid universalism. Not being a universalist, he was forced to adopt the view that there were two unions with Christ, one in which all humanity is engaged (carnal union) and one in which only believers are engaged (spiritual union).[61] He said that the connection between these was a 'mystery'.

Two former doctoral students of J. B. Torrance, Trevor Hart and Baxter Kruger, have expounded in more detail this view of the relationship of human beings to Christ. Like Torrance, Hart opposed the 'benefit centred' understanding of Western theology, in both its Catholic and Protestant forms.[62] Instead he sought an incarnational and ontological understanding of the atonement. As regards the Adam–Christ parallel, he seeks to develop his position out of a starting point in the Christology of Irenaeus.[63] Hart is not a universalist either and he sees in Irenaeus a way of expressing the gospel which recognizes that not all will be saved: 'The fact that the new humanity has already been realized for us in the person of Christ does not, therefore, imply that there is no response to be made on the part of others, or that their own behaviour has become a matter of indifference.'[64] The gospel message is that we must become in ourselves what we are already in Christ. He does not use Torrance's notion of two different unions with Christ but does argue that 'There is, therefore, a first order sanctification of our humanity in its assumption by the Son of God, in which we share by virtue of our union and

---

60. Of course it is possible to hold the view that Christ took fallen humanity without accepting Torrance's understanding of incarnational redemption. See J. D. G. Dunn, *Christology in the Making: A New Testament Inquiry into the Origins of the Doctrine of the Incarnation* (2nd ed., Grand Rapids, MI: Eerdmans, 1989), pp. 110–111.
61. W. D. Rankin, 'Carnal Union with Christ in the Theology of T. F. Torrance', PhD thesis, University of Edinburgh, 1997.
62. T. A. Hart, 'Humankind in Christ and Christ in Humankind: Salvation as Participation in Our Substitute in the Theology of John Calvin', *SJT* 42, no. 1 (1989), pp. 67–74.
63. T. A. Hart, 'Irenaeus, Recapitulation and Physical Redemption', in T. A. Hart and D. P. Thimell (eds.), *Christ in Our Place: The Humanity of God in Christ for the Reconciliation of the World*, (Exeter: Paternoster, 1989), pp. 152–181.
64. Hart, 'Irenaeus, Recapitulation and Physical Redemption', p. 177.

communion with him; but there is also a second order sanctification in which we are conformed to his likeness.'[65]

Kruger, on the other hand, has no qualms about adopting a universalist position. In his article 'Jesus Christ and the Undoing of Adam' he argues that all humanity is saved in and through Christ.[66] The sin of Adam which brought sin into the world did not call forth the wrath of God but only his love. God was not angry with our first parents, simply determined that his best for them, which is to be incorporated into the very life of the Trinity, should be realized despite their wrong choice. As to the Adam–Christ parallel, he argues that Christ's reversal of Adam's work means that he entered into the reality of Adam's sin and disobedience and took it up into himself. He then went through life and death bearing that sinful nature, fundamentally changing and converting Adamic humanity and emerging victorious at the other side, the side of the resurrection. Christ did this on behalf of all human beings.

Some of this is similar to the way in which James Dunn interprets the passages under consideration. Like Torrance, Hart and Kruger, it is important for him that Christ took 'fallen humanity' rather than the humanity of Adam before the fall. He notes that, 'whatever ομοιωμα means exactly, the phrase "precise likeness of sinful flesh" must denote Jesus in his oneness with sinful man, in his complete identity with fallen Adam'.[67] That is to say, '*before he became last Adam Jesus shared wholly the lot of the first Adam*'.[68] Christ having thus taken fallen humanity upon himself, his death 'is the death of all humanity'.[69] Hence he can say that 'The divine programme for man which broke down with Adam has been run through again in Jesus – this time successfully'.[70] In spelling this out he writes, 'This total solidarity with men "in every respect" (κατα παντα) was indispensable if his glory beyond death was to be something man could share too (Heb. 2:10–18). In short, Christ could not become last Adam, progenitor of a new manhood beyond death, if he had not first been Adam, one with the manhood which the first Adam begot.'[71]

---

65. Hart, 'Irenaeus, Recapitulation and Physical Redemption', p. 177.
66. See C. Baxter Kruger, *Jesus Christ and the Undoing of Adam* (Jackson, MS: Perichoresis Press, 2001; available at http://www.perichoresis.org/downloads/jesusandundoingofadam.pdf).
67. Dunn, *Christology*, p. 112.
68. Dunn, *Christology*, pp. 112–113.
69. J. D. G. Dunn, *The Theology of Paul the Apostle* (Edinburgh: T & T Clark, 1998), p. 210.
70. Dunn, *Christology*, p. 110.
71. Dunn, *Christology*, pp. 110–111.

Dunn goes on to speak of Jesus bursting 'through the cul-de-sac of death into life'. By this he means that Christ

> went all the way with the first Adam to the end of Adam in death. But beyond death he re-emerged as a new Adam whose hallmark is life from the dead. By sinking to the depths with man in death, the depths of his present plight, he was able to catch up man in resurrection, to make it possible for God's original intention for man to be fulfilled at the last.[72]

Dunn expands on this later, saying that Christ 'becomes one with man in his sinfulness in order that by the power of his life-giving Spirit he might remould man in God's righteousness. He becomes what Adam fell to by his disobedience in order that Adam might become what Christ was exalted to by his obedience.'[73]

The problem with the views expressed by Torrance, Hart and Kruger is that what Christ has done is expressed in such universal categories that either one has to adopt desperate measures to avoid universalism (carnal and spiritual union with Christ) or one has to embrace universalism and thus reject a large element of biblical teaching. With Dunn, the problem is that one remains unsure as to precisely what he means. It is very dramatic to speak of Christ bursting through death and so on but what precisely is the connection of that event to my humanity and my life? In what sense did the one act of the one man bring justification?

Conclusions

In the light of our analysis of the critique of covenant theology offered by Barth, the Torrances and others, there are perhaps two things to be said. First, Barth's theology remains the most serious challenge to the tradition of covenant theology, not least because it seeks to integrate the doctrine of God with the exposition of reconciliation in Christ, which covenant theologians have often failed to do. Second, while there are clearly aspects of Barth's thinking on covenant which we believe to be mistaken, nevertheless there are lessons to be learned from Barth and the Torrances and others in their theological tradition, lessons which act as a useful corrective to some expressions of covenant theology.

---

72. Dunn, *Christology*, p. 111.
73. Dunn, *Christology*, p. 113.

3. JOHN MURRAY

Introduction

In the twentieth century there was a dispute within covenant theology which centred on issues of law and grace. The disputants were John Murray and Meredith Kline. Murray served as Professor of Systematic Theology at Westminster Theological Seminary. He was opposed, however, by his pupil (and later his colleague) Meredith Kline.

It is our intention to summarize and assess the views of these two men (and two schools) within Westminster Theological Seminary. We do this in order to demonstrate that the key issue between these two schools of thought within covenant theology amounts to the relative place given in the system of doctrine to law and to grace. We shall consider John Murray's view in this chapter and Meredith Kline's in the next.

John Murray

John Murray was born in the Highlands of Scotland, in Badbea, near Bonar Bridge. His schooling was at Dornoch Academy. He then served as a soldier in the First World War with the Black Watch, until he was injured and discharged in 1918, having lost an eye to a shrapnel wound. On his return he went to

Glasgow University, from which he graduated with an MA in 1923. He was also accepted as a candidate for the ministry by his own denomination, the Free Presbyterian Church of Scotland (FPC). In 1924, the FPC sent him to Princeton for further theological study, to prepare him for a future role as tutor to theological students.

When he returned from Princeton in 1927, however, he found himself embroiled in a controversy within the denomination regarding the Sabbath. The Synod of the FPC had ruled that anyone who used public transport to get to church on the Lord's Day was in breach of the fourth commandment. Murray disagreed, arguing that, although he himself did not feel able to use public transport on the Lord's Day, the desire to get to church was a worthy motive and such people should not be disciplined by the denomination. The Synod would not change its view and Murray's candidature for the ministry was terminated.

Murray took up the offer of a scholarship which he had won while at Princeton, which enabled him to do a year of postgraduate study at New College in Edinburgh. He then accepted a position as an instructor in systematic theology at Princeton Theological Seminary, as assistant to Caspar Wistar Hodge, with the proviso that he would remain only one year. At that stage he fully intended to return to Scotland. After his year in Princeton (1929–30) he was invited by Dr J. Gresham Machen to become Professor of Systematic Theology at the newly established Westminster Theological Seminary. In 1937 he became a minister of the newly formed Orthodox Presbyterian Church, also established on the initiative of Machen. Murray served at Westminster for thirty-seven years, until he retired back to Scotland at the end of 1966. In retirement he married, had a son and a daughter, preached widely and spoke at conferences and theological gatherings all over the UK and overseas. He also continued to write. He died in 1975.

Murray and the covenants

Murray was one of the finest theologians Scotland has produced and, although clearly Reformed or Calvinistic in his thinking, he was always ready to challenge the Reformed tradition if it did not conform to the Scriptures. There are some today who appear to regard the WCF as immutable and who treat it almost as if it were Scripture but Murray was not of this ilk. He recognized that theology did not end in 1647 and understood that through the Scriptures God, by his Holy Spirit, would continue to shed light on our understanding. He was convinced that covenant theology, like other aspects of Reformed theology, must always be subject to scrutiny in the light of Scripture. He wrote,

> It would not be . . . in the interests of theological conservation or theological progress for us to think that the covenant theology is in all respects definitive and that there is no further need for correction, modification, and expansion. Theology must always be undergoing reformation. The human understanding is imperfect. However architectonic may be the systematic constructions of any one generation or group of generations, there always remains the need for correction and reconstruction so that the structure may be brought into closer approximation to the Scripture and the reproduction be a more faithful transcript or reflection of the heavenly exemplar. It appears to me that the covenant theology, notwithstanding the finesse of analysis with which it was worked out and the grandeur of its articulated systematization, needs recasting. We would not presume to claim that we shall be so successful in this task that the reconstruction will displace and supersede the work of the classic covenant theologians. But with their help we may be able to contribute a little towards a more biblically articulated and formulated construction of the covenant concept and of its application to our faith, love, and hope.[1]

In other words, we are not bound to the formulations of an earlier generation if we can show that Scripture can usefully be understood in a different way. The principle *semper reformanda* (always reforming) is important in Reformed theology although it must be understood properly. We hear the language of 'reforming' a good deal today from those of a more liberal persuasion, when they produce teaching which is entirely at odds with the plain teaching of Scripture. They are inclined to justify their departure from Scripture on the grounds that they are 'listening to the Holy Spirit' or that they are following the *semper reformanda* principle. This shows a complete misunderstanding of the principle. The *semper reformanda* principle involves reforming 'according to the Scriptures' and not otherwise. Murray not only believed in the principle but he also practised it. As we shall see below, the interpretation of Genesis 2 was one of these areas where he challenged the traditional covenant theology on the basis of Scripture. Those who are resistant to any change in the formulations of Reformed theology must learn from Murray. In terms of our present discussion, for example, they must remember that the expressions 'covenant of works', 'covenant of grace' and 'covenant of redemption' do not appear in Scripture and hence are not sacrosanct. We must be open to the possibility that other ways of expressing the teaching of Scripture might be found to be more useful and accurate.

As a Scottish theologian in the Reformed tradition, it is clear that Murray was significantly influenced by Thomas Boston and his theology demonstrates

---

1. J. Murray, *The Covenant of Grace* (London: Tyndale Press, 1954), pp. 4–5.

evidence of dependence on the earlier writer. There are many similarities between these two theologians and many points of common interest. To give one example: John Murray is well known for his distinction between 'definitive' and 'progressive' sanctification[2] but, over two hundred years earlier, Boston had spoken of 'initial' sanctification and 'progressive' sanctification,[3] making essentially the same point.

In the area of covenant theology, Murray also showed some dependence on Boston. Significantly, he followed Boston in indicating that grace was at the very heart of the covenants which God made. Murray spelled out his understanding of the grace of God in the scriptural covenants, as well as his conviction regarding the fundamental unity of the covenants, in an important lecture which he delivered in Cambridge entitled 'The Covenant of Grace'. It was the Tyndale Biblical Theology Lecture for 1953 and was subsequently published in 1954.[4] Since Murray was both a systematic theologian and a fine exegete, this lecture remains an important contribution to our understanding of the covenants and of covenant theology. Noting that many of the earlier covenant theologians viewed the covenants as mutual pacts or agreements, Murray stated the purpose of his lecture in this way: 'the question is whether biblico-theological study will disclose that, in the usage of Scripture, covenant (*bĕrît* in Hebrew and *diathēkē* in Greek) may properly be interpreted in terms of a mutual pact or agreement.'[5]

With that as his starting point, Murray went on to argue that all covenants between God and human beings are unilateral (not bilateral) and are concerned with the administration of grace:

> From the beginning of God's disclosures to men in terms of covenant we find a unity of conception which is to the effect that a divine covenant is a sovereign administration of grace and of promise. It is not compact or contract or agreement that provides the constitutive or governing idea but that of dispensation in the sense of disposition. This central and basic concept is applied, however, to a variety of situations and the precise character of the grace bestowed and of the promise given differs in the differing covenant administrations. The differentiation does not reside

---

2. J. Murray, *Collected Writings of John Murray*, ed. I. Murray, vol. 2 (Edinburgh: Banner of Truth, 1977), pp. 277–317.
3. T. Boston, *The Complete Works of the Late Rev Thomas Boston*, ed. S. McMillan (London: William Tegg & Co., 1853), 1:653–661.
4. Murray, *The Covenant of Grace*.
5. Murray, *The Covenant of Grace*, p. 8.

in any deviation from this basic conception but simply consists in the differing degrees of richness and fullness of the grace bestowed and of the promise given.[6]

Murray recognizes that there were biblical covenants between human beings which were bilateral but does not believe that these provide a model for the divine–human covenants. He mentions a number of these which seem to be mutual pacts or bonds but notes, 'This does not mean the divine–human covenants are of the same type';[7] 'even should it be true that in these [human] covenants the idea of mutual compact is central, it does not follow that the idea of compact is central in or essential to the covenant relation which God constitutes with man'.[8]

He also notes that the LXX translates *bĕrît* as *diathēkē* and not as *synthēkē*, a more natural word for a mutual compact or contract.[9] In fact, he argues that even most human covenants do not have mutual compacts or contracts at their heart:

> when all the instances of merely human covenants are examined, it would definitely appear that the notion of sworn fidelity is thrust into prominence in these covenants rather than that of mutual contract. It is not the contractual terms that are in prominence so much as the solemn engagement of one person to another. To such an extent is this the case that stipulated terms of agreement need not be present at all. It is the giving of oneself over in the commitment of troth that is emphasized and the specified conditions as those upon which the engagement or commitment is contingent are not mentioned. It is the promise of unreserved fidelity, of whole-souled commitment that appears to constitute the essence of the covenant.[10]

Murray demonstrates that covenants made by human beings with God also avoid ideas of compact or contract. He writes,

> what we find in these instances is solemn, promissory commitment to faith or troth on the part of the people concerned. They bind themselves in bond to be faithful to the Lord in accordance with His revealed will. The covenant is solemn pledging of devotion to God, unreserved and unconditional commitment to His service. We are

---

6. Murray, *The Covenant of Grace*, pp. 30–31.
7. Murray, *The Covenant of Grace*, p. 9.
8. Murray, *The Covenant of Grace*, p. 9.
9. Murray, *The Covenant of Grace*, pp. 9–10.
10. Murray, *The Covenant of Grace*, p. 10.

far away from the idea of a bond as sealed on the acceptance of certain prescribed stipulations and the promise of fulfilment of these stipulations on the condition that other parties to the contract fulfil the conditions imposed upon them. The thought is rather that of unreserved, whole-souled commitment.[11]

Murray was also at pains to demonstrate that those who view the covenants principally in terms of a compact or agreement between parties have misunderstood the Scriptures. As we saw in the last chapter, J. B. Torrance consistently argued that covenant theology is misguided in that it changed covenants into contracts. Murray recognizes that some have made this mistake but emphatically neither he nor Boston did so, providing a paradigm for a covenant theology which is centred on grace.

In this lecture Murray goes through the various covenants in the Old Testament, demonstrating their fundamental continuity. As he gradually builds up the picture, he is able to define the key elements of covenant as 'a dispensation of grace to men, wholly divine in its origin, fulfilment, and confirmation'.[12]

Murray shows that the covenant with Noah was gracious, universal, unconditional, monergistic and everlasting.[13] He sums this up in these marvellous words:

these features of covenant plainly evince that this covenant is a sovereign, divine administration, that it is such in its conception, determination, disclosure, confirmation, and fulfilment, that it is an administration or dispensation of forbearance and goodness, that it is not conditioned by or dependent upon faith or obedience on the part of men. It is an administration of grace which emanates from the sovereign good pleasure of God and continues without any modification or retraction of its benefits by the immutable promise and faithfulness of God.[14]

He calls this covenant with Noah 'dispensation of grace'.[15] It is also a 'sovereign disposition'[16] since Noah's cooperation 'is quite foreign to that of pact or convention. It is the co-operation of response which the grace of the covenant constrains and demands.'[17]

---

11. Murray, *The Covenant of Grace*, p. 11.
12. Murray, *The Covenant of Grace*, p. 15.
13. Murray, *The Covenant of Grace*, pp. 12–14.
14. Murray, *The Covenant of Grace*, p. 14.
15. Murray, *The Covenant of Grace*, p. 15.
16. Murray, *The Covenant of Grace*, p. 16.
17. Murray, *The Covenant of Grace*, p. 16.

When Murray comes to consider the Abrahamic covenant he finds 'no deviation from the idea of covenant as a sovereign dispensation of grace'.[18] With regard to the possibility of 'breaking' the covenant, Murray agrees that there are 'conditions' attached to the covenant. He then says, 'but the conditions in view are not really conditions of bestowal. They are simply the reciprocal responses of faith, love and obedience, apart from which the enjoyment of the covenant blessing and of the covenant relation is inconceivable. In a word, keeping the covenant presupposes the covenant relation as established rather than the condition upon which its establishment is contingent.'[19] This means that the breaking of the covenant 'is not the failure to meet the terms of a pact nor failure to respond to the offer of favourable terms of contractual agreement. It is unfaithfulness to a relation constituted and to grace dispensed.'[20]

We might imagine that, when Murray comes to the Mosaic covenant, he will have much more difficulty in avoiding the notion of compact or mutual agreement; but not so. He is quite clear that, in its fundamental disposition, the Mosaic covenant has the same general character as the Abrahamic covenant. He does recognize that obedience is required but he notes that this is true of all the covenants. The issue is rather whether this obedience is meritorious or is necessary for the covenant to be established. He thinks not: 'Undoubtedly there is a conditional feature to the words, "If ye will obey my voice indeed, and keep my covenant". But what is conditioned upon obedience and keeping of the covenant is the enjoyment of the blessing which the covenant contemplates.'[21] Murray is able then to conclude in these words: 'we find that the Mosaic covenant also is a sovereign administration of grace, divinely initiated, established, confirmed, and fulfilled.'[22]

He notes that some have argued for the conditionality of the Mosaic covenant and have seen it 'in sharp contrast both with the Abrahamic covenant and the New Testament'.[23] Murray rejects this interpretation and notes that the deliverance from Egypt was a direct result of the Abrahamic covenant (Exod. 2:24). He agrees that, at first glance, Exodus 19:5–6 and Exodus 24:7–8 might give the impression that the covenant is conditional but denies that this can be sustained exegetically. He concludes, 'in reality there is nothing that is principally

---

18. Murray, *The Covenant of Grace*, p. 18.
19. Murray, *The Covenant of Grace*, p. 19.
20. Murray, *The Covenant of Grace*, p. 19.
21. Murray, *The Covenant of Grace*, p. 21.
22. Murray, *The Covenant of Grace*, p. 22.
23. Murray, *The Covenant of Grace*, p. 20.

different in the necessity of keeping the covenant and of obedience to God's voice, which proceeds from the Mosaic covenant, from that which is involved in the keeping required in the Abrahamic.'[24]

In respect of the Davidic covenant, Murray notes that, although God's relationship with David is not called a covenant in 2 Samuel 7:12–17, it is so called in Psalm 89 and in Psalm 132:11–12. David himself uses covenant language in 2 Samuel 23:5. Murray writes, 'No example of covenant in the Old Testament more clearly supports the thesis that covenant is sovereign promise, promise solemnized by the sanctity of an oath, immutable in its security and divinely confirmed as respects the certainty of its fulfilment.'[25]

Murray notes that the Davidic covenant promises of an 'eternal covenant' are messianic[26] and he quotes various passages from Isaiah to support this. He also quotes Malachi 3:1 and says of the Messiah, 'He comes in pursuance of the covenant promise and purpose, and He is Himself the covenant because the blessings and provisions of the covenant are to such an extent bound up with Him that He is Himself the embodiment of these blessings and of the presence of the Lord with His people which the covenant insures.'[27] Murray quotes Isaiah 54:9–10 and writes, 'This passage shows that the post-diluvian Noahic covenant provides the pattern or type of what is involved in God's covenant of peace with His people, namely, that it is an oath-bound and oath-certified assurance of irrevocable grace and promise.'[28]

In discussing covenant in the New Testament, Murray notes the significance of Zacharias's words, especially Luke 1:72–73, where the events surrounding redemption are linked to Abraham. Also the deliverance language is reminiscent of the exodus. Murray says of Zacharias, 'it is apparent that he construes the redemptive events which form the subject of his doxology as a fulfilment of the Abrahamic covenant'.[29] Murray then concludes,

> We cannot escape the inference that the redemptive accomplishment signalized by the coming of Christ found its historical prototype in the redemption from Egypt. In Zacharias' esteem it is the same fidelity to covenant promise and oath that is exemplified in the accomplishment of redemption through Christ and in the redemption from

---

24. Murray, *The Covenant of Grace*, p. 22.
25. Murray, *The Covenant of Grace*, p. 23.
26. Murray, *The Covenant of Grace*, p. 23.
27. Murray, *The Covenant of Grace*, p. 24.
28. Murray, *The Covenant of Grace*, p. 25.
29. Murray, *The Covenant of Grace*, p. 25.

Egypt by the hand of Moses and Aaron. This indicates that the undergirding principle of the thought of pious Israelites at this time was the unity and continuity of God's covenant revelation and action, a principle which came to spontaneous expression in the thanksgiving of Zacharias and bears the imprimatur of the Holy Spirit.[30]

Murray notes that in Romans 9:4 and Ephesians 2:12 the word used is 'covenants' (plural) and the Ephesians reference calls these 'covenants of promise'. Murray supports this with Galatians 3:15, 17. Thus he argues that the Abrahamic covenant is only *one* of the covenants of promise and the Mosaic covenant is another.[31]

When Murray turns to the 'new covenant', he is able to conclude that all the covenants which have gone before have a fundamental unity. He examines the language used by Jesus in relation to the Lord's Supper as a covenant in his blood (Matt. 26:28; Mark 14:24; Luke 22:20; and 1 Cor. 11:25), as well as the new-covenant language used by Paul in 2 Corinthians 3:6 and by the writer to the Hebrews in Hebrews 8:6–13. Murray sees the new covenant as the 'expansion and fulfilment of the Abrahamic' and writes, 'The new covenant in respect of its being a covenant does not differ from the Abrahamic as a sovereign administration of grace, divine in its inception, establishment, confirmation, and fulfilment.'[32] Indeed, he sees the new covenant not only as being in unity with the covenants of the Old Testament but as representing the peak and consummation of God's covenant relationship with his people:

> To whatever extent the old covenant was the means of establishing the peculiar relation of the Lord to Israel as their God and their relation to Him as His people, the new covenant places this older intimacy of relation in the shadow. For it is the new covenant *par excellence* which brings to realization the promise 'I will be to them a God, and they shall be to me a people' (Heb. viii. 10).[33]

Then Murray turns to address what could be conceived as a problem for the case he is making, namely, the contrast between the old covenant and the new covenant in Hebrews 8:6–13. How, in the light of this passage, can he sustain the argument that all of the covenants flow from grace? Murray argues that the contrast drawn in Hebrews 8 cannot be between law and grace because the old

---

30. Murray, *The Covenant of Grace*, p. 25.
31. Murray, *The Covenant of Grace*, p. 26.
32. Murray, *The Covenant of Grace*, p. 27.
33. Murray, *The Covenant of Grace*, p. 28.

covenant was gracious. How then are we to understand the contrast? Murray writes, 'the spiritual relationship which lay at the centre of the covenant grace disclosed in both the Abrahamic and Mosaic covenants reaches its ripest fruition in the new covenant. So grace is the enhancement that a comparative contrast can be stated as if it were absolute.'[34] Thus Murray can write, 'Again, the new covenant is not indifferent to law. It is not contrasted with the old because the old had law and the new has not. The superiority of the new does not consist in the abrogation of that law but in its being brought into more intimate relation to us and more effective fulfilment in us.'[35] In short, the contrast between the old and the new covenants, for Murray, appears to be between the level of blessing received. The new covenant is the 'dispenser of forgiveness of sin' (Heb. 8:12) and it 'universalizes the diffusion of knowledge' (Heb. 8:11).[36]

In emphasizing the unity of the covenants, Murray was following John Calvin, who wrote, 'The covenant made with all the patriarchs is so much like ours in substance and reality that the two are actually one and the same. Yet they differ in the mode of dispensation.'[37]

As he draws the threads of his argument together, Murray writes,

> This brings to a close our review of the evidence bearing upon the nature of God's covenant with men. From the beginning of God's disclosures to men in terms of covenant we find a unity of conception which is to the effect that a divine covenant is a sovereign administration of grace and of promise. It is not compact or contract or agreement that provides the constitutive or governing idea but that of dispensation in the sense of disposition.[38]

Driving the point home, he writes, 'The new covenant does not differ from the earlier covenants because it inaugurates this peculiar intimacy. It differs simply because it brings to the ripest and richest fruition the relationship epitomized in that promise.'[39] He then concludes by arguing that there can be no further enhancement, nor any other covenant:

---

34. Murray, *The Covenant of Grace*, p. 28.
35. Murray, *The Covenant of Grace*, p. 28.
36. Murray, *The Covenant of Grace*, pp. 28–29.
37. J. Calvin, *The Institutes of the Christian Religion*, tr. F. L. Battles, ed. J. T. McNeill, Library of Christian Classics, vols. 20 and 21 (Philadelphia, PA: Westminster Press, 1977), 2/10/2.
38. Murray, *The Covenant of Grace*, p. 30.
39. Murray, *The Covenant of Grace*, p. 31.

In this respect also the new covenant is an everlasting covenant – there is no further expansion or enrichment. The mediator of the new covenant is none other than God's own Son, the effulgence of the Father's glory and the express image of His substance, the heir of all things. He is its surety also. And because there can be no higher mediator or surety than the Lord of glory, since there can be no sacrifice more transcendent in its efficacy and finality than the sacrifice of Him who through the eternal Spirit offered Himself without spot unto God, this covenant cannot give place to another.[40]

Murray's exegesis thus leads him to affirm the unity and graciousness of God's covenantal dealings with his people. From the *protoevangelion* of Genesis 3:15 until the *eschaton* itself, God has sovereignly administered his grace and saved his people by that same grace, through faith.

The Adamic administration

Having considered Murray's general approach to the biblical covenants, as representing God's sovereign administration of grace, we must now focus in on an area where Murray offered a new interpretation of covenant theology, namely, God's dealings with humanity in Adam.

In his article 'The Adamic Administration'[41] Murray notes that Adam was created 'in the image of God, a self-conscious, free, responsible, religious agent'.[42] He was created good and righteous, such that he was 'approved and accepted by God'.[43] In other words, he stood in a right relationship to God. This righteous state would have continued indefinitely, so long as Adam had maintained his obedience to God and fulfilled his obligation 'to love and serve God with all the heart, soul, strength, and mind'.[44]

Nevertheless, as Murray points out, there were two respects in which Adam's relationship to God might be regarded as falling short of a 'higher' situation. First, Adam's position was 'a contingent situation, one of righteousness but mutably so, and likewise of justification and life. There is always the possibility of lapse on man's part and, with the lapse, loss of integrity, justification, life.'[45]

---

40. Murray, *The Covenant of Grace*, pp. 31–32.
41. Murray, *Collected Writings*, vol. 2, pp. 47–59.
42. Murray, *Collected Writings*, vol. 2, p. 47.
43. Murray, *Collected Writings*, vol. 2, p. 47.
44. Murray, *Collected Writings*, vol. 2, p. 47.
45. Murray, *Collected Writings*, vol. 2, p. 47.

The second problem is that in Adam's natural condition 'There is the absence of full-orbed communion with God in the assurance of permanent possession and increasing knowledge'.[46]

Murray notes that the specific command not to eat of the tree of the knowledge of good and evil was intended to create a new and better situation for our first parents. Effectively, they were on probation and, if they had obeyed God perfectly during that period of probation, they would have taken of the tree of life and received the gift of eternal life, from which state it would no longer have been possible to fall into sin.[47]

Like Boston, Murray also makes the point that Adam 'acted in a public capacity'.[48] Drawing attention to Romans 5:12–19 and 1 Corinthians 15:22, 45–46 Murray shows that, just as Adam's sin brought judgment and death upon the human race, so his obedience would have brought life to the human race. He puts it like this:

> Analogy is drawn between Adam and Christ. They stand in unique relations to mankind. There is none before Adam – he is the first man. There is none between – Christ is the second man. There is none after Christ – he is the last Adam (1 Cor. 15:44–49). Here we have an embracive construction of human relationships. We know also that in Christ there is representative relationship and that obedience successfully completed has its issue in righteousness, justification, life for all he represents (1 Cor. 15:22). So a period of obedience successfully completed by Adam would have secured eternal life for all represented by him.

Murray calls the relationship established by God with Adam in Genesis 2 the 'Adamic administration'. He speaks of this administration as the means through which God, 'by a special act of providence, established for man the provision whereby he might pass from the status of contingency to one of confirmed and indefectible holiness and blessedness'.[49] In other words, Adam would have been confirmed in a state in which it would have been impossible for him to sin.

Adam having disobeyed God, however, the consequences of that disobedience came upon all human beings. Only thus can we properly explain why it is that human beings are born with a sinful nature. As Murray says, 'We are sinners

---

46. Murray, *Collected Writings*, vol. 2, p. 47.
47. Murray, *Collected Writings*, vol. 2, p. 48.
48. Murray, *Collected Writings*, vol. 2, p. 49.
49. Murray, *Collected Writings*, vol. 2, p. 49.

and come into the world as such. This situation demands explanation. It cannot stand as an empirical fact. It requires the question: Why or How? It is the Adamic administration with all its implications for racial solidarity that alone provides the answer. This is the biblical answer to the universality of sin and death.'[50]

There are many points of agreement between Boston's view of the covenant of works and John Murray's Adamic administration, of which we must highlight two. The first significant point of agreement is their shared conviction that what God did in Genesis 2 (whether we call it a covenant or an administration) was an act of grace. That is to say, the establishment of this covenant or administration involved God's unmerited favour, the gracious action of a gracious God. Boston was quite clear that the covenant of works was a legal covenant and that Adam's successful completion of his probationary period would have obliged God to grant him the benefits implied in the covenant. He writes that God '[made] over to him a benefit by way of a conditional promise, which made the benefit a debt upon the performing of the condition'.[51] Yet Boston was also clear that the very decision of God to establish such a covenant was an act of grace. Notice that he is not saying that the covenant made with Adam was a covenant of grace; he is saying that God's decision to establish the covenant was itself an act of grace.

The second significant point of agreement concerned imputation. Boston and Murray are quite clear that our relationship to Adam and our relationship to Christ, as spelled out in Romans 5 and 1 Corinthians 15, are vital if we are to maintain imputed sin and imputed righteousness.

There were, however, significant disagreements between Boston and Murray and these take us to the heart of Murray's position, which we shall shortly set against the position of Meredith Kline. The first significant point of disagreement between Boston and Murray concerns whether or not it is right to call what happened in Genesis 2 a covenant. Boston, as we have seen, following the WCF, called it a covenant of works. Murray, on the other hand, called it the 'Adamic administration'. Murray clearly believed that it was possible to conceive of the headship of Adam without a covenant of works as the basis for this headship.

Boston lays out his argument in these words:

> Now it is true, we have not here the word *covenant*; yet we must not infer, that there is no covenant in this passage, more than we may deny the doctrine of the Trinity and sacraments, because those words do not occur where these things are treated of in

---

50. Murray, *Collected Writings*, vol. 2, p. 58.
51. Boston, *Complete Works*, 11:178.

scripture, nay, are not to be found in the scripture at all. But as in those cases, so here we have the thing; for the making over of a benefit to one, upon a condition, with a penalty, gone into by the party it is proposed to, is a covenant, a proper covenant, call it as you will.[52]

Murray disagrees with this argument and states his position in this way:

This administration has often been denoted 'The Covenant of Works'. There are two observations. (1) The term is not felicitous, for the reason that the elements of grace entering into the administration are not properly provided for by the term 'works'. (2) It is not designated a covenant in Scripture. Hosea 6:7 may be interpreted otherwise and does not provide the basis for such a construction of the Adamic economy. Besides, Scripture always uses the term covenant, when applied to God's administration to men, in reference to a provision that is redemptive or closely related to redemptive design. Covenant in Scripture denotes the oath-bound confirmation of promise and involves a security which the Adamic economy did not bestow.[53]

The second significant area of disagreement concerns the Mosaic law, given on Mount Sinai. One of the problems faced by covenant theologians is to interpret what Paul meant in Galatians 4:24, when he says that there are two covenants, one of which is 'from Mount Sinai'. Those who have structured their theology round a covenant of works and a covenant of grace have to explain the relationship between these covenants and this covenant from Mount Sinai. To put this in another way: when the New Testament writers speak of the 'old covenant' they are clearly referring to the Mosaic covenant and not to what happened in Genesis 2. What then is the relationship between the so-called covenant of works and the Mosaic covenant? Two main possibilities present themselves, one represented by Boston and the other by Murray.

Boston, following Herman Witsius[54] and other Reformed theologians on this matter, takes the view that Sinai was a republication of the covenant of works. Commenting on Galatians 4:24 he writes,

This covenant from Mount Sinai was the covenant of works as being opposed to the covenant of grace, namely, the law of the ten commandments, with promise and

---

52. Boston, *Complete Works*, 11:180.
53. Murray, *Collected Writings*, vol. 2, p. 49.
54. H. Witsius, *The Economy of the Covenants between God and Man: Comprehending a Complete Body of Divinity*, vol. 2 (London: T. Tegg & Son, 1837), p. 187.

sanction, as before expressed. At Sinai it was renewed indeed, but that was not its first appearance in the world.[55]

Murray, on the other hand, is not satisfied exegetically with this interpretation. He writes,

> The view that in the Mosaic covenant there was a repetition of the so-called covenant of works, current among covenant theologians, is a grave misconception and involves an erroneous construction of the Mosaic covenant, as well as fails to assess the uniqueness of the Adamic administration. The Mosaic covenant was distinctly redemptive in character and was continuous with and extensive of the Abrahamic covenants. The Adamic had no redemptive provision, nor did its promissory element have any relevance within a context that made redemption necessary.[56]

In other words, the proper way to interpret Paul's argument in Galatians 3 and 4 is to view the Mosaic covenant as a spelling out of the obligations of the Abrahamic covenant, rather than as republication of a covenant of works.

Conclusion

The covenant theology of John Murray has been taken forward and given further expression in the writings of various scholars but particularly by O. Palmer Robertson[57] and Thomas E. McComiskey.[58] These scholars have adopted the general tenor of Murray's work, especially the emphasis on grace and the unilateral nature of the divine covenants, with some development and refinement. Each of these scholars makes a contribution to the overall direction of Murray's thought. At the same time, there is some disagreement with Murray and attempts to refine his position at certain points. The details are relatively minor, however, and do not affect the overall argument.

There are, then, three significant and distinctive elements in Murray's covenant theology. First, he believes that grace comes before law, in the very act of God

---

55. Boston, *Complete Works*, 11:181.
56. Murray, *Collected Writings*, vol. 2, p. 50.
57. O. P. Robertson, *The Christ of the Covenants* (Phillipsburg, NJ: Presbyterian & Reformed, 1980).
58. T. E. McComiskey, *The Covenants of Promise: A Theology of the Old Testament Covenants* (Nottingham: IVP, 1985).

in entering into a relationship with Adam. Second, he does not like the language of a 'covenant of works', preferring instead to speak of an 'Adamic administration'. Third, he regards the Mosaic covenant as flowing out of the Abrahamic covenant as a further expansion of God's sovereign administration of grace and rejects the idea that the Mosaic covenant is a republication of a covenant of works.

4. MEREDITH KLINE

Introduction

Having considered the covenant theology of John Murray, we now turn to consider the covenant theology of Meredith Kline. This, as we shall see, stands in sharp contrast to the theology of his former teacher. We shall provide a summary of Kline's theology and then turn to the work of Michael Horton, who has been the principal theological advocate of Kline's covenant theology in recent years. Kline was an Old Testament scholar with a particular interest in the second millennium BC and so wrote in the context of those biblical and extra-biblical studies. Horton, on the other hand, is a systematic theologian. By viewing them together, we obtain a more complete picture of this particular expression of covenant theology.

Meredith Kline

Meredith G. Kline was born in 1922 in Pennsylvania and did his undergraduate work at Gordon College, from which he graduated with a BA degree. He then went to Westminster Theological Seminary from which, in 1947, he graduated with ThB and ThM degrees. In 1948 he was ordained as a minister of the Orthodox Presbyterian Church by the Presbytery of New Jersey and served for two years as Minister of Calvary OPC in Ringoes, New Jersey. In 1948 he was also appointed to teach Old Testament at Westminster Theological Seminary in Pennsylvania on a part-time basis. This became a full-time position in 1950. He completed a PhD in Assyriology and Egyptology from Dropsie College in 1956. Kline remained at Westminster until 1965, when he accepted a post at Gordon Divinity School (now Gordon-Conwell Theological Seminary), serving until 1993. From 1981 to 2003 he taught in the spring semester at Westminster Seminary California. He died in 2007.

Like Murray, Kline was a scholar who was committed to *semper reformanda* and was thus willing to disagree with the received Reformed teaching if he believed that Scripture required this. For example, with respect to the 'days' of Genesis, Kline adopted what has been called 'the framework interpretation',[1] a view he shared with other significant scholars, such as Henri Blocher.[2] This and other attempts to challenge received wisdom on the basis of Scripture attracted significant criticism. As his son, Meredith M. Kline, said at his funeral:

> Some of his ideas are not popular. He agreed with my atheist high school classmates who successfully petitioned the Supreme Court to eliminate required corporate prayer from public schools. He argued that the days of Genesis 1 were heavenly and not earthly 24-hour days. He wrote that the sabbath does not apply outside a theocracy. Some in the presbytery where he held his church membership wanted to bring charges against him, even while chemotherapy was emaciating him. He was kept from teaching where he had taught before and from publishing in normal Reformed channels.[3]

Kline's main academic work, however, was to centre on covenant theology, where he saw himself as continuing in the 'biblical theology' tradition of Geerhardus Vos. His most significant contribution to the study of covenant theology came through his interest, as an Old Testament scholar, in Ancient Near Eastern studies (henceforth ANE), particularly in the second millennium BC. His key interest was in the parallel between the Hittite suzerainty treaties and the biblical covenants. He built on the work of earlier scholars who

---

1. 'Space and Time in the Genesis Cosmogony', *Perspectives on Science and the Christian Faith* 48, no. 1 (March 1996), pp. 2–15.
2. H. Blocher, *In the Beginning: The Opening Chapters of Genesis* (Leicester: IVP, 1984).
3. http://www.opc.org/os.html?article_id=54, accessed 28 July 2015.

had explored this area of ANE studies, particularly G. E. Mendenhall and D. J. Wiseman.[4] In his *Treaty of the Great King*, Kline spells out this parallel and then constructs a theological argument concerning the nature of the biblical covenants.[5] It is a significant and scholarly work which impacted ANE studies and is highly respected even by those who do not agree with Kline's conclusions.

Kline identified three elements in the Hittite suzerainty treaties. First, there was the identification of the suzerain or lord. Second, there was an historical statement indicating the previous relationship between the suzerain and the vassal. Finally, there was a statement of the treaty obligations.[6] Kline believed that the biblical covenants followed the same pattern. At Sinai, for example, God identifies himself, 'I am the LORD your God', and then states the historical connection, 'I brought you up out of Egypt'. Finally, the two tablets of the law are given, being the covenant obligations.[7]

From this parallel with the Hittite suzerainty treaties, Kline goes on to argue that we must understand the biblical covenants as functioning in the same way. He asserts that the book of Deuteronomy was clearly written by Moses in the form of a suzerainty treaty. This enables him to argue for the integrity of the book of Deuteronomy in its present form, in opposition to many of the higher-critical theories of its origins and development. Kline also goes so far as to say that God deliberately chose to use the Hittite treaty model in devising a covenant with his chosen people:

> It would seem indisputable that the Book of Deuteronomy, not in the form of some imaginary original core but precisely in the integrity of its present form, the only one for which there is any objective evidence, exhibits the structure of the ancient suzerainty treaties in the unity and completeness of their classic pattern. That there should be a measure of oratorical and literary enrichment of the traditional legal form is natural, considering the calibre of the author and the grandeur of the occasion. And, of course, there is the conceptual adaptation inevitable in the adoption of common formal media for the expression of the unique revelation of God in the

---

4. G. E. Mendenhall, 'Covenant Forms in Israelite Tradition', *The Biblical Archaeologist* 17 (1954), pp. 3, 50–76; D. J. Wiseman, *The Vassal-Treaties of Esarhaddon* (London: British School of Archaeology in Iraq, 1958).
5. See M. G. Kline, *The Treaty of the Great King* (Grand Rapids, MI: Eerdmans, 1963).
6. M. G. Kline, 'The Two Tables of the Covenant', *WTJ* 22 (1960), pp. 133–134.
7. Kline, 'The Two Tables of the Covenant', pp. 133–134.

Scriptures. What is remarkable is the detailed extent to which God has utilized this legal instrument of human kingdoms for the definition and administration of his own redemptive reign over his people.[8]

The parallel with the Hittite suzerainty treaties also led Kline to conclude that all of the biblical covenants were bilateral, conditional law covenants, like these ancient suzerain–vassal treaties. This was one of the points of departure from those on whose work he had built, since he rejected Mendenhall's view that the covenant made with Abraham was 'different in kind' from the Mosaic covenant.[9] In his *By Oath Consigned* he spells this out in more detail. As well as rejecting Mendenhall's distinction between the Abrahamic and Mosaic covenants, Kline also rejected Murray's attempt to view all of the biblical covenants as 'promise covenants'. Kline argued that 'promise covenant' was an inadequate description of the biblical covenants:

> Historical priority belongs incontestably to law covenant since pre-redemptive covenant administration was of course strictly law administration without the element of guaranteed, inevitable blessings. By the same token promise covenant is disqualified from the outset as a systematic definition of covenant because it is obviously not comprehensive enough to embrace the pre-redemptive covenantal revelation. It remains, however, to show that law constitutes the ground structure of redemptive covenant administration and thus that a definition of covenant as generically law covenant would be applicable over the whole range of history as is necessary in a systematic theology of the covenant.[10]

In developing his theological position, not least on the basis of his ANE studies, Kline adopted three key themes: first, a particular interpretation of the biblical covenants; second, the contrast between law and grace; and third, the idea that the Mosaic covenant was a 'republication' of the covenant of works. We shall consider these in turn.

There are, however, two important points to make at the outset. First, although Kline's central focus appears to be on the covenants, this actually stems from a deeper conviction that the kingdom of God is the central motif in Christian theology. The covenants are viewed as the means (or instruments) by

---

8. M. G. Kline, 'Dynastic Covenant', *WTJ* 23 (1960), p. 14.
9. Kline, 'The Two Tables of the Covenant', p. 143.
10. M. G. Kline, *By Oath Consigned: A Reinterpretation of the Covenant Signs of Circumcision and Baptism* (Grand Rapids, MI: Eerdmans, 1968), pp. 29–30.

which God works out his kingdom.[11] Second, Kline sees the covenantal structure as underlying everything, not just the Adam–Christ parallel or the old covenant–new covenant parallel. His book *By Oath Consigned* sought to demonstrate the significance of the Hittite suzerainty treaties for the biblical covenants, not least the covenant signs of circumcision and baptism. Then, when he came to write *The Structure of Biblical Authority*,[12] a book on the authority of Scripture, one of his pressing concerns was to show that what we learn from those ancient treaties helps us in developing a theology of the canon of Scripture on a covenantal basis.

The covenants

Kline began his analysis of the biblical covenants by considering the meaning of the Hebrew word *bĕrît*, usually translated as 'covenant' and hence the equivalent of the Greek *diathēkē*. This etymological study, supported by what he learned from his ANE studies, underlined his conviction that the fundamental structure of the biblical covenants was a legal arrangement. He writes,

> Clearly a *berith* is a legal kind of arrangement, a formal disposition of a binding nature. At the heart of a *berith* is an act of commitment and the customary oath-form of this commitment reveals the religious nature of the transaction. The *berith* arrangement is no mere secular contract but rather belongs to the sacred sphere of divine witness and enforcement.[13]

There are indications that he would prefer not to use the translation 'covenant' for *bĕrît*, since that can have the connotation of 'relationship' rather than that of 'testament' (used for *diathēkē* and which he argues is closer to the real meaning of *bĕrît*). Nevertheless, for various secondary reasons, not least its widespread use, he opts to continue with 'covenant' as an appropriate translation.[14]

Without naming him, Kline rejects Murray's definition of covenant as a 'sovereign administration of grace and promise'.[15] He argues that this definition

---

11. M. G. Kline, *Kingdom Prologue: Genesis Foundations for a Covenantal Worldview* (Eugene, OR: Wipf & Stock, 2006), p. 1.
12. M. G. Kline, *The Structure of Biblical Authority* (Grand Rapids, MI: Eerdmans, 1972).
13. Kline, *Kingdom Prologue*, p. 1.
14. Kline, *Kingdom Prologue*, pp. 3–4.
15. Kline, *Kingdom Prologue*, p. 5.

is inadequate because 'there are *berith* arrangements in the Bible that are informed by the principle of works, the opposite of grace. One of these is the original order in Eden.'[16] This idea that there are some covenants which might well be described as involving 'a sovereign administration of grace' and others that are based on 'the principle of works' is a good place to begin in examining Kline's general description of the various biblical covenants. It is in *By Oath Consigned* that he provides an initial outline of his overall theological programme in relation to the covenants. Later, however, in his *Kingdom Prologue*, which might rightly be regarded as his magnum opus, he spells this out in more detail and also offers a 'revision' of some of his earlier views.[17]

In seeking to provide an overview of the entire structure of covenantal relationship, bearing in mind the priority Kline gives to the kingdom of God as the primary motif for interpreting God's relationship to his creation, he writes,

> If a general unifying term were desired it might then be Covenant of the Kingdom. For the two major divisions of the Covenant of the Kingdom our suggestions would be Covenant of Creation and Covenant of Redemption. Since the terms 'creation' and 'redemption' call attention to God's position in relation to his covenant people as their Maker and Owner-Possessor, they effectively unfold the concept of God's lordship. Moreover, these terms point to a fundamental distinguishing feature of each covenant in the distinctive kind of divine action by which each covenantal order was established.[18]

This is slightly confusing to those who are familiar with the traditional terminology of covenant theology as that has developed since the sixteenth century. What Kline here calls the 'covenant of redemption' is what might normally be called the 'covenant of grace'. The expression 'covenant of redemption' was historically used to refer to the intra-trinitarian agreement between God the Father and God the Son, to the effect that, if the Son took the place of God's elect, lived a sinless life and paid the penalty for their sins, the Father would accept his sacrifice and impute his righteousness to the elect, thereby justifying them (declaring them to be righteous) and pardoning their sins. Kline prefers to call this simply the intra-trinitarian covenant or the 'eternal covenant'.

From this starting point, Kline then speaks about the covenant of creation. He is quite happy with the terminology of a 'covenant of works' made with

---

16. Kline, *Kingdom Prologue*, p. 5.
17. Kline, *Kingdom Prologue*, p. 312.
18. Kline, *By Oath Consigned*, p. 37.

Adam, emphasizing as it does the 'principle of works', but he wants to stress that God was in covenant with humanity from the point of creation. This is partly to avoid the argument of those who 'superimpose' a covenant with Adam, as a later step, after the creation. Many covenant theologians have argued that God first created all things, including our first parents, gave them the Garden of Eden in which to live and blessed them richly, giving them all good things to enjoy. Then, at some later point, God came to Adam (described in Gen. 2:15–17) and made a covenant with him (and all humanity in him). Kline rejects this two-stage process and argues that Adam was in covenant with God from the moment of his creation and indeed that creation itself was a covenantal act of God.[19]

This covenant of creation involved a covenant of works with Adam by which, if he had obeyed the commandment not to eat of the forbidden tree, he and his posterity would have received the blessing of eternal life. This would have been achieved by his own obedience and thus by his own merit. Kline also speaks of a covenant of conferment, which represents the instrument or mechanism by which the righteousness of Adam (had he fully obeyed) would have been conferred on his posterity.

When Christ came, he too was under the covenant of works. Happily, where Adam failed, he succeeded: where Adam disobeyed, Christ was fully obedient. Through his active obedience he merited righteousness, which was passed, by a covenant of conferment, to all those whom he represented in the covenant of works, namely, the elect. His obedience to the Father was meritorious in the same way that Adam's would have been, had he remained faithful to God and obeyed the command. Through his passive obedience, Christ paid the penalty for the sins of the elect committed under the law.

The covenant with Noah is regarded as having two parts. The first part refers to the period before the flood when Noah, by his obedience, merited the favour of God. This was an aspect of the covenant of redemption. After the flood, however, God made a common-grace covenant with Noah, with humanity and with the whole of creation (including the animals). This provided the foundation for the re-establishment of the cultural mandate given to Adam in Genesis 1, by which he was given authority and dominion over the earth.

The covenant of redemption was intimated in the *protoevangelion* of Genesis 3:15 and takes a number of forms, not least the covenant with Abraham, in which the blessing comes in the form of a promise, and the covenant with the elect in Christ, when the blessings of the covenant promised to Abraham are realized and applied to God's elect.

---

19. Kline, *Kingdom Prologue*, p. 17.

Law and grace

As we have seen, Kline distinguished two types of biblical covenants: law covenants and promise covenants. The different types are distinguished by the 'oath' which forms part of the covenant-making event. Thus Kline writes,

> First, however, notice must be taken of a feature which law covenants and promise covenants have in common but which, nevertheless, being more closely analyzed, serves to distinguish clearly between the two. Every divine–human covenant in Scripture involves a sanction-sealed commitment to maintain a particular relationship or follow a stipulated course of action. In general, then, a covenant may be defined as a relationship under sanctions. The covenantal commitment is characteristically expressed by an oath sworn in the solemnities of covenant ratification. Both in the Bible and in extra-biblical documents concerned with covenant arrangements the swearing of the oath is frequently found in parallelistic explication of the idea of entering into the covenant relationship, or as a synonym for it.
>
> It is this swearing of the ratificatory oath that provides an identification mark by which we can readily distinguish in the divine covenants of Scripture between a law covenant and one of promise. For it is evident that if God swears the oath of the ratification ceremony, that particular covenantal transaction is one of promise, whereas if man is summoned to swear the oath, the particular covenant thus ratified is one of law. In view of questions that have emerged in the course of the development of Covenant Theology, it is especially to be observed that precisely because it is sworn commitment that constitutes these particular transactions 'covenants', a relationship ratified by a human oath of allegiance is a 'covenant' because of that human oath, and it is a 'covenant', therefore, quite irrespective of whether or not the arrangement happens to be at the same time an administration of divine grace and promise.[20]

This dichotomy between law and grace was vital to the overall structure of Kline's theology. We might say that he wanted to emphasize the starkness of the contrast between law and grace. He insisted that a covenant of works was established by God with Adam and that this covenant was a legal covenant. Had Adam obeyed God perfectly during his probationary period he would have merited eternal life. This would not have involved grace at any point, merely obedience to the law and the specific command of God. Thus, in the pre-fall

---

20. Kline, *By Oath Consigned*, p. 16.

period, human beings were related to God by law; only afterwards was a relationship of grace necessary. On this view, we may speak of grace only after the fall and never before. Kline did believe that we can speak of God's love and benevolence prior to the fall but that this was not grace, in the sense of being a response to demerit.

Above all, Kline's view of the relationship between law and grace was intended to protect the integrity of the doctrine of justification. Kline insists that the radical dichotomy between a law covenant and a gracious promise covenant, undergirded by the radical dichotomy between law and grace, is vital in maintaining the doctrine of justification by faith. According to Kline, where grace and law are confused, a mixture of faith and works in justification ensues, as he saw in the innovations of Norman Shepherd.[21]

Republication

When he comes to discuss the Mosaic covenant established at Sinai, Kline argues that this was a law covenant. Indeed, following a number of earlier covenant theologians, including the English Puritan John Owen,[22] he argued that the law given at Sinai was a republication of the covenant of works. To this end he believed that there was a radical discontinuity between the Abrahamic covenant and the Mosaic covenant. Having said that, he recognized that the law did not annul the promise and said that 'the law was administratively compatible with the promise':

> Paul, of course, taught that the Mosaic revelation of law made its contribution within the history of redemption to the fulfillment of the promises (Gal. 3:15ff.). The law covenant did not make the promise covenant of no effect. Somehow the law was administratively compatible with the promise. We have already had to say something about this compatibility, and it will be necessary to say more presently. But even when this compatibility has been affirmed the difference between the two covenants is not denied but rather assumed. The Sinaitic law covenant was consistent with the earlier promise, but as a covenant it did not consist in promise.[23]

---

21. See chapter 5 below.
22. J. Owen, *An Exposition of the Epistle to the Hebrews*, vol. 7, in *Works*, vol. 22 (Edinburgh: Banner of Truth, 1998), p. 78.
23. Kline, *By Oath Consigned*, p. 25.

This 'compatibility' prompted Kline, even while distinguishing the Abrahamic and Mosaic covenants, to assert with the WCF (7.5) that the Mosaic covenant was an administration of the covenant of grace.

All of Kline's teaching on the covenants moves forward to a conclusion in the new covenant made with Christ and those who are 'in him'. It is in Christ that the promises and the law are seen in their starkest contrast and where 'wrath and mercy meet'. We might express it like this: the promise covenants, such as that made with Abraham, are all fulfilled and completed in Christ, for he is the promised one to whom all of the promises from Genesis 3:15 onwards point. At the same time, the law covenants are also concluded in Christ, in the sense that he perfectly keeps the law and so obtains by his own merit that righteousness which is then imputed to the elect. Kline speaks of this as the 'law inheritance principle':

> Moreover, we distinguish between law-inheritance through human works (the inheritance principle as expressed in the Mosaic Covenant viewed as a covenant ratified exclusively by human oath and by which, as Paul affirms, man cannot actually secure the inheritance) and the expression of the law-inheritance principle that centers in the work which Christ, the covenant mediator, performs in declaration of the inherent righteousness of God as he justifies believers. It is in Christ that the principles of law and promise co-operate.[24]

Meredith Kline, one of the most significant covenant theologians of the twentieth century, through his ANE studies, his biblical theology and his convictions about law and grace, has made a massive contribution to the study of the biblical covenants. It is a contribution which puts law before grace, which emphasizes the notion of 'merit' and which brings everything together in the person and work of Christ. It is indeed a tour de force on an epic scale.

It is clear, however, that the covenant theology of Meredith Kline stands in marked contrast to that of John Murray. They shared many things in common: a commitment to Reformed theology, stemming from Calvin and the Reformed confessions; a commitment to biblical theology in the tradition of Geerhardus Vos; and a commitment to presuppositional apologetics in the tradition of Cornelius Van Til. Nevertheless, on this matter of the covenants they disagreed, with Murray emphasizing the continuity of the biblical covenants and Kline emphasizing a certain discontinuity, Murray emphasizing grace and Kline urging the importance of law.

---

24. Kline, *By Oath Consigned*, p. 30.

Michael Horton

The theology of Meredith Kline has been taken forward by a number of scholars, not least some of the academics at Westminster Seminary California. In particular, Michael Horton has become the standard-bearer for Kline's covenant theology. In his more academic books, Horton has done great service to evangelical theology by engaging with the major theologians of the day and by bringing Reformed theology into discussion with other strands of modern theology.[25] He is one of the few Reformed scholars the quality of whose work has been recognized by scholars such as John Webster, Colin Gunton, David Kelsey and others.

It is, however, in a more popular book, *Introducing Covenant Theology*, that Horton most clearly expounds his understanding of covenant theology.[26] In this book we have a faithful representation of the covenant theology of Meredith Kline. Horton is persuaded by Kline's view that everything must be viewed covenantally and traces the whole idea of covenant back into the Trinity. He writes, 'God's very existence is covenantal: Father, Son, and Holy Spirit live in unceasing devotion to each other, reaching outward beyond the Godhead to create a community of creatures serving as a giant analogy of the Godhead's relationship.'[27]

Horton also takes Kline's view that there was no period of time between the creation of human beings and the giving of the covenant. Rather, human beings were in covenant with God from the moment of their creation. His argument is that, having been created in the image of God, we are by nature in relationship with God:

> We were not just created and then *given* a covenant; we were created *as* covenant creatures – partners not in deity, to be sure, but in the drama that was about to unfold in history. As covenant creatures by nature, every person has a relationship with God. What exactly the nature of that relationship happens to be after the Fall will be taken up at some length in this book, but there can be no doubt: everyone has a relationship with God, and that relationship is covenantal.[28]

---

25. M. S. Horton, *Covenant and Eschatology: The Divine Drama* (Louisville, KY: Westminster John Knox Press, 2002); *Lord and Servant: A Covenant Christology* (Louisville, KY: Westminster John Knox Press, 2005); *Covenant and Salvation: Union with Christ* (Louisville, KY: Westminster John Knox Press, 2007).
26. M. S. Horton, *Introducing Covenant Theology* (Grand Rapids, MI: Baker, 2006).
27. Horton, *Introducing Covenant Theology*, p. 10.
28. Horton, *Introducing Covenant Theology*, p. 10.

Meredith Kline

We have already noted that Kline based a good deal of his interpretation of the biblical covenants on his work in ANE studies, notably the Hittite suzerainty treaties. We also noted that he viewed the Mosaic covenant as a republication of a covenant of works made with Adam. Not only are these two convictions at the centre of Horton's book but the very structure of the book is designed to promote them. Horton begins with the treaties of the ANE, then goes on to talk about the Mosaic covenant on Sinai and only after that does he turn his attention to the Abrahamic covenant. By dealing with the Mosaic covenant before dealing with the Abrahamic covenant, he effectively sets up a system where law comes before grace. This stands in marked contrast to the work of John Murray, who carefully and systematically worked through the biblical covenants in the precise order in which they are found in Scripture, thus showing their continuity and development.

After an introductory chapter, Horton begins chapter 2 by dealing with various ANE treaties, particularly the Hittite suzerainty treaties.[29] He uses these treaties as the template for interpreting the biblical covenants but the problem is that, having begun with the ANE treaties, he then fits the Old Testament into that background.[30] Now it is legitimate to say that the context in which a particular portion of Scripture was written is important to understanding that Scripture. The problem here is that, having begun with these treaties and having identified them as essentially law treaties, when he comes to the biblical covenants he goes straight to Sinai because that is the covenant which is most easily identifiable as a law covenant. He does not at this stage deal with the covenant with Noah or the covenant with Abraham; he goes straight to the Mosaic covenant.

If Horton's view was simply that the ANE treaties provide a useful background to help us understand the biblical covenants, then we might agree or disagree. What Horton says, however, is that when God decided to make a covenant with his people, he modelled that covenant on these ANE treaties! Thus he can write, 'it is not surprising then that God adapted the international treaty as the template for his relationship to creatures.'[31]

Horton's programme becomes clear when he then writes, 'beginning with the law, we will move through the prophets and the period between the two testaments into the New Testament era in an effort to survey the specific covenant forms that we find in Scripture'.[32] I find it astonishing that he should

---

29. Horton, *Introducing Covenant Theology*, pp. 24–28.
30. Horton, *Introducing Covenant Theology*, p. 29.
31. Horton, *Introducing Covenant Theology*, p. 29.
32. Horton, *Introducing Covenant Theology*, p. 31.

begin with the law and the prophets and then go into the New Testament, without looking at the first two covenants mentioned in Scripture, the covenants with Noah and with Abraham. It is clear that he wants to begin with law so that he can later develop a strong law/gospel contrast, in order to move forward into discussions of justification and other related doctrines. The problem with this approach, of course, is that the Scriptures do not begin with the law and they do not begin with Sinai.

Following Kline, Horton takes the view that the covenant made at Sinai was in fact a republication of the covenant made with Adam. He expresses it this way:

> after all, the covenant of works made with Adam and his posterity still requires fulfillment if anyone is to be saved. There must be a second Adam, not just a second Israel. There are both continuities and discontinuities between the covenant of works made with Adam and the republication of the works-covenant at Sinai, differences that are determined largely by changing historical contexts.[33]

Horton later expands upon this idea by making a further distinction. He writes, 'I will return to this point below in my analysis of the differences between the Suzerainty Treaty and the Royal Grant Treaty (also known as patron covenant): the former is conditional, while the latter is an unconditional promise on the part of the suzerain.'[34]

When Horton does come to the Abrahamic covenant he interprets it in the light of what he has already said about the Mosaic covenant, rather than the other way round. We shall spell out in chapter 7 our view of the relationship between the biblical covenants; suffice it to say here that, as Paul makes clear in Galatians 3, the covenant at Sinai was a spelling out of the obligations of the covenant made with Abraham. Therefore, contra Kline and Horton, we do not interpret the covenant with Abraham in the light of the covenant at Sinai, as if law was primary and grace was secondary; rather we look at Sinai in the light of the covenant with Abraham as Paul does in Galatians 3:15–18. This means, of course, that the Mosaic covenant is not a republication of the covenant of works made with Adam but rather a spelling out of the obligations of the Abrahamic covenant.

When Horton does get to Abraham (and Noah) he has to agree that the situation is completely different from that at Sinai. Having begun with ANE treaties, then moved on to Sinai and law, the Abrahamic covenant is then

---

33. Horton, *Introducing Covenant Theology*, pp. 32–33.
34. Horton, *Introducing Covenant Theology*, p. 33.

regarded as some kind of anomaly![35] If Horton had begun with Noah and Abraham, as John Murray does in his booklet *The Covenant of Grace*, this need not have happened.

It is interesting to note that, when Horton begins to speak about the fact that there two covenants in the Old Testament, one with Abraham and one on Mount Sinai, he turns to Galatians 4 rather than to Galatians 3. Having taken Galatians 4 out of the context of Galatians 3, which precedes it, he speaks of two mountains and two mothers and then says,

> a covenant of law is established at Mount Sinai, engendering an earthly Jerusalem, which is identified with Hagar the slave; and a covenant of promise is given to Abraham and his seed, engendering a heavenly Jerusalem, which is identified with Sarah the free woman. Confusion of these two covenants, Paul believed, lay at the heart of the Galatian heresy, a charge repeated by the Protestant reformers in the 16th century.[36]

This interpretation of Galatians 4 is open to challenge. Indeed, if Galatians 4 is read in the light of Galatians 3, where Paul argues for a certain continuity between the Abrahamic covenant and the Mosaic covenant, we might offer a different interpretation. Indeed, we might argue that Paul's concern was that people were treating the covenant at Sinai precisely the way that Horton does, namely, as if it were primary and not secondary. When the law is separated from its context in the Abrahamic covenant (as spelled out in Gal. 3) people then try to live according to Sinai, instead of recognizing that the key point is faith and the promise given to Abraham in the earlier covenant. If this view is correct (we shall spell it out in more detail later), then Horton's strong emphasis on law as primary is in fact precisely the problem that Paul was trying to deal with in Galatians and so Horton, instead of solving the problem, is in fact making it worse.

Even when Horton is discussing Galatians 4 he persistently puts law before grace and deals with the covenant of law before the covenant of promise. Horton's conclusion is that, 'while there certainly are more than two explicit covenants in Scripture, they can all be grouped around two *kinds* of arrangements: conditional covenants that impose obligations and unconditional covenants that announce a divine promise.'[37] Then, strikingly, Horton says, 'we

---

35. Horton, *Introducing Covenant Theology*, p. 33.
36. Horton, *Introducing Covenant Theology*, p. 35.
37. Horton, *Introducing Covenant Theology*, p. 36.

will first look at the precise nature of the Sinai covenant (a covenant of law) and then the Abrahamic covenant (a covenant of promise).'[38] The question remains: why does Horton persist in dealing first with the Mosaic covenant and only second with the Abrahamic covenant, since the Scripture has it precisely the other way round? Horton, by the very structure of his book, has trapped himself into a law/grace discussion which forces him to put Sinai before Abraham, which is precisely the wrong way round. It could be argued that this emphasis on law as the primary relationship which human beings sustain to God was one of the principal factors which led to the development of 'two-kingdom theology' among the supporters of Kline's position – but that is an argument for another day.[39]

It is not our purpose here to offer a complete review and critique of Horton's book, merely to observe that his whole approach to the covenants is so determined by, first, the Hittite suzerainty treaties and, second, the priority of law over grace that the whole picture is contrary to the clear and chronological exposition of the covenants as we find them in Scripture.

Theology of merit

In the debate between Murray and Kline, the concept of 'merit' is at the centre. Was Kline right to argue that the merit of Christ required as its implication and corollary the merit of Adam (had he remained faithful)? Is it possible to trust in the work of Christ without using 'merit' language in respect of Adam? One of Kline's disciples, Mark Karlberg, has argued that Kline's position on merit is not only correct but is vital to the doctrine of salvation.[40]

---

38. Horton, *Introducing Covenant Theology*, p. 37.
39. There is an increasing literature on this subject. See, for example: D. VanDrunen, *Living in God's Two Kingdoms: A Biblical Vision for Christianity and Culture* (Wheaton, IL: Crossway, 2010); D. VanDrunen, *Natural Law and the Two Kingdoms: A Study in the Development of Reformed Social Thought*, Emory University Studies in Law and Religion (Grand Rapids, MI: Eerdmans, 2010); D. VanDrunen, *Divine Covenants and Moral Order: A Biblical Theology of Natural Law*, Emory University Studies in Law and Religion (Grand Rapids, MI: Eerdmans, 2014); R. C. McIlhenny (ed.), *Kingdoms Apart: Engaging the Two Kingdoms Perspective* (Phillipsburg, NJ: P&R, 2012); J. Frame, *Escondido Theology: A Reformed Response to Two Kingdom Theology* (Lakeland, FL: Whitefield Media, 2011).
40. M. W. Karlberg, 'Reformed Theology as the Theology of the Covenants: The Contributions of Meredith G. Kline to Reformed Systematics', in H. Griffith and

Kline's use of the word 'merit' is very important in understanding his position, although his position has been challenged by other theologians. Indeed, it received a significant challenge from another Westminster theologian, David B. McWilliams, the first Professor of Systematic Theology at Westminster Theological Seminary's Dallas campus, which is now an independent seminary known as Redeemer Seminary.[41]

In answering the question 'Does the merit of Christ stand or fall on the merit of Adam?' McWilliams notes that Meredith Kline 'would answer the question affirmatively'.[42] McWilliams rejects this idea on several counts, most notably that God's promise and God's action far outweighed anything required of Adam. McWilliams prefers to place the meritorious obedience of the last Adam in contrast with the demerit occasioned by the fall. He writes,

> It seems that the idea of merit becomes a vital element by virtue of sin. *Demerit* was created by the Fall. Therefore, the idea of merit is *absolutely requisite* in relation to the obedience of the last Adam. It does not seem, however, that the parallelism of merit is essential to federalism and this fact does not eclipse the active obedience of Christ in the least. Since demerit comes into consideration through the Fall, the active obedience of Christ is meritorious. His active obedience is accomplished in the context of demerit.[43]

In this way, McWilliams is able to reject any notion of human merit in respect of what was required of Adam or what he might have achieved had he sustained obedience during the period of 'probation', while at the same time maintaining that the word 'merit' is appropriate for use in respect of the last Adam, Jesus Christ. This is a most helpful solution to one of the difficulties posed when considering the headship of Christ in relation to the headship of Adam. At the same time, we might well want to follow Calvin, who wished fervently that the word 'merit' had never been brought into theological discourse at all![44]

J. R. Muether (eds.), *Creator, Redeemer, Consummator: A Festschrift for Meredith G. Kline* (Eugene, OR: Wipf & Stock, 2000), pp. 235–252.

41. D. B. McWilliams, 'The Covenant Theology of the *Westminster Confession of Faith* and Recent Criticism', *WTJ* 53 (1991), pp. 109–124.
42. McWilliams, 'The Covenant Theology', p. 120.
43. McWilliams, 'The Covenant Theology', p. 121.
44. J. Calvin, *The Institutes of the Christian Religion*, tr. F. L. Battles, ed. J. T. McNeill, Library of Christian Classics, vols. 20 and 21 (Philadelphia, PA: Westminster Press, 1977), 3/15/2.

Conclusion

The view which will be presented in the remainder of this book is that, on the disputed issues, John Murray's argument is more persuasive than that of Meredith Kline. We shall take the view that Murray greatly advanced the cause of Reformed theology in three specific ways. First, Murray demonstrated that the relationship between God and Adam, together with the headship of Adam over all humanity, could be established without the necessity of a covenant to undergird and sustain it (hence our language of 'headship theology' rather than 'covenant theology'). Second, Murray showed that the key relationship is not between the so-called covenant of works and the Mosaic covenant (as a republication of the covenant of works) but rather between the Abrahamic covenant and the Mosaic covenant, the one building on the other, as described in Galatians. Third, Murray showed that grace always has priority over law and demonstrated the dangers of making law and merit to have priority. Later, we shall press that idea further and answer questions about Paul and the law.

5. THE FEDERAL VISION

Introduction

Having stated our conviction that, on the key issues between Murray and Kline, Murray's view is to be preferred, we are then faced with something of a problem. There has arisen in recent years a version of covenant theology which, in many respects, seems initially to follow in the footsteps of John Murray and to identify with some of his key concerns, yet which has been rejected by many of those who claim to stand in the Murray school of Reformed theology.

This new version of covenant theology was originally called the 'Auburn Avenue Theology' for reasons that will become apparent. More generally, it is now known as the Federal Vision (FV). In this chapter we shall provide an outline of this view and offer a critique of its key elements. It must be said at the outset, however, that there are two problems in assessing the FV. The first problem is that the FV is not a clearly defined theological perspective to which all its adherents subscribe. Rather it is a broad movement of thought with many strands, some of which contradict each other. Indeed, two particular schools of thought are now emerging within the movement, one centred around Douglas Wilson and one around Peter Leithart.

The other problem in seeking to understand the FV is that it is a modern movement which makes significant use of electronic communication. That is to say, it has carried out much of its internal debate and development not primarily in books (although there are some significant books) but at conferences, on websites and in social media. The fact that people can post a view on a blog and then change it under debate, or take a position on Facebook only later to develop it further and clarify the view previously taken, makes for an exciting, growing and constantly evolving movement. It does, however, make it difficult to assess. At best, any summary and critique will be a snapshot in time.

The reinterpretation of Reformed theology set out by proponents of the FV has been so strongly opposed by some conservative Presbyterians that heresy trials have taken place within the Presbyterian Church in America. The advocates of the FV have been accused not only of furthering the theology of Norman Shepherd but also of incorporating into their position much of the 'New Perspective' teaching, particularly as represented by N. T. Wright. The proponents of the FV have responded by saying that they are seeking to allow the text of Scripture to inform their thinking, even when this leads them away from traditional formulations and categories.

One of the problems in this debate has been that some of those who are opposed to the FV have been so determined to defend covenant theology against what they see as an attack on its fundamental principles that they have overreacted in the direction of a covenant theology which is legalistic, meritorious and ultimately contrary to a biblical doctrine of God.

Federal Vision: the key themes

Many would trace the origins of the FV as a movement to the Auburn Avenue Pastors' Conference (AAPC), which took place at Auburn Avenue Presbyterian Church in Monroe, Louisiana, in 2002. This conference initiated discussion on a series of issues within Reformed theology, including election, justification, baptism, covenant, regeneration and the church. At the AAPC in 2003 these themes were explored a little further and some of the implications of this new direction in Reformed theology were spelled out. This began to cause significant controversy within the Reformed community.

Calvin Beisner, who had close friends and respected colleagues on both sides of the emerging debate, had attended the 2003 AAPC and listened to the debate which took place there between those who were identified with the new ideas and four Reformed theologians who rejected these ideas. Beisner decided to call both sides of the controversy together, to a colloquium at Knox Theological Seminary in August 2003. At this colloquium, there was a debate between a number of the FV proponents[1] and those who thought that the FV had moved away from orthodox theology.[2] The papers of this colloquium were subsequently published and provide us with a good summary of the key issues as they were articulated at this early stage in the life of the FV.[3]

It is not possible to highlight every argument which was offered on either side in this debate but we shall consider some of what later proved to be the key issues for the FV.

Justification

Perhaps the most significant criticism of the FV was that it denied the doctrine of justification by faith 'alone'. Joseph Pipa, quoting Steve Schlissel, wrote that the proponents of the FV hold that the instrument of justification in the Old Testament is covenant faithfulness.[4] Morton Smith presented the same argument, highlighting the theology of Norman Shepherd, clearly arguing that this was the same position held by the proponents of the FV. This would later become the key issue in seeking to argue that the proponents of the FV were in breach of their confessional commitments.

It is certainly true that one of the key figures in the early days of the FV was Norman Shepherd, Murray's successor as Professor of Systematic Theology at Westminster Theological Seminary. Norman Shepherd was ultimately removed from his position at the seminary. No charge of doctrinal error was brought against him, either by the seminary or by his church, but his views caused considerable controversy within the Westminster community and its wider constituency. Ultimately his removal was on the grounds that he was 'unclear' in his teaching on justification, with particular respect to the relative place of 'faith' and 'works' in salvation.[5]

---

1. Douglas Wilson, Steve M. Schlissel, Peter J. Leithart, Rich Lusk, John Barach and Tom Trouwborst.
2. Joseph A. Pipa Jr, Chris Hutchinson, R. Fowler White, Richard D. Phillips, Morton H. Smith, Carl D. Robbins and George W. Knight.
3. E. C. Beisner, *The Auburn Avenue Theology Pros and Cons: Debating the Federal Vision* (Fort Lauderdale, FL: Knox Theological Seminary, 2004).
4. Beisner, *Auburn Avenue Theology*, p. 17.
5. For an analysis of the controversy surrounding Norman Shepherd by someone who believed that Shepherd was right and his critics were wrong, see I. A. Hewitson, *Trust and Obey: Norman Shepherd and the Justification Controversy at Westminster Theological Seminary* (distributed by Minneapolis, MN: NextStep Resources, 2011).

Shepherd later spelled out his views in more detail, setting out his understanding of what it means to be in covenant with God and the implications of this for our understanding of justification and salvation.[6] His opponents argued that his emphasis on the place of works or obedience in relation to salvation undermined the Reformed conviction that faith was the sole instrument of justification.[7] His supporters argued that he was orthodox and that he was merely laying emphasis on important scriptural themes which had been neglected in the Reformed tradition. For example, throughout Scripture there is an emphasis on obedience but Reformed theologians, afraid of falling into the categories of Roman Catholic theology, often emphasized grace to the exclusion of the need for obedience. Also, Reformed theologians have clung tenaciously to the 'solas' of the Reformation, insisting that we are saved 'by faith alone'. Shepherd wanted to take seriously the fact that the words 'faith' and 'alone' appear together in Scripture in only one place, James 2:24, which reads: 'You see that a person is justified by what he does and not by faith alone.' Reformed theologians have typically drawn their doctrine of justification 'by faith alone' from Romans and then treated this passage in James as a problem to be solved. What if they were to begin with James? Shepherd recognized the danger of falling into legalism, whereby our works become meritorious and contribute towards our salvation (a view he attributed to Roman Catholic theology), but he was also aware of the danger within Reformed theology of falling into the categories of antinomianism. His desire was to recognize the significance of passages like James 2:24 and Galatians 5:6, while holding on to faith as the sole instrument of justification.[8]

Throughout the controversy, Shepherd insisted that he believed in the orthodox doctrine of justification by faith and was merely insisting that faith is always accompanied by obedience. It is faith 'working through love' (Gal. 5:6, ESV) or, as WCF 11.2 puts it, 'Faith, thus receiving and resting on Christ and His righteousness, is the alone instrument of justification; yet is it not alone in the person justified, but is ever accompanied with all other saving graces, and is no dead faith, but worketh by love.' Shepherd's teaching has been influential among many of those who have adopted the theology of the FV.

---

6. N. Shepherd, *The Call of Grace: How the Covenant Illuminates Salvation and Evangelism* (Phillipsburg, NJ: P&R, 2000).
7. For the case that Shepherd's views were contrary to the Reformed faith and that his removal from Westminster was legitimate, see M. W. Karlberg, *The Changing of the Guard: Westminster Theological Seminary in Philadelphia* (Unicoi, TN: The Trinity Foundation, 2001).
8. Shepherd, *Call of Grace*, pp. 59–62.

Union with Christ

It is clear from the first chapter of Beisner's book that proponents of the FV hold the doctrine of union with Christ to be critical in Reformed theology. One of the disputed issues in the debate over the FV concerns the imputation of Adam's sin and the imputation of Christ's righteousness. For the FV, however, union with Christ is a more significant way of describing how we 'become the righteousness of God' (2 Cor. 5:21) than is imputation. Proponents of the FV would support the illustration, attributed to Martin Luther, that a poor woman who marries a rich man thereby becomes rich. The man does not have to transfer money to her, for the very act of union brings her a share in his riches. Some of the FV proponents do maintain a strong doctrine of imputation but the general tendency is to focus on union with Christ as serving the function which imputation serves in more traditional Reformed theology. In this regard, there is some similarity with the views of Karl Barth and of N. T. Wright.[9] In Beisner's book Pipa later criticizes those who would base our restoration on union with Christ rather than on forensic justification.[10]

Lusk later deals with the 'imputation or union with Christ' debate.[11] He does not accept Pipa's view that the choice is between union with Christ and forensic justification. He wants to insist on the forensic character of justification, while advocating a strong doctrine of union. He uses what might be regarded as very provocative language: 'my in-Christ-ness makes imputation redundant.'[12] He demonstrates that, for Calvin, the model is union not imputation and he also calls in Richard Gaffin in support of this position.[13]

When we ask regarding the nature of this union with Christ, we find Douglas Wilson arguing that union with Christ means 'inclusion in the life of the Trinity'.[14] He also says that union with Christ means union with the church: 'union with His body as it is in the world today, blemishes and

---

9. In chapter 9 we shall demonstrate the difference between Barth's understanding of union with Christ and that of Richard Gaffin and others. The primary difference is that the latter group of theologians hold to a high view of union with Christ but also a high view of imputation, refusing to see these as alternatives.
10. Beisner, *Auburn Avenue Theology*, p. 274.
11. Beisner, *Auburn Avenue Theology*, pp. 141–143.
12. Beisner, *Auburn Avenue Theology*, p. 142. As we shall see in chapter 9, however, Gaffin holds to both union with Christ and imputation, not setting these against one another.
13. Beisner, *Auburn Avenue Theology*, p. 143.
14. Beisner, *Auburn Avenue Theology*, p. 5.

all'.[15] Peter Leithart later develops this idea by expanding on what is meant by the church. He believes that the distinction between the 'visible church' and the 'invisible church' has led to the undermining of what it means to be part of the visible church on earth.[16] Leithart thus develops a very 'high' view of church membership, arguing that salvation comes through being incorporated into the saved community.[17]

Baptism

The third theme which would later be developed is the idea that baptism is the means by which believers are incorporated into Christ. Joseph Pipa, in responding to the opening statement made by Wilson at the colloquium, says that the real problem with the proponents of FV, when it comes to the doctrine of union with Christ, is the means by which this is effected. Pipa argues that the FV regards baptism as the means by which men and women are united to Christ. Pipa contrasts the covenantal union of the visible church with the saving union of the invisible church and believes that the FV confuses these.

Pipa does seem accurately to have assessed the view taken by at least some of the proponents of the FV. For example, Leithart argues that through baptism we are brought into the church and thus united to Christ as an external, objective fact.[18] This leads him to an even more controversial point (at least in Reformed circles), namely, that being united to Christ and incorporated into the church does not guarantee final salvation. He writes,

> None of this means that every one of the baptized will necessarily be part of the saved community forever. Children may rebel against the Father and be disinherited; branches may be cut from the vine; some may grieve the Spirit so that he departs from them, leaving the house desolate. Those who trust in their loving Father, abide in Christ, and keep in step with the Spirit – those who by pure grace endure to the end improving on their baptisms – they will be eternally saved.[19]

This raises the further question of how we understand the relationship between the covenant and being 'in Christ'. Schlissel touches on this matter when he speaks about the fact of the breaking of the covenant. He comes

---

15. Beisner, *Auburn Avenue Theology*, pp. 5–6.
16. Beisner, *Auburn Avenue Theology*, p. 69.
17. Beisner, *Auburn Avenue Theology*, p. 70.
18. Beisner, *Auburn Avenue Theology*, pp. 70–71.
19. Beisner, *Auburn Avenue Theology*, p. 71.

to the nub of the matter when, having noted that there were people who broke the covenant, he asks whether or not they were truly in the covenant of grace in the first place.[20] The FV proponents would say 'yes' and most of their opponents would say 'no'. That is to say, the opponents of the FV are forced to say that if someone breaks the covenant, he or she was never truly in the covenant in the first place. The FV proponents reply by asking how you can break a covenant if you were not included in it.

The issue here is whether the new covenant has both blessings and curses, as did the old covenant. Interestingly, Fowler White, writing as one of the opponents of the FV, agrees with the FV at this point. He recognizes the 'tendency toward reducing covenant to election or guaranteed promise'.[21]

On the question of the nature of baptism and what it achieves, Wilson quotes Calvin's Catechism to powerful effect:[22]

Q. My child, are you a Christian in fact as well as in name?
A. Yes, my father.
Q. How is this known to you?
A. Because I am baptized in the name of the Father, and
   of the Son and of the Holy Spirit.

Phillips is very critical of Wilson's view of baptism and provides his own understanding as to why we baptize our children. Among other things it is 'to placard God's covenant offer of salvation'.[23] Perhaps, however, Phillips' key statement in his critique of Wilson is this: 'the sacramental theology he espouses forces him to say that one may be in covenant relationship with the saving God without being saved.'[24] This becomes one of the most critical issues in the FV debate. The response to Phillips might be that Abraham's sons were 'in covenant' relationship with God, even if they were not both ultimately saved, as Romans 9:6–13 seems to teach.

In his chapter, Wilkins draws together significant biblical evidence to demonstrate that to be 'in the covenant' by baptism is to be 'in Christ'.[25] He concludes, 'covenant, therefore, is a gracious relationship, not a "potentially" gracious

---

20. Beisner, *Auburn Avenue Theology*, p. 37.
21. Beisner, *Auburn Avenue Theology*, p. 207.
22. Beisner, *Auburn Avenue Theology*, p. 234.
23. Beisner, *Auburn Avenue Theology*, p. 250.
24. Beisner, *Auburn Avenue Theology*, p. 251.
25. Beisner, *Auburn Avenue Theology*, pp. 259–265.

relationship.'[26] He then says, 'but the covenant is not "unconditional". It requires persevering faithfulness.'[27]

The covenant of works

The fourth area of dispute concerns the covenant of works. Pipa says that the denial of the covenant of works in FV theology is fraught with difficulty. He recognizes that some leading Reformed theologians have rejected the idea of a covenant of works, including John Murray, although Pipa does not name Murray.[28] Why is Pipa so strong on this point? It is because he believes that a covenantal structure is necessary to ensure the passing to all humanity of the sin of Adam. He touches on this later, in response to a chapter by Wilkins: 'by neglecting the formal arrangement of the covenant of works, he has no basis for the imputation of that sin to Adam's posterity.'[29]

Morton Smith also argues very strongly in defence of a covenant of works. Although a student of Murray, Smith seems, in this matter, to follow Meredith Kline.[30] Like Kline he argues for the priority of law over grace, speaking of 'the covenant of works (law) and the covenant of Grace (gospel)'.[31] He argues that Norman Shepherd was wrong to see the covenant of works as 'gracious' in character.[32] Yet, as we have seen, this was also the view of Boston and Murray.

Interestingly, Smith does not say that Christ fulfilled the covenant of works, as others have argued. Instead, he says, 'Christ rendered the full obedience that was demanded of man, though it was not specifically to the command of Eden. It was the same quality of obedience that was to have been exemplified in the covenant of works (Romans 5:12–21).'[33] Smith goes on to say that it is Christ's active obedience which is the 'ground of our acceptance with God' and which is imputed to us.[34] This having been imputed to us, in justification we are then 'declared' to be righteous.[35] The view presented here by Smith, that it is the 'active obedience of Christ' which is imputed to us, rather than simply

---

26. Beisner, *Auburn Avenue Theology*, p. 265.
27. Beisner, *Auburn Avenue Theology*, p. 266.
28. Beisner, *Auburn Avenue Theology*, p. 17.
29. Beisner, *Auburn Avenue Theology*, p. 274.
30. Beisner, *Auburn Avenue Theology*, p. 97.
31. Beisner, *Auburn Avenue Theology*, p. 98.
32. Beisner, *Auburn Avenue Theology*, p. 101.
33. Beisner, *Auburn Avenue Theology*, p. 104.
34. Beisner, *Auburn Avenue Theology*, p. 109.
35. Beisner, *Auburn Avenue Theology*, p. 112.

'the righteousness of Christ', would later become a very controversial point. Even as early as this colloquium we find Lusk challenging this concept.[36]

Lusk denies that a covenant of works is necessary to the gospel. He quotes Kline to the effect that to deny a pre-fall meritorious covenant of works is 'an assault on the foundations of the Gospel' and then points out that no-one pre-Reformation held this position![37] In response to the suggestion that the doctrine of justification is damaged if we deny a meritorious covenant of works, Lusk points out that John Piper rejects the covenant of works, as do most Lutherans and many Dutch Reformed theologians.[38] He goes on to provide a list of theologians who believed in a gracious Adamic covenant.[39] Lusk does believe in a covenant made with Adam, not least on the basis of Hosea 6:7, although not a covenant of 'works' and certainly not one involving 'merit'.[40] Indeed, on the question of merit, which as we saw was critical for Kline and Horton, Lusk quotes Bavinck, who opposes the idea of merit.[41] Lusk also says that to speak of Christ fulfilling the covenant of works is a very inadequate understanding of what Christ was doing[42] and comments on the 'much more' achieved by Jesus.[43]

Covenant membership

The fifth theme which was thrown up by this debate concerned covenant membership. Phillips says that a covenant is not a relationship but is rather a treaty or contract, a means of entering into a relationship. He goes further and states we cannot be 'in the covenant' but only in the covenant community.[44] He then makes a deliberately provocative statement: 'The Federal Vision says we are saved by the covenant; Reformed theology says we are saved by Christ. The Federal Vision says the covenant itself conveys a relationship of life and blessing with God; the Reformed faith says the covenant offers salvation upon the condition of faith in Christ and his gospel.'[45] Whatever criticisms might be made

---

36. Beisner, *Auburn Avenue Theology*, pp. 139–141.
37. Beisner, *Auburn Avenue Theology*, pp. 118–119.
38. Beisner, *Auburn Avenue Theology*, pp. 119–120.
39. Beisner, *Auburn Avenue Theology*, p. 120.
40. Beisner, *Auburn Avenue Theology*, p. 121.
41. Beisner, *Auburn Avenue Theology*, p. 125.
42. Beisner, *Auburn Avenue Theology*, pp. 136–137.
43. Beisner, *Auburn Avenue Theology*, p. 139.
44. Beisner, *Auburn Avenue Theology*, p. 78.
45. Beisner, *Auburn Avenue Theology*, p. 79.

of the FV, the idea that its proponents do not believe that we are saved by Christ is the kind of 'playing to the gallery' overstatement which has increasingly marked this debate. This is to say nothing of the fact that, by contrasting 'the FV says' with 'Reformed theology says', the decision has already been reached that the FV is not seen as a variation within Reformed theology, a debate within the family, but as something else altogether. We shall see the same approach below in the work of Guy Waters.

Phillips goes on to insist that the word 'Christian' should be applied only to the regenerate.[46] He does not answer the FV point (supported by Calvin's Catechism) that we cannot 'see' regeneration and that we must presume that someone is a Christian if that person is a baptized member of the church and act accordingly. He uses the language of being 'offered' the covenant, which seems to undermine the unilateral nature of the covenant. This point is taken further when Phillips says that the covenant has 'conditions' and adds, 'Until the conditions of the covenant are fulfilled' the baptized child is not in relationship with God and needs to be evangelized.[47]

To say that baptized children are not in relationship with God is an astonishing statement. It is a far cry from John Murray's view of the work of God's grace in the lives of children. He wrote,

> The argument for infant baptism rests upon the recognition that God's redemptive action and revelation in this world are covenantal. In a word, redemptive action is covenant action and redemptive revelation is covenant revelation. Embedded in this covenantal action of God is the principle that the infant seed of believers are embraced with their parents in the covenant relation and provision.[48]

After considering a number of passages of Scripture concerning children, especially where Jesus says, 'of such is the kingdom of heaven', Murray sums up their teaching in a few principles:

> These principles are: (1) that little children, even infants, are among Christ's people and are members of his body; (2) that they are members of his kingdom and therefore have been regenerated; (3) that they belong to the church, in that they are to be received as belonging to Christ, that is to say, received into the fellowship of the saints.[49]

---

46. Beisner, *Auburn Avenue Theology*, p. 79.
47. Beisner, *Auburn Avenue Theology*, p. 80.
48. J. Murray, *Christian Baptism* (Nutley, NJ: Presbyterian & Reformed, 1977), p. 2.
49. Murray, *Christian Baptism*, p. 65.

Phillips by contrast can write, 'Baptism presents God's offer of salvation within the covenant community of the church.' It 'does not itself create a new relationship with God or convey any grace that has not previously been received through faith'.[50]

Covenant, election and regeneration

Another contested issue concerns the relationship between the covenant and election and regeneration. Barach opens up a discussion on the relationship between covenant and election.[51] He challenges the view that only the elect are really in the covenant and suggests that such a view is even narrower than the position of the Westminster Confession of Faith. He also makes some interesting points on the relationship of all this to baptism and he refers to Abraham Kuyper, who taught that not every baptism is genuine. If the person is elect it is a real baptism but if the person is not elect it is a mere sprinkling with water. Barach disagrees with Kuyper and shows the theological and pastoral problems associated with this view.[52] Barach rejects the Arminian view as well as the 'truly reformed' position.[53] Having cleared the ground, he finally gives his own position: 'there is another view of the relationship between God's covenant and God's predestination. In the Bible we regularly see that God makes his covenant with believers and their households (e.g. Genesis 17).'[54] In other words, Barach wants to separate covenant from election. This is very similar to the position we shall argue for in the next chapter, when we seek to separate covenant from headship.

Barach sums up his view in this way: 'We need, then, to hold three things together. First, God has eternally predestined an unchanging number of people (but not everyone) to eternal glory with Christ. Second, God's covenant includes some who have not been predestined to eternal salvation but who will apostatize. Third, God addresses his people – including each member personally – as his chosen ones.'[55] Barach says that this is Calvin's view and also the view of the Heidelberg Catechism, as expressed in Q. and A. 54.[56]

Robbins, in response to Barach, argues that the proponents of the FV are simply representing views on the covenant which were held by Klass Schilder

---

50. Beisner, *Auburn Avenue Theology*, p. 82.
51. Beisner, *Auburn Avenue Theology*, p. 149.
52. Beisner, *Auburn Avenue Theology*, p. 150.
53. Beisner, *Auburn Avenue Theology*, p. 149.
54. Beisner, *Auburn Avenue Theology*, p. 150.
55. Beisner, *Auburn Avenue Theology*, p. 153.
56. Beisner, *Auburn Avenue Theology*, pp. 153–155.

and others in the 'liberated' churches in the Netherlands.[57] He criticizes Barach for saying that those in the covenant are 'elect'.[58]

When the discussion is extended to take in the relationship between covenant and regeneration, the issues are sharpened. Trouwborst asks a series of key questions concerning covenant children and then goes on to insist (again quoting Calvin and the Heidelberg Catechism in support) that covenant children are considered regenerate, or hold title to regeneration.[59] He then contrasts this with the view of James Henley Thornwell, who argued that covenant children are to be treated like the reprobate! He describes how Thornwell believed the church should treat covenant children:

> how is she to treat them? Precisely as she treats all other impenitent and unbelieving men – she is to exercise the power of the keys, and shut them out from the communion of saints. She is to debar them from all the privileges of the inner sanctuary . . . they are to be dealt with as the Church deals with all the enemies of God.[60]

Church and covenant

One of the most important doctrines in seeking to understand the FV is the doctrine of the church: more specifically, the doctrine of the church as the covenant people of God. In one sense it can be argued that everything centres around this doctrine. One of the most significant figures in the FV movement is Douglas Wilson and in his book *Reformed Is Not Enough* he brings together many of the themes explored in the Beisner colloquium. Part of what Wilson is trying to achieve in this volume is the defence of his own orthodoxy and that of other supporters of the FV. He insists that the proponents of the FV hold to the doctrines of the Westminster Confession of Faith, the problem being that the opponents of the FV read the WCF with Enlightenment eyes, rather than with Reformed and medieval eyes.[61]

It is interesting for our purposes, however, to note his view of the church. Wilson's key theme is the objectivity of Christian faith and the Christian church. In seeking to define what the word 'Christian' means, he says, 'membership in the Christian faith is objective – it can be photographed and

---

57. Beisner, *Auburn Avenue Theology*, p. 157.
58. Beisner, *Auburn Avenue Theology*, p. 159.
59. Beisner, *Auburn Avenue Theology*, pp. 188–195.
60. Beisner, *Auburn Avenue Theology*, p. 198.
61. D. Wilson, *Reformed Is Not Enough: Recovering the Objectivity of the Covenant* (Moscow, ID: Canon Press, 2002), pp. 7–9.

fingerprinted.'[62] Part of the problem, he argues, is the use which has been made of the 'visible church/invisible church' distinction. He writes, 'We know there is only one Church, so which is the real one? Modern evangelical Protestants have tended to say that the invisible Church is the real one, which is why we tend to have such a low view of the churches we can actually see.'[63]

Wilson speaks of the means of grace in the Old Testament and New Testament and says this: 'God never commanded men to save themselves. He always commands them to come, in sincere faith, to the means He has established. If they do so, they receive blessing through His means. If they come in unbelief they receive covenant curses. But in all ordinary cases, they are dealing with the means established by God.'[64] This leads him to say that there is no such thing as a nominal Christian: 'so there are no nominal Christians, but there are wicked and faithless Christians. These faithless Christians incur the displeasure of God because they trample underfoot the blood of the covenant by which they were sanctified.'[65]

Wilson argues that baptism saves, based on 1 Peter 3:21 and the expression in the Nicene Creed: 'one baptism for the remission of sins'. He goes to some length to justify this view on the basis of various passages of Scripture, including Acts 2:38; Acts 22:16; Titus 3:5; and Hebrews 10:19–22.[66] This, of course, combined with his high view of the church, requires him to answer questions as to how someone could be saved through baptism and membership in the church but later turn away. To that end he has an interesting chapter on apostasy, which he describes as 'a real sin'.[67] He argues that people can be Christians and then, at a later stage, apostatize. In Reformed theology more generally, with a high view of predestination, the typical response when people fall away is either to say that they were never true believers in the first place, or that they are backsliding and will return to Christ in due course.

Wilson points to all the warnings about the dangers of falling away, especially in the letter to the Hebrews, and insists that we take these seriously. He is very critical of the Reformed exegesis of these passages which sees them as hypothetical and not real warnings. He writes, 'But the Reformed have their own set of problems here. One such problem is to assume that all such warnings are

---

62. Wilson, *Reformed Is Not Enough*, p. 21.
63. Wilson, *Reformed Is Not Enough*, p. 70.
64. Wilson, *Reformed Is Not Enough*, p. 88.
65. Wilson, *Reformed Is Not Enough*, p. 97.
66. Wilson, *Reformed Is Not Enough*, pp. 100–107.
67. Wilson, *Reformed Is Not Enough*, pp. 131–140.

hypothetical. In other words, God warns His elect away from something that cannot happen to them – something like erecting a giant "beware of the cliff end" sign in the middle of Kansas.'[68] He presses the point home: 'The Reformed need to hear some other Words of Christ: "If a man abide not in me, he is cast forth as a branch." The one cast out as a branch *was a branch*, and not some bit of tumbleweed caught in the branches. So there is such a thing as genuine covenantal connection to Christ which is not salvific at the last day.'[69]

By separating election from being in the covenant, Wilson is able to take seriously the warnings in Hebrews, while at the same time recognizing that God will preserve his elect and enable them to persevere to the end. Hence he can write, 'It is important to note that the doctrine of preservation applies to the elect, not to all and sundry covenant members. Both are equally in the covenant, and both have means of preservation near at hand. The elect may neglect them, but only for a time. The nonelect neglect them at a profound level.'[70] In order to sustain this view, it is necessary for proponents of the FV to argue for a distinction between 'covenantal election' and 'special election'. That is to say, those who are in the covenant are all 'elect' in one sense but those who will ultimately be saved are 'elect' in a way which guarantees their final destiny.[71]

In terms of the day-to-day life of the church, however, we must engage with the objectivity of Christian faith and hence 'we must receive everyone who is lawfully baptized in the name of the Father, the Son, and Holy Ghost as a fellow Christian. This means that they are counted as a member of the covenant, which is not the same thing as saying that they are faithful to it.'[72] This enables Wilson to argue that there are people in the covenant who are not elect in the final eschatological sense. They are, however, in the covenant of grace, albeit under a curse. He quotes approvingly from Greg Bahnsen:

> The Covenant of Grace curses people who have the privilege of being among God's people on earth distinguished from the world and yet don't live up to what He teaches. That's why the church sometimes has to intervene, lest the church profane God's covenant and its seals. My only point is you couldn't write that unless you believed that the non-elect, who were being disciplined, are in the covenant.[73]

---

68. Wilson, *Reformed Is Not Enough*, p. 132.
69. Wilson, *Reformed Is Not Enough*, p. 133.
70. Wilson, *Reformed Is Not Enough*, p. 136.
71. Wilson, *Reformed Is Not Enough*, pp. 138–139.
72. Wilson, *Reformed Is Not Enough*, p. 142.
73. Wilson, *Reformed Is Not Enough*, p. 160.

To examine further the relationship between church and covenant, it is useful to consider a volume of essays simply entitled *The Federal Vision*. Steve Wilkins says that the purpose of the book 'is to introduce (or, more properly, to re-introduce) the modern Church to covenantal reading and thinking'.[74] Given the title, we might have expected the introduction to say that the purpose of the book was to introduce the church to the Federal Vision but not so. This highlights an important point, namely, that the proponents of the FV see themselves as simply teaching covenant theology. It is a full-blooded covenant theology, covering every aspect of life and salvation. As Wilkins writes,

> Covenant is the central teaching of the Word of God; it describes a relationship with the Triune God through Jesus Christ, His only Begotten Son. To be in covenant is to be in real communion with God, attendant with real privileges and real blessings. It is to be brought into the circle of the eternal fellowship that has always existed between Father, Son, and Spirit (John 14:23–24; 17:20–23). It is to be made partaker of the divine nature (2 Peter 1:2–4). It is to be beloved of the Father for the sake of His Son and is founded upon union with Christ (John 17:20–23).[75]

It is, however, a covenant theology which challenges traditional expressions of that theology. Wilkins goes on to say this:

> Sadly, most Christians have lost sight of the glorious reality of covenant and consequently ended up (inadvertently) looking more to their own experiences for assurances of salvation than they have to Christ. The Gospel has been abstracted and reduced to a collection of propositional statements about Christ which require intellectual assent. The Church has been reduced to an institution that is merely a place of potential blessing rather than the Spirit-filled, blessing-filled body of Christ. The sacraments have become nothing more than mere symbols that visibly picture the Gospel but do not actually accomplish anything when they are administered according to the Scriptures. To many in the Church, the covenant is a meaningless, indefinable concept which merely allows infants to be baptized (for some unknown reason).[76]

Barach, in the same volume, underlines the importance of people understanding that if they profess faith in Christ, they are part of the covenant with

---

74. S. Wilkins and D. Garner (eds.), *The Federal Vision* (Monroe, LA: Athanasius Press, 2004), p. 11.
75. Wilkins and Garner, *The Federal Vision*, p. 11.
76. Wilkins and Garner, *The Federal Vision*, p. 11.

all that this entails. They should not be asking the question, 'Am I elect?' but should rather recognize that being in the church means being in the covenant and therefore a beneficiary of all that the covenant offers. In this context, he highlights the problem of non-attendance at the Lord's Supper:

> There are churches where perhaps twenty people out of seven hundred partake of the Lord's Supper because they are taught that they need to wait to find out if they are *really* elect. They aren't sure that they are in the covenant. All God's promises are only for the covenant and the covenant, they say, is made with the elect only and they don't know if they are elect. They are given the impression that they need to wait for some kind of experience of God's grace and love to know that they are elect before they can even be confident that they were really baptized, that they are really God's covenant people, that Jesus really died for them. They need to wait for some kind of experience apart from Scripture. That is not a caricature. I wish to God that it were.[77]

Barach traces this problem to a false understanding of the covenant status of believers. He notes that

> there is another view more popular in our circles which says that only the elect, that is, only those whom God has predestined to eternal glory with Christ, are really in the covenant. Others may be in the *sphere* of the covenant. They may be *externally* in the covenant, but only those predestined to eternal glory with Christ are *really* in the covenant or *internally* in the covenant. God makes no promises, then, to those who are not predestined to eternal salvation.[78]

To resist this view, Barach uses the same argument as we saw in Douglas Wilson: namely, that there are non-elect people in the covenant. After considering some passages of Scripture, including John 15 and Hebrews 10:29, he writes this:

> Jesus teaches us that some who are in Him get cut off and burned. They apostatize and they go to Hell. Scripture tells us that not all who are in the covenant have been predestined to eternal glory with Christ. They don't end up in eternal glory, and they don't end up there because they have not been predestined to end up there.[79]

---

77. Wilkins and Garner, *The Federal Vision*, p. 19.
78. Wilkins and Garner, *The Federal Vision*, p. 20.
79. Wilkins and Garner, *The Federal Vision*, p. 22.

The Federal Vision

In a later essay, Lusk says the same thing. In a section on his view of baptism and parenting, he says very bluntly, 'a baptized person is a Christian until and unless he apostatizes.'[80]

Barach then lays out his conclusion:

> What, then, is the relationship between covenant and election? As we read Scripture we discover that the covenant includes believers and their children. Abraham and his seed are included, even the hypocrites. There are people in the covenant and in the Church who will not be in the Church on the last day but will have been cut off and burned. There are people in the covenant and in the Church whom God has not predestined to persevere to the end and to inherit eternal glory with Christ forever.[81]

Different strands

As indicated at the beginning of the chapter, those who hold to the key components of the theology of the FV also have some significant differences between them. In recent times there seem to have emerged two main strands, the one clustered around Douglas Wilson and the other around Peter Leithart.[82]

Douglas Wilson is Minister of Christ Church in Moscow, Idaho and president of the denomination to which his congregation belongs, the Communion of Reformed Evangelical Churches (CREC). He is very involved in the Christian classical education movement, both at high school and college level. He has also been involved in public debates with leading atheists. A prolific writer, although with no formal theological qualifications, he has published a number of books, writes a blog (Blog & Mablog) and is editor of *Credenda/Agenda*, a magazine which explores Reformed theology and is published both in print and online formats.

The various quotations from Wilson earlier in this chapter demonstrate that Wilson was at the very centre of the theological development of the FV. It would seem, however, that he is concerned about the direction being taken by other proponents of the FV. In particular, he is concerned that the FV view of the sacraments be solidly rooted in Scripture and in the WCF. In his earlier writings he wanted to emphasize the 'high' view of the sacraments which he

---

80. Wilkins and Garner, *The Federal Vision*, p. 112.
81. Wilkins and Garner, *The Federal Vision*, p. 23.
82. I am grateful to Steffen Jenkins for helping me to understand some of the issues surrounding these two strands of the FV.

saw in the WCF and accused Reformed Presbyterians from various denominations of playing down the efficacy of the sacraments for fear of falling into the categories of Roman Catholicism. In his *Reformed Is Not Enough* he argued that the teaching of the WCF and other confessional documents has been read through the eyes of the Enlightenment and hence its original meaning has been distorted: 'We believe ourselves to be in the process of recovering what our fathers taught from the Reformation down to the Enlightenment – that is, a Reformed and medieval mindset. We believe our opponents to be sincere Christians, but men who have erroneously made a bad truce with modernity and who have accommodated their theology to the abstract dictates of the Enlightenment.'[83]

He also argued that this was particularly true of their opponents' understanding of the sacraments as taught by the WCF. His argument was that a form of 'rationalism' had crept into Reformed Presbyterian interpretations of the WCF which undermined what it actually says: 'rationalism has made considerable inroads into the conservative wing of the Reformed faith, and the clear tendency of this rationalism is a reductionist one. Instead of a robust supernaturalism that applies to all of life (seen and understood by faith only), the clear tendency of the rationalist system is to disparage the means of grace.'[84]

Wilson then applied this critique of the influence of rationalism in Reformed theology to baptism. He quoted 1 Peter 3:18–22, in which Peter speaks of the way in which Noah and his family were 'saved through water'. Peter then says, 'and this water symbolises baptism that now saves you also – not the removal of dirt from the body but the pledge of a good conscience towards God. It saves you by the resurrection of Jesus Christ, who has gone into heaven and is at God's right hand – with angels, authorities and powers in submission to him.' For Wilson, this means what it says: that baptism saves. He writes, 'baptism in water is objective, and it establishes an objective covenant relationship with the Lord of the covenant, Jesus Christ.'[85] At the same time, he stressed that 'baptism does *not* automatically save the one baptized' and rejected both Roman Catholic teaching of baptismal regeneration and Protestant reductionism.

In more recent days, however, Wilson has been concerned that some of the FV proponents have gone a step further and seem now to be arguing that baptism does save and does bring regeneration. He seems to have in mind the work of Peter Leithart.

---

83. Wilson, *Reformed Is Not Enough*, p. 9.
84. Wilson, *Reformed Is Not Enough*, p. 85.
85. Wilson, *Reformed Is Not Enough*, p. 99.

Peter J. Leithart is President of the Theopolis Institute for Biblical, Liturgical, & Cultural Studies in Birmingham, Alabama, and formerly taught at New St Andrews College, Moscow, Idaho. He previously served as Minister of Reformed Heritage Presbyterian Church in Birmingham, Alabama, from 1989 to 1995 and of Trinity Reformed Church, Moscow, Idaho, from 2003 to 2013. Leithart is perhaps the most academically gifted and qualified of the FV proponents, with a Cambridge PhD and many publications. He has a significant interest in literary as well as in theological studies and also seeks to be a voice in the public square on the public life of America. Like Wilson he has a blog (at firstthings.com) and is a prolific writer at both academic and popular levels.

Leithart previously served as a minister in the Presbyterian Church in America (PCA) and was the subject of a heresy trial due to his advocating FV theology. At the 2007 General Assembly of the PCA a Study Committee on the Federal Vision reported and its findings were approved by the General Assembly. The report included nine declarations and five recommendations. Among other things, this report said that proponents of the FV theology should submit their views for examination by their own presbyteries, to see if they were in line with the doctrinal standards of the denomination. Peter Leithart duly submitted his own responses to the nine declarations to his presbytery, the Pacific Northwest Presbytery, and requested that presbytery conduct such an examination. In the course of this, a number of charges were laid against him. In 2011 the presbytery exonerated him of all charges.

This decision was challenged at General Assembly level and the Standing Judicial Commission (SJC) of the PCA then examined the matter. After reviewing the case, the SJC said that the Pacific Northwest Presbytery should revisit the case and reconsider its verdict. The presbytery did so and concluded once again that Leithart's views were in line with the denomination's standards, although urging that he and others should be more careful in their use of language. Complaints were raised against this decision of the Pacific Northwest Presbytery and against Leithart's theology. In 2013 the SJC agreed to deny the complaint and affirm the decision of Pacific Northwest Presbytery, hence Leithart was found not guilty of all charges.

When Leithart moved to Birmingham, Alabama, to work at the Trinity House Institute (now called the Theopolis Institute for Biblical, Liturgical, & Cultural Studies), he requested permission to 'labour outwith the bounds', in other words, to serve an institution within the bounds of the PCA Evangel Presbytery which was not an institution of the presbytery. His request was refused, hence his ordination credentials are now with the Communion of Reformed Evangelical Churches (CREC).

The key difference between Wilson and Leithart seems to be on what baptism is and what it does. Wilson argues that baptism brings us into covenantal union with Christ but regeneration and spiritual union with Christ are only for the elect. Leithart argues that baptism unites us to Christ and regenerates us and some 'branches' will later be broken off which were in fact regenerate.

In his recent book *Against the Church* Wilson makes his own position clear.[86] Having argued that baptism is the means by which people are brought into covenant with God, Wilson is careful to insist that this does not necessarily involve regeneration and spiritual union with Christ. There will be within the covenant those who are reprobate but clearly not regenerate. In pursuing this argument, he makes the distinction between 'baptism' and 'true baptism': 'True baptism is of the internal man, by the Holy Spirit, and if that is missing you do not have a Christian inwardly. You do not have a true Christian, but rather a wet member of the visible covenant.'[87] Later he says that to be in the covenant while not regenerate brings even greater condemnation. He writes, 'But the natural man, the unconverted man, the unregenerate man, is the same kind of man whether he is inside the covenant or outside it, with the difference that reprobates inside the covenant have greater condemnation.'[88]

Wilson is conscious of the problem the FV theology faces: that if you hold to a 'high' view of baptism as a means of bringing people into the covenant, yet at the same time do not accept the notion of baptismal regeneration, you must define union with Christ and regeneration very carefully. He puts it like this:

> If there are only two final destinations, Heaven or Hell, and there are, and if it is possible for baptized Christians, who have been communing since they were 'so high', with all their external papers in order, to go to Hell, and it is, and if God is sovereign over all history (which includes every biography), which He is, then we must have a robust doctrine of heart regeneration. It is the only way to make sense of the basic data.[89]

Leithart takes a somewhat different view and wants to insist that baptism not only brings people into the covenant but unites them spiritually with Christ. Whether or not it brings regeneration is less clear in his writings. Baptism has been a significant theme in Leithart's work. His 1998 PhD thesis at the University of Cambridge was entitled 'The Priesthood of the Plebs: The Baptismal

---

86. D. Wilson, *Against the Church* (Moscow, ID: Canon Press, 2013).
87. Wilson, *Against the Church*, p. 18.
88. Wilson, *Against the Church*, p. 143.
89. Wilson, *Against the Church*, pp. 34–35.

Transformation of Antique Order'. This was later published as *The Priesthood of the Plebs: A Theology of Baptism*.[90]

In his book *The Baptized Body* Leithart makes it clear that those who have been baptized are brought into union with Christ and participate in the Spirit. In answer to the question why some of the baptized continue in Christ and some do not, he points to the significance of faith:

> Everyone who is baptized – every one – is brought into the body of Christ, ordained to be a priest before God, married to Jesus, and brought into the family of the Father, into the circle of God's personal favour. Everyone who is baptized is shown favor simply by the fact of their being baptized, for being named with the Triune name and being planted in the body of Christ are undeserved favors. But that favor does not last, or it does not produce fruit, without faith. Only those who respond in faith fulfill their priestly role rightly, persevere in the marriage covenant with Christ, stay in the family, remain in the circle of God's favor. Faith is the proper response to the favor of being baptized, the proper response from first to last. It is only by faith that we remain in the body of Christ, and only by faith that the water of baptism poured out on the earth of our bodies will bear fruit.[91]

Leithart quotes some of the passages which speak of apostasy and notes that the typical Reformed response to apostasy is to say that such people were never Christians in the first place and never truly experienced the grace of God in the gospel. He points out, however, that in these various biblical quotations, those who are said to have abandoned their faith did indeed appear to have a real, if temporary, experience of God. He writes,

> Yet, all of these passages describe a real, although temporary, experience of favor, fellowship, and knowledge of God. These reprobates really were joined to Christ, really were enlightened and fed, really shared in the Spirit, and yet they did not persevere and lost what they had been given. Ultimately, these blessings and gifts are no help. Like the exorcized man who is infested with seven demons, their last state, Peter says, is worse than the first (2 Pet. 2:20). But the New Testament says pretty plainly that they have lost something real, which includes a relationship with the Spirit, union with Christ, and knowledge of the Savior.[92]

---

90. P. J. Leithart, *The Priesthood of the Plebs: A Theology of Baptism* (Eugene, OR: Wipf & Stock, 2003).
91. P. J. Leithart, *The Baptized Body* (Moscow, ID: Canon Press, 2007), p. 84.
92. Leithart, *The Baptized Body*, p. 91.

It may be too strong to suggest that the proponents of the FV are dividing into two camps but there do seem to be, at the very least, two emphases which are rather different, as represented by Wilson and Leithart.

Guy P. Waters

The most sustained critique of the FV to date is a book written by Guy Waters, now of Reformed Theological Seminary.[93] In this book Waters attempts to analyse the FV and he says that he is going to do it by comparing it with the WCF and with Scripture; the truth, however, is that really he compares the FV only with the WCF. This may be because his work originated as a study paper for the Mississippi Valley Presbytery of the Presbyterian Church in America, where the key issue was whether exponents of the FV were in breach of their ordination vows in respect of the WCF and therefore whether action could be taken against them. Let us see some examples of this method of examination.

On merit

Waters engages with the FV on the issue of merit, both the merits of Christ and the supposed merit that Adam might have achieved had he remained faithful and not fallen into sin. Unfortunately, he simply quotes from the WCF and the Larger Catechism and he does not answer the question whether or not the argument being presented by the FV people is biblical, which is surely the key point.[94] Having stated the FV view, he says, 'This is a departure from the Standards.'[95] It is the same when he engages with Peter Leithart on the question of imputation. He believes that Leithart denies the imputation of Adam's sin to his posterity. In response to Leithart's doubts whether Romans 5:12–14 actually teaches 'the historic Reformed doctrine of the imputation of Adam's sin to his posterity', Waters says that Leithart's position is not true to the historic Reformed understanding of these matters.[96] His conclusion is, 'At least one FV proponent seriously questions whether the Adamic covenant entailed the imputation of Adam's sin to his posterity in the way that the Standards frame

---

93. G. P. Waters, *The Federal Vision and Covenant Theology: A Comparative Analysis* (Phillipsburg, NJ: P&R, 2006).
94. Waters, *The Federal Vision*, pp. 40–41.
95. Waters, *The Federal Vision*, p. 57.
96. Waters, *The Federal Vision*, pp. 55–58.

The Federal Vision

that doctrine.'⁹⁷ There it is again: critique purely on the basis of the teaching of 'the Standards'.

On the New Perspective

Waters argues that the FV people are following the New Perspective on Paul (NPP) in relation to justification, instead of historic Reformed doctrine. He quotes Lusk to the effect that the NPP view of justification, particularly as seen in N. T. Wright, merely has a different way of arguing towards the same objective. Using N. T. Wright as an example, Lusk says that Wright 'uses union with Christ to do in his theology what imputation does for traditional Reformed systematics'.⁹⁸ In his critique of Lusk, Waters makes no attempt to analyse the scriptural arguments. Instead, he posits the 'traditional' view over against the 'NPP' view. That is to say, he once again opts for tradition (meaning the view of the Standards), rather than Scripture, to argue against any deviation. Waters is correct in recognizing the significance of union with Christ in FV theology and the FV proponents' conviction that union with Christ is the key element in our justification and salvation. He is also correct to recognize that, for some of them, this obviates the need for imputation. He does not, however, offer any biblical rationale for rejecting their position.

On justification

Waters quotes Lusk as saying,

> works do not justify in their own right since they can never withstand the scrutiny of God's inspection. But we will not be justified without them either. They are not merely evidential 'e.g., of our faith', but even causal or instrumental ('means') in our final salvation. Faith is the sole instrument of initial justification, but faith comes to be perfected by good works. At the last day, faith, as the solitary instrument of union with Christ, and obedience, as the fruit of our union with Christ, will be one and the same – distinguishable, yes, but separable, no.⁹⁹

Waters criticizes Lusk's view in this way:

> Lusk appears to understand our good works to be necessary to our justification. Had he said that our good works are necessary *evidences* of our justification, we could not

---

97. Waters, *The Federal Vision*, p. 58.
98. Waters, *The Federal Vision*, p. 69.
99. Waters, *The Federal Vision*, p. 89.

quibble. But Lusk explicitly uses the language of means or causality in relating our works to our justification. He argues that the language of 'evidence' is insufficient to relate works to our final justification.[100]

Waters does not consider those passages of Scripture which argue for the significance of works in relation to justification (Jas 2:24) nor does he consider those passages which say that final judgment is on the basis of works (Matt. 16:27; 25:31–46; Rom. 2:6; 1 Cor. 3:12–15; 2 Cor. 5:10; Rev. 20:12; 22:12). Simply to argue that the FV goes against the 'tradition' or the 'historic Reformed understanding' is simply not good enough.

On baptism
Waters is also critical of Norman Shepherd (whom he seems to regard as being part of the FV), particularly when Shepherd argues that,

> instead of looking at covenant from the perspective of regeneration, we ought to look at regeneration from the perspective of the covenant. When that happens, baptism, the sign and seal of the covenant, marks the point of conversion. Baptism is the moment when we see the transition from death to life and the person is saved.
>
> This is not to say that baptism accomplishes the transition from death to life, or that baptism causes a person to be born again. That is the doctrine of baptismal regeneration, which is rightly rejected by Reformed churches.[101]

In order to defend his critique of FV on baptism Waters is driven to some very questionable statements. For example, he writes, 'it is doubtful, for instance, whether such passages as Romans 6:1–3 and Galatians 3:27 have primary reference to the physical application of water baptism.'[102] This is very difficult to defend exegetically but, of course, Waters does not attempt to do so.

Critique of Waters
There are several points that we must make in relation to Waters' book. First, Waters does not always appear to know his own 'Reformed tradition'. For example, he argues that Douglas Wilson has an unacceptable understanding of the doctrine of assurance. He writes, 'at very best, Wilson has outlined in this chapter a doctrine of assurance containing two unreconciled components,

---

100. Waters, *The Federal Vision*, p. 93.
101. Waters, *The Federal Vision*, p. 104.
102. Waters, *The Federal Vision*, p. 137.

namely, subjective and objective assurance.'[103] Now it may be that the emphasis is on the word 'unreconciled' but he should at least have recognized that many of the best Reformed theologians, including Thomas Boston, have seen assurance in this two-sided manner.

The second point to make is that Waters seems to be interested in the 'Reformed tradition' only when it suits his argument. For example, Waters refers to Lusk's argument on baptism and then says,

> Lusk's argument is filled with quotations from Calvin, other 16th-century Reformers, and certain 17th-century divines. He points to these quotations as evidence that his position has some pedigree and precedent in the Reformed tradition. To engage each of these quotes *seriatim* would distract us from our primary concern: to offer an exposition and a biblical, theological, and confessional critique of the distinguishing doctrines of the FV.[104]

Having argued all the way through about the importance of the 'Reformed tradition' he now dismisses it summarily, since it does not seem to support his position.

If Waters had said that he was simply offering a 'confessional critique' of the FV, this might be justified, since there is a place for ecclesiastical assessment of a theological position against doctrinal standards. Waters asserts, however, that he is offering 'a biblical, theological, and confessional critique' and hence his dismissal of quotations from Calvin and others in this rather cavalier manner is very disappointing.

The third point follows from this and it is simply, as we have said, that the final court of appeal in every argument is the Westminster Standards and not Scripture. For example, Waters goes on to accuse Lusk of proof-texting of Calvin and other sixteenth- and seventeenth-century writers, while admitting that on a prima facie reading these quotations from Calvin and the others support Lusk's position. Despite this, Waters simply refuses to engage with them. His conclusion to this section of the argument underlines precisely the point we have been making throughout this analysis:

> to return to our main point, we have bypassed these quotations and have restricted ourselves to a single argument, the argument from the Westminster Standards. Our interest is in establishing whether Lusk's views are in accord with the teaching of the

---

103. Waters, *The Federal Vision*, p. 143.
104. Waters, *The Federal Vision*, p. 211.

Standards. Since it is *this* theological document to which ministers, elders, and members of a number of Reformed and Presbyterian confessional dominations subscribe, this document is most vital for providing a benchmark of comparison – not debatable quotations from Calvin or later writers.[105]

This is an astonishing argument, suggesting that you can pinpoint one snapshot in time (the WCF) and judge the entire Reformed position purely on that basis. Surely it is impossible to ignore those whose work led to that Confession? In any case, how can he be so sure that the WCF was right and that the earlier authors were wrong, without biblical analysis?

This is a deeply disappointing book. Waters has locked in to a very modern way of doing theology which seems to be uninterested in assessing any doctrine as over against Scripture but merely as over against the Westminster Standards. This approach severely weakens the book because it leaves the unanswered question: since the Westminster Divines were fallible human beings, how do we know if they were right on every matter? If they were not right on every matter, how can we judge that? The answer of course is that only the Scriptures have infallible authority and therefore everything must be judged against Scripture. Waters' failure to do this makes the book very weak indeed. He and others have been concerned largely with matters of discipline, which is to say that they wanted those who affirm the FV to be removed from the PCA for their lack of 'orthodox theology'.

A major weakness in modern conservative Presbyterian theology (particularly in America) is that, in many of the most controversial debates in recent years, the WCF has been the trump card, whatever Scripture might say. One might argue that the WCF has come to function in conservative Presbyterian theology in the same way as 'tradition' functions in Roman Catholic theology. This is a functional denial of the Reformation principle of the authority of Scripture.

Critique of the Federal Vision

Expressing this criticism of Waters' book does not mean that we are defending the views of the FV; we are merely asking that they be judged according to Scripture. There are some areas on which we can agree with the FV, or at least respect its proponents' attempts to bring to the centre certain biblical truths

---

105. Waters, *The Federal Vision*, p. 212.

which have often been neglected in Reformed theology. Here are some of the points where their contribution has been valuable:

First, we appreciate the recognition that modern Reformed theology, particularly in the northern hemisphere, has been more influenced by Enlightenment rationalism than it often realizes.[106] This has had two unfortunate effects on Reformed theology. One effect is that an unashamed biblical supernaturalism has been replaced by a suspicion of anything which cannot be 'explained'. Despite a commitment to believing in the miraculous, as described in Scripture, there has developed an anti-supernaturalism when faced with claims of the miraculous today. We need to listen to our brothers and sisters in the southern hemisphere who have not been affected to the same extent by rationalism (except where Western missionaries have exported it). The other unfortunate effect is that faith has become associated with assent to propositions and theology has been built on a propositional method.

Second, we can appreciate the strong emphasis in the FV theology on the doctrine of the church and the view that the church is the covenant people of God. The doctrine of the church is the weakest area in Reformed theology. It sometimes appears as if, at the Reformation, we gained a doctrine of justification but lost the doctrine of the church. The fact that any small group of Christians believe that they can rent a room and be 'a church' is a striking departure from both biblical and early church teaching. The constant splits in Protestant churches are a disgrace and the idea of 'denominations' (nowhere mentioned in Scripture but justified by arguments about 'maintaining our distinctives') is a curse. The FV theology of the church is a refreshing and encouraging view.

Third, the emphasis on a 'high' doctrine of the sacraments is a welcome alternative to the dismissive attitude to the sacraments in many Reformed churches. To hear Reformed people talk about a service of worship as if the sermon were the only thing that mattered (propositions again) and sometimes even speaking of the remainder of the service as 'the preliminaries' is deeply disturbing, especially when worship is the primary duty of the believer. To see baptism in a more biblical sense, as that which brings us into covenant with God, is refreshing. The emphasis on a more regular administration of the Lord's Supper is also to be welcomed. Calvin wanted the Lord's Supper every week, whereas in most of our Reformed churches it is a quarterly event.

Fourth, the emphasis on grace as opposed to the use of 'merit' language is most welcome and chimes with the theology of John Murray. There has

---

106. See R. Lusk, 'Paedobaptism and Baptismal Efficacy: Historic Trends and Current Controversies', in Wilkins and Garner, *The Federal Vision*, pp. 76–83.

undoubtedly crept into Reformed theology a legalism which emphasizes law instead of grace, wants to insist on 'merit' as an appropriate way of speaking about God's relationship with Adam and insists that the covenant with Moses was a 'republication of the covenant of works'. This language and these ideas are difficult to reconcile with Scripture.

At the same time, we must question some of the tenets of the FV theology and ask that further debate and dialogue take place. Among the matters which are less welcome are the following:

First, we reject the proposal that there was a covenant made with Adam and that it was a covenant of grace. We have already demonstrated the cogency of Murray's argument against viewing God's relationship with Adam in covenantal terms. Also, Murray's insistence on grace before law is most helpful but it does not mean that he would speak of a covenant of grace with Adam.

Second, the theological underpinning of the FV theology of the covenant proposes that the Trinity is a covenant community. This is far too close to social trinitarianism and undermines the unity of the persons in the Trinity and their unity of purpose and action. There are no biblical grounds whatsoever for suggesting that there was a 'covenant' relationship between Father, Son and Holy Spirit. Instead, we affirm the *opera trinitatis ad extra sunt indivisa* (the external works of the Trinity are undivided). This affirms that the whole Godhead is present in whatever God does and helps us to maintain the unity of the persons in the Trinity.

Third, it is one thing to say that baptism brings us into covenant with God but to say that it unites us with Christ is more problematic and insufficient biblical evidence has been brought forward to support this. You can break the covenant and be a branch broken off but surely you cannot be disunited from Christ. The further idea that baptism regenerates is one which most of the FV proponents reject but has been flirted with, not least by Leithart.

Fourth, the relationship between being in the covenant and being elect is one that has caused much confusion. The FV proponents argue that the covenant of grace is objective, which is to say that all covenant members are in the family of God whether or not they are elect. Thus a distinction is sometimes mooted between being elect and being covenantally elect. This needs a more substantial biblical defence before it could be considered.

Fifth, the question of imputation as over against union with Christ does seem to move in a direction more associated with neo-orthodox theology. As we shall see in our concluding chapter, it is perfectly possible to maintain, as Richard Gaffin and others have done, both union with Christ and imputation. The FV theology may be correct to reject the imputation of the active obedience of Christ but perhaps wrong to reject the imputation of the righteousness of Christ (which incorporates both his active and passive obedience).

Sixth, the most significant problem with the FV is that the emphasis on obedience and good works, however qualified and explained, does tend towards a weakening of the truth that justification is by faith alone. The best of the FV writers are very careful to insist on *sola fide* but much of the language of FV, seeking to emphasize the importance of 'obedient faith', can easily be read as undermining the doctrine of justification.

Conclusion

It may be that the proposal of this book will help alleviate some of the controversy over the FV. For example, if we argue that 'headship' is what incorporates us into either Adam or Christ but that 'covenant' is the description of God's ongoing relationship with his people, then we may be able to solve some of the difficulties associated with 'apostasy' without resorting to a visible/invisible church distinction. In other words, if we separate headship from covenant we can make sense of those passages of Scripture which suggest that some of the covenant people were rejected by God, some of them broke the covenant and therefore some of them fall away and will ultimately be lost.

PART 2:

THE PROPOSAL

In this part of the book we offer a proposal which we believe to be in keeping with the core objectives of the older covenant theology but which offers various refinements. The proposal consists of three main parts.

First, we shall argue that the language of 'covenant of works', 'covenant of redemption' and 'covenant of grace', as a division of themes around which to structure Reformed theology, is inadequate. In this we follow John Murray, who rejected the language of a 'covenant of works'.

Second, we shall argue that the parallel between Adam and Christ in 1 Corinthians 15 and Romans 5 is the key idea around which the whole Bible revolves. We shall further argue that this does not require a covenantal underpinning. The key theme is the headship of Adam and the headship of Christ, such that those who are 'in Adam' will die and those who are 'in Christ' will be made alive. Hence we advocate a 'headship theology' rather than a 'covenant theology'.

Third, we shall argue that the 'covenant' theme ought to be separated from the 'headship theology' theme. This allows the covenants to function as they do in Scripture, as representing God's relationship with his people. In particular, it allows us to argue that the Mosaic covenant is a spelling out of the obligations of the gracious Abrahamic covenant, rather than involving the 'republication' of a primal Adamic 'covenant of works'.

6. HEADSHIP THEOLOGY: ADAM AND CHRIST

Introduction

When we step back and ask what it is about the covenant of works and covenant of grace which was so central to Reformed theology as it developed in the late sixteenth century, we have to conclude that it is the parallel between Adam and Christ as recorded in 1 Corinthians 15 and Romans 5. The vital element of covenant theology is that all human beings are either 'in Adam' or 'in Christ' and that death or salvation come by means of our relationship with one or other of these 'representative heads'. In this chapter we shall argue that it is perfectly possible to maintain this representative headship without the need for a covenantal underpinning to make it work. We shall further argue that, in covenant theology, the representative headship has been smothered by the felt need to subsume it under various covenants, thus undermining rather than enhancing its importance. We shall seek to liberate this key theological concept from these strictures by demonstrating a way in which Reformed theology can retain the relationship between Adam and Christ at the centre of its understanding of creation and redemption and keep most of the strengths of covenant theology, while at the same time moving beyond the current expressions of that theology and avoiding many of its problems and mistakes. The system of theology which emerges from this partial reconstruction we are calling 'headship theology'.

In order to achieve these objectives, this chapter is divided into three parts. First, we shall consider the relevant passages in Scripture which describe the Adam–Christ parallel, namely, 1 Corinthians 15:21–22, 45–49 and Romans 5:12–21. Second, we shall review several of the most significant attempts to interpret this biblical theme theologically. Third, we shall offer 'headship theology' as an alternative to these.

The exegetical evidence

In the New Testament, various titles are given to Jesus of Nazareth, the title 'Christ' being the most significant of these. The titles 'second man' and 'last Adam', which are accorded to Jesus in 1 Corinthians 15:45–49, have, however, been somewhat neglected. One possible reason for this neglect concerns the range of opinion among scholars as to the importance for Christology of the passages in which Paul expounds this theme. Some commentators, such as Anthony Thiselton, have strongly emphasized their significance. Commenting on 1 Corinthians 15:21–22 he writes, 'The implications for Christology are startling'[1] and he notes that a number of scholars regard 15:20–28 as the most significant section in the whole epistle.[2]

Others, however, are less convinced. Commenting on the later passage, 1 Corinthians 15:45–49, Gordon Fee argues that one of the 'crucial contextual matters' to keep in mind when interpreting these verses is that 'the concern is *not* christological'.[3] Fee does not deny that Paul had what James Dunn has called an 'Adam Christology';[4] indeed he argues that 'His varied use of this theme suggests that it is a commonplace with Paul, for whom Christ stands at the beginning of the new humanity in a way analogous to, but not identical with, the way Adam stood at the beginning of the old order, both temporally and causally'.[5] Nevertheless, he does not believe that Paul has any Christological purpose in this passage. It is true, of course, that the focus in chapter 15 is on

---

1. A. C. Thiselton, *The First Epistle to the Corinthians: A Commentary on the Greek Text*, New International Greek Text Commentary (Grand Rapids, MI: Eerdmans, 2000), p. 1228.
2. Thiselton, *First Corinthians*, p. 1226.
3. G. D. Fee, *The First Epistle to the Corinthians*, New International Commentary on the New Testament (Grand Rapids, MI: Eerdmans, 1987), pp. 787–788.
4. J. D. G. Dunn, *The Theology of Paul the Apostle* (Edinburgh: T & T Clark, 1998), p. 200.
5. Fee, *The First Epistle to the Corinthians*, p. 751.

the resurrection and the resurrection body but it is very difficult to believe that Paul could use the language of these verses, especially the titles 'second man' and 'last Adam', without having *some* Christological intention. The same debate takes place over the related passage, Romans 5:12–21. Douglas Moo describes these verses as a 'passage that rivals 3:21–26 for theological importance'[6] but points out that opinions on this point vary. Whereas some see 5:12–21 as 'the logical centre of the Epistle', others see it as 'a digression'.[7]

James Dunn is in no doubt that these passages are highly significant for Christology, arguing for a recognition of Paul's 'Adam Christology'. In addition to the key 1 Corinthians and Romans passages where this 'Adam Christology' is spelled out in detail, he also sees traces of it in Hebrews 2:5–9; Romans 8:3; Galatians 4:4–5; and Philippians 2:6–8. His conclusion is that 'There does seem to have been abroad in first generation Christianity an already quite sophisticated Adam Christology'.[8] In his commentary on Romans, he goes so far as to say that Paul's 'Adam Christology' may already have been well established among the first generations of Christians, 'hence the fact that here Paul can assume the typological Adam/Christ correlation without pausing to prove it'.[9]

In order to assess whether or not Dunn, Thiselton, Moo and others are correct in their assertions of the significance of Paul's 'Adam Christology', we shall consider the key passages, beginning with 1 Corinthians 15:21–22 and 45–49.

1 Corinthians 15:21–22

In 1 Corinthians 15:21–22 Paul uses what Simon Kistemaker calls 'typical semitic parallelism' to demonstrate a relationship between Adam and Christ.[10] In fact, it is a 'double parallelism', the first parallel coming in verse 21: 'For since death came through a man, the resurrection of the dead comes also through a man.' Then the second parallel comes in verse 22: 'For as in Adam all die, so in Christ all will be made alive.'

Taken together, these two verses can be understood as saying that just as death comes to human beings through (or because of) the one man Adam, so

---

6. D. Moo, *The Epistle to the Romans*, New International Commentary on the New Testament (Grand Rapids, MI: Eerdmans, 1996), p. 314.
7. Moo, *The Epistle to the Romans*, p. 315.
8. Dunn, *The Theology of Paul the Apostle*, p. 203.
9. J. D. G. Dunn, *Romans 1–8*, Word Biblical Commentary, vol. 38a (Dallas, TX: Word, 1988), p. 279.
10. S. J. Kistemaker, *Exposition of the First Epistle to the Corinthians*, New Testament Commentary (Grand Rapids, MI: Baker, 1993), p. 22.

resurrection comes to human beings through (or because of) the one man Christ. Paul makes no attempt at this point to explain precisely how the relationship between Adam and humanity, or the relationship between Christ and humanity, is constituted, nor does he explain how these relationships operate. Clearly, however, he is seeking to expound the significance of Genesis 3 and at the same time to assert that Christ has overturned the death which comes through Adam, bringing instead resurrection. There are, however, two questions which arise from these verses. The first question relates to the double use of the word 'all' (παντες) in verse 22: 'in Adam all die . . . in Christ all will be made alive.' The second question concerns the historicity of Adam. Do these verses require us to believe in a literal, historical Adam?

Universalism?
First, then, the interpretation of Paul's use of the word 'all' in verse 22. Does this teach or imply universal salvation? Is Paul saying that all humanity will die because of Adam but that all humanity will be resurrected because of Christ? It is true that Scripture teaches a general resurrection of the dead but the commentators are almost unanimous that this is not what is being argued here. The subject of this passage is not the bodily resurrection of all human beings prior to judgment but rather the resurrection of the faithful to eternal life and blessedness. This interpretation is supported by the verse which immediately follows, where Paul identifies those who will experience resurrection as 'those who belong to Christ' (οι του Χριστου).

Commenting on the use of the word 'παντες' Kistemaker writes, 'the adjective occurs twice following the names of Adam and Christ respectively. The prepositional phrases *in Adam* and *in Christ* limit the scope of the adjective, so that all in Adam face death and all in Christ receive life through him.' This enables him to conclude, 'The adjective *all* should not be interpreted to mean that Paul teaches universal salvation. Far from it. The meaning of verse 22 is that as all those who by nature have their origin in Adam die, so all those who by faith are incorporated in Christ shall be made alive.'[11]

Geerhardus Vos makes the point that it is the universality of the modus operandi, rather than universal salvation, which is being affirmed. He writes,

> Vs.22 serves to elucidate vs.21, and in the latter verse the point of the statement is that both death and resurrection are through a man. Consequently in Vs.22 not 'παντες' by itself, but 'παντες' jointly with 'in Adam' and 'in Christ' has the emphasis; there is no

---

11. Kistemaker, *First Corinthians*, p. 550.

dying outside of Adam, there is no quickening apart from Christ. With abstract, absolute universalism this has nothing to do whatsoever.[12]

Nevertheless, some have argued otherwise. Joachim Jeremias, for example, in his exegesis of the related passage, Romans 5:12–21, attempted a universalist interpretation of justification on the basis of the Adam–Christ parallel. This was resisted by Herman Ridderbos, who noted that in Paul's preaching 'it is unthinkable to refer justification to all men without distinction'.[13]

In this chapter, following Kistemaker, Vos and Ridderbos, we take the position that the most sustainable exegesis of 1 Corinthians 15:22 can be expressed in the following paraphrase: 'all those in Adam will die, all those in Christ will be made alive.'

Historicity of Adam
The second question concerns the historicity of Adam. This is a matter much debated by the commentators, although there is a growing consensus that Paul built the parallel with Christ on the basis that both were historical figures. The position taken by Hans Conzelmann, that Paul was dependent upon Philo and was therefore referring to 'primal man' rather than to an historical Adam,[14] is no longer held to be persuasive, despite the influential appendix to his commentary on 1 Corinthians entitled 'Excursus: Adam and Primal Man'.[15] Anthony Thiselton is typical of most modern commentators when he says that 'Paul's eschatological Adam is *not* the "second" Adam of Philo; he does not allude to a myth of a primal man'.[16]

Today most commentators take the view that Paul believed Adam to be an historical individual, even if they themselves do not hold to this position. For example, C. K. Barrett notes that Paul assumed the historicity of Adam yet argues that this is 'unimportant' to the argument. The weakness of Barrett's view is perhaps revealed by the fact that he immediately felt the need to say, 'It is impossible to draw the parallel conclusion that the historicity of Christ is equally unimportant.'[17]

---

12. G. Vos, *The Pauline Eschatology* (Grand Rapids, MI: Eerdmans, 1972), p. 241.
13. H. Ridderbos, *Paul: An Outline of His Theology* (London: SPCK, 1977), p. 341 n. 32.
14. H. Conzelmann, *A Commentary on the First Epistle to the Corinthians*, tr. J. W. Leitch (Philadelphia, PA: Fortress Press, 1975), p. 269.
15. Conzelmann, *First Epistle to the Corinthians*, pp. 284–286.
16. Thiselton, *First Corinthians*, p. 1227.
17. C. K. Barrett, *The First Epistle to the Corinthians*, Black's New Testament Commentaries (2nd ed., London: A & C Black, 1971), p. 353.

In response to Barrett, we might usefully note the point made by Douglas Moo in his commentary on the related passage in Romans 5. Moo addresses the assertion that Adam is a mythical figure in this way:

> But there is every reason to think that Paul read Gen. 2 – 3 as a historical account of real people, and no reason at all for us to think we must 'demythologize' what Paul took to be real. Indeed, it is difficult to see how Paul's argument in Rom. 5:12–21 hangs together if we regard Adam as mythical. For Adam and Christ are too closely compared in this passage to think that one could be 'mythical' and the other 'historical'. We must be honest and admit that if Adam's sin is not 'real', then any argument based on the presumption that it is must fall to the ground.[18]

Some commentators not only believe that Paul is referring to an historical Adam but argue that this is required by the text. Kistemaker, for example, makes the case for an historical Adam in this way: 'In the Greek text, he placed a definite article before each name to confirm that they represent historical persons.'[19] In support of this view, he references the respected commentators Robertson and Plummer, who say that 'The article before Αδαμ and before Χριστω points to both as historical persons, each producing an effect'.[20]

There has been much recent debate on this subject of an historical Adam.[21] This has come about not least because of the developments in science and the desire of Christians to relate their theology to their understanding of the scientific discoveries made in our modern world. Peter Enns has argued that the evidence for evolution, not least the evidence which has come out of the Human Genome Project, is overwhelming and convincing. He writes, 'The Human Genome Project, completed in 2003, has shown beyond any reasonable scientific doubt that humans and primates share common ancestry.'[22] The answer to the issue which Enns proposes is to recognize that Genesis was written prior to the development

---

18. Moo, *The Epistle to the Romans*, p. 325.
19. Kistemaker, *First Corinthians*, p. 550.
20. A. Robertson and A. Plummer, *A Critical and Exegetical Commentary on the First Epistle of St Paul to the Corinthians*, International Critical Commentary (2nd ed., Edinburgh: T & T Clark, 1963 [1911]), p. 352.
21. For example, see P. Enns, *The Evolution of Adam: What the Bible Does and Doesn't Say about Human Origins* (Grand Rapids, MI: Brazos Press, 2012); William VanDoodewaard, *The Quest for the Historical Adam: Genesis, Hermeneutics and Human Origins* (Grand Rapids, MI: Reformation Heritage Books, 2015).
22. Enns, *The Evolution of Adam*, p. ix.

of a modern scientific worldview and that we should interpret it accordingly. He writes, 'It is important for future generations of Christians to have a view of the Bible where its rootedness in ancient ways of thinking is embraced as a theological positive, not a problem to be overcome.'[23] In other words, we must establish what Genesis was really saying, in the context of its ancient worldview, rather than setting it against the modern worldview as if it were speaking the same language and answering the same questions.

Others have sought to diminish the problem of conflict between Genesis and the scientific worldview in other ways, for example, by following a 'framework hypothesis' interpretation of Genesis 1 – 2. As we noted in chapter 4, this was the view taken by Meredith Kline. It is also the position adopted by Henri Blocher.[24] This enables them to recognize the scientific, particularly geological, evidence for an old earth, while at the same time maintaining that God is Creator and asserting the historicity of Adam. Blocher is able to write,

> The liquidation of sin 'once for all' in the datable, localizable event of Golgotha, on the contrary, presupposes the teaching of Genesis. Twice the same structure, instituted by God, has come into play: the organic solidarity which united the members of one humanity under its Head, and gives him power to be its representative. On both occasions it had to be a real act, otherwise the second Adam would not have been able to put right the work of the first. The obedience of the unique Man on that Good Friday has set free a great multitude because the evil which held us enslaved had its origin in history, and we all contracted it through the offence of the first man, on that first evil day. For a historical sin there is a historical redemption.[25]

This approach is deeply unsatisfying to those who hold to a literal hermeneutical interpretation of Genesis, in which they advocate a young earth and reject any form of evolution. The most recent advocate of the literal hermeneutic is William VanDoodewaard. He traces the history of the discussion over the literal, historical interpretation of Genesis and takes his stand firmly on the literal view, rejecting the consensus of modern scientific findings as contrary to Scripture and therefore invalid, either because the science is wrong or because the scientists have not taken account of cataclysmic events such as the flood.[26]

---

23. Enns, *The Evolution of Adam*, p. 145.
24. H. Blocher, *In the Beginning: The Opening Chapters of Genesis* (Leicester: IVP, 1984).
25. Blocher, *In the Beginning*, p .170.
26. VanDoodewaard, *Quest for the Historical Adam*, pp. 313–316.

In this chapter we take the position that, in order to maintain the significance of the parallel between Adam and Christ, it is necessary to follow Paul in recognizing both Adam and Christ as historical figures. This does not imply that we hold to 'young earth' theories, nor that we do not respect the findings of science. We believe, however, that we are able to maintain historicity without holding to the literal view of VanDoodewaard.

1 Corinthians 15:45–49

So far, then, based on 1 Corinthians 15:21–22, we are able to say that death comes to human beings who are 'in Adam' and resurrection comes to human beings who are 'in Christ', although Paul does not spell out the implications of this teaching. If we now move on to verses 45–49 we find that Paul develops the analogy and gives us a more detailed explanation of its meaning and significance.

In 1 Corinthians 15:45 Paul quotes the LXX version of Genesis 2:7, 'The first man Adam became a living being', and then adds the words, 'the last Adam, a life-giving spirit'. This addition to (or commentary on) the Genesis text helps to deepen and strengthen the parallel between Adam and Christ begun earlier in the chapter. It also emphasizes the overwhelming superiority of what Christ has done as over against what Adam has done. Adam 'became a living being' but Christ is the one who is 'life-giving'. The natural may have come first (v. 46) but the spiritual is much greater and more powerful. That is to say, Christ did not simply undo what Adam had done but rather has brought inestimable benefits to those who are in him.

This contrast between 'the first man Adam' (πρωτος ανθρωπος Αδαμ) and 'the last Adam' (εσχατος Αδαμ) is echoed in verse 47 where we have the contrast between 'the first man' (πρωτος ανθρωπος) and 'the second man' (δευτερος ανθρωπος). The first man, we are told, was 'earthy' or 'of the dust', whereas the second man is 'from heaven' (v. 47). Human beings are like one of these two men, because we are all either 'of the dust' or 'of heaven' (v. 48). Those who are of the earth have borne the image of the first man and those who are of heaven will bear the image of the second man (v. 49).

These verses strengthen the key element in the parallel between Adam and Christ, namely, the notion of representation. As Barrett notes, 'Neither of the two men whom he has mentioned was simply a private individual. Each was an *Adam*, a representative man; what each was, others became.'[27] Dunn refers to this 'representative significance of Jesus in Paul's theology'[28] and notes that in

---

27. Barrett, *First Epistle to the Corinthians*, pp. 376–377.
28. Dunn, *The Theology of Paul the Apostle*, p. 199.

both Romans 5 and 1 Corinthians 15 Adam and Christ are understood in a representative capacity, such that 'Christ is the eschatological counterpart of primeval Adam. Adam is the pattern or "prototype" of Christ in that each begins an epoch, and the character of each epoch is established by their action. Hence all who belong to the first epoch are "in Adam", and all who belong to the second are "in Christ" (1 Cor. 15:22).'[29]

Romans 5:12–21

If we now turn to Romans 5:12–21 we find the same parallel between Adam and Christ but used differently. As Calvin noted, in the 1 Corinthians passage Paul's concern is to use the parallel to speak of the resurrection 'in Christ' as the reward of the spiritual life, whereas 'In the fifth chapter of Romans he uses the same contrast, but with this difference, that there he is dealing with spiritual life and death'.[30] Here Paul expands even more significantly the parallel which he had earlier developed in 1 Corinthians 15. In these verses we are told that through the one act of the one man Adam, sin and death came into the world and many died because of this one man's trespass, since judgment led to condemnation. In parallel to this, we are told that through the one act of the one man Christ, the grace of God abounded for many, leading to the free gift of justification.

This is, in some respects, a very difficult passage to interpret as can be seen from the range of positions taken by the commentators. The most difficult question concerns the nature of the relationship between human beings and the two representatives and the implications of this for the transmission of sin and righteousness. No matter how we express it, there can surely be no doubt that Adam stands in a certain relationship to human beings which leads to the transmission of sin and death. Moo makes the interesting, if rather obvious, point that the entry of sin into the world is attributed by Paul to Adam not Eve. He comments: 'The fact that Paul attributes to Adam this sin is significant since he certainly knows from Genesis that the woman, Eve, sinned first (cf. 2 Cor. 11:3; 1 Tim. 2:14). Already we see that Adam is being given a status in salvation history that is not tied only to temporal priority.'[31]

John Murray argues that Adam and Christ stand as representative heads of the human race and that only by understanding this solidarity between human

---

29. Dunn, *The Theology of Paul the Apostle*, p. 200.
30. J. Calvin, *The First Epistle of Paul the Apostle to the Corinthians*, in *Calvin's Commentaries*, tr. J. W. Fraser, ed. D. W. Torrance and T. F. Torrance (Carlisle: Paternoster, 1996), p. 323.
31. Moo, *The Epistle to the Romans*, p. 319.

beings and the two 'heads' can we understand the imputation of sin and the imputation of righteousness and hence the doctrine of justification.[32] He argues that the sequence of events which lead to sin and death, together with the sequence of events which lead to righteousness and eternal life, cannot be understood outwith the context of this 'solidaric relationship'. He goes so far as to say that 'This passage is eviscerated of its governing principle if these two solidaric relationships are not appreciated, and it is futile to try to interpret the passage except in these terms'.[33]

Yet how precisely does Adam affect future humans? Some, like Fee, argue that we are affected by Adam's sin simply because we are part of the human race and hence are affected by the sin and death which is an integral part of that humanity.[34] Others want to say much more than this. The key to the problem lies in the interpretation we place on verse 12, where we are told that 'death came to all men, because all sinned'. At face value this suggests that death is the result of each human being's individual sin but this seems to be at odds with verses 18 and 19, where we are told that it was because of the one man's sin that many were made sinners. In other words, do we become sinners because of what Adam did or because of what we do?

Some, like Cranfield, take the latter view. He writes, 'The many have not been condemned for someone else's transgression, for Adam's sin, but because, as a result of Adam's transgression, they have themselves been sinners.'[35] Others, like Murray, take the former view. According to Murray the first half of 5:12 refers to the 'entrance' of sin and death, whereas the second half deals with the permeation of sin. He writes, 'It *entered* through the sin of the *one man*; it permeated through the sin of *all*.'[36] Still others, like Fitzmyer, do not believe that the question can be answered. Speaking of Paul's use of the 'causal connection between Adam's sin and the sinfulness of human beings', he says that 'Paul never explains how that causality works or how Adam's sin is transmitted'.[37]

---

32. J. Murray, *The Epistle to the Romans: The English Text with Introduction, Exposition and Notes*, vol. 1 (London: Marshall, Morgan & Scott, 1960), p. 206.
33. Murray, *Romans*, p. 179.
34. Fee, *The First Epistle to the Corinthians*, p. 751.
35. C. E. B. Cranfield, *A Critical and Exegetical Commentary on the Epistle to the Romans*, International Critical Commentary (Edinburgh: T & T Clark, 1975), vol. 1, p. 290.
36. Murray, *Romans*, p. 182.
37. J. A. Fitzmyer, *Romans*, The Anchor Bible (London: Chapman, 1992), p. 409.

Headship theology: Adam and Christ

There are, however, factors which can help us towards a conclusion. In particular, we can interpret verse 12 in the light of verses 18 and 19. Since the passage speaks of the 'one sin' of the 'one man', Murray is sure that 'there must be some kind of solidarity existing between the "one" and "the all" with the result that the sin of the one may at the same time and with equal reference be regarded as the sin of all'.[38] Moo agrees with Murray, despite recognizing the risk involved in basing the exegesis of verse 12 so heavily on the later verses. He does, however, believe that the 'popularity of conceptions of corporate solidarity in the Jewish world of Paul's day' gives us good reason to suppose that Paul would understand the notion of corporate figures.[39] In any case, as Moo says, the sinfulness of humanity clearly 'demands an explanation' and no matter which view we take of humanity's relation to Adam, 'this, the biblical, explanation for universal human sinfulness, appears to explain the data of history and experience as well as, or better than, any rival theory'.[40]

Having spoken of Adam's corporate act in bringing sin upon mankind, we must turn to think of Christ. What are we to make of the 'one act of righteousness' (v. 18) which brings justification? Murray's interpretation of 'one act of righteousness' is that it refers to the righteousness of Christ[41] by which we are 'constituted righteous'. He says, 'we must not tone down the formula "constituted righteous" to any lower terms than the gracious judgement on God's part whereby the obedience of Christ is reckoned to our account and therefore reckoned as ours with all the entail of consequence which righteousness carries with it.'[42] He also insists that the future tense used in 5:19 does not imply that justification is in the future, as argued by N. T. Wright.[43]

We would conclude with Moo that:

> The perspective is corporate rather than individual. All people, Paul teaches, stand in relationship to one of two men, whose actions determine the eternal destiny of all who belong to them. Either one 'belongs to' Adam and is under sentence of death because of his sin, or disobedience, or one belongs to Christ and is assured of eternal life because of his 'righteous' act, or obedience.[44]

---

38. Murray, *Romans*, p. 186.
39. Moo, *The Epistle to the Romans*, pp. 321–328.
40. Moo, *The Epistle to the Romans*, p. 329.
41. Murray, *Romans*, pp. 201–202.
42. Murray, *Romans*, p. 206.
43. Murray, *Romans*, p. 206.
44. Moo, *The Epistle to the Romans*, p. 315.

Theological interpretation

How then are we to interpret theologically the exegetical material which we have considered? In particular, how are we to interpret the solidarity between human beings and the respective 'heads'? Moo points out that, historically, this solidarity has been interpreted either in a 'realist' way or in a 'representative' (or federalist) way. He comments: 'Perhaps, indeed, Paul has not provided us with enough data to make a definitive decision; and we should probably be content with the conclusion that Paul affirms the reality of a solidarity of all humanity with Adam in his sin without being able to explain the exact nature of that union.'[45]

The early Fathers typically used the Adam–Christ parallel to emphasize the real humanity of Christ in opposition to various heresies. Tertullian, for example, exegetes 1 Corinthians 15 in order to demonstrate that the 'second man' has flesh and soul just like the 'first man', as part of his argument in favour of a physical (or bodily) resurrection. His docetic and gnostic opponents, being strongly influenced by a Hellenistic dualism which separated flesh and spirit, believed that resurrection applies only to the 'soul'.[46]

Irenaeus was the first writer to make significant theological use of the Adam–Christ parallel in his work *Against Heresies*.[47] Following the earlier Fathers, Irenaeus argued, on the basis of the analogy between Christ and Adam, that the flesh of Christ, which he took from his mother, was real and that there had been a true incarnation.[48] The originality of his position comes when he treats his understanding of recapitulation, by which the life and death of Christ are seen as a means of redeeming and sanctifying every stage of life.[49] He argued that Christ became a child for children, a youth for young people and so on, even going to great lengths to prove that Christ was around fifty when he died, so he could also argue that Christ had become an old man for old men! He also made much of the notion that Christ died on the same day as Adam: that is to

---

45. Moo, *The Epistle to the Romans*, p. 328.
46. Tertullian, 'On the Resurrection of the Flesh', in *Ante-Nicene Fathers*, vol. 3: *Latin Christianity: Its Founder, Tertullian*, ed. A. Roberts and J. Donaldson (Peabody, MA: Hendrickson, 1994), pp. 582–587.
47. Irenaeus, 'Against Heresies', in *Ante-Nicene Fathers*, vol. 1: *The Apostolic Fathers, Justin Martyr, Irenaeus*, ed. A. Roberts and J. Donaldson (Peabody, MA: Hendrickson, 1994), pp. 309–567.
48. Irenaeus, 'Against Heresies', Book 3, ch. 22.
49. Irenaeus, 'Against Heresies', Book 2, ch. 22.

say, Adam died on the sixth day of creation and Jesus died on the sixth day (Friday).[50] For Irenaeus, the key mediatorial role of Christ was to unite human beings to God in his own person. As he writes, 'unless man had been joined to God, he could never have become a partaker of incorruptibility.'[51] He argues that the very purpose of the coming of the Son was 'that man, having been taken into the Word, and receiving the adoption, might become the son of God'. He then repeats the statement that only through being united to incorruptibility (and this time he adds 'immortality') could human beings obtain these blessings.[52] To this end, the Mediator 'passed through every stage of life, restoring to all communion with God'.[53] In this work, Christ unites human beings to the Spirit and causes the Spirit to dwell in them. He also wages war against the enemy and crushes the head of the serpent (Satan) in fulfilment of Genesis 3:15.[54]

It is on the basis of this overall theory that Irenaeus approaches the Adam–Christ parallel. Indeed, he uses the parallel to explain the birth of Christ: 'so did He who is the Word, recapitulating Adam in Himself, rightly receive a birth, enabling Him to gather up Adam [into Himself], from Mary, who was as yet a virgin.'[55] Irenaeus even extends the parallel to include Mary. Just as what Adam did is recapitulated and healed by what Christ did, so what Eve did was 'balanced in the opposite scale' by Mary. Thus the Virgin Mary becomes the 'patroness (*advocata*) of the virgin Eve'.[56]

The position argued by Irenaeus has been taken up and developed in recent years, for example, by Hans Boersma.[57] In his work on the atonement, Boersma attempts to get behind the disputes which have taken place since the Reformation in order to develop a coherent and catholic, ecumenical approach. In doing so, the primary move is to take Irenaeus's notion of recapitulation and N. T. Wright's notion of 'reconstitution' (the two main influences upon his work) and add to this a reinvigorated 'Christus Victor' theme, the whole being set in a Reformed context where the penal aspect of atonement is

---

50. Irenaeus, 'Against Heresies', Book 5, ch. 23.
51. Irenaeus, 'Against Heresies', Book 3, ch. 18.
52. Irenaeus, 'Against Heresies', Book 3, ch. 19.
53. Irenaeus, 'Against Heresies', Book 3, ch. 18.
54. Irenaeus, 'Against Heresies', Book 5, chs. 20–21.
55. Irenaeus, 'Against Heresies', Book 3, ch. 21.
56. Irenaeus, 'Against Heresies', Book 5, ch. 19.
57. H. Boersma, *Violence, Hospitality, and the Cross: Reappropriating the Atonement Tradition* (Grand Rapids, MI: Baker, 2004).

viewed in the light of a new understanding of the positive teaching about violence.

The problem with the position advocated by Irenaeus (less so as amended and developed by Boersma) is that the recapitulation theory on its own leaves one not quite sure of the precise relationship between the action of Christ and the salvation of individual sinners.

Augustine comes to 1 Corinthians 15 in the context of a discussion concerning whether or not Adam would have died had he not sinned, a view being expressed by his Pelagian opponents. Augustine spells out clearly his view that if Adam had not sinned he would not have died. He does this in his 'A Treatise on the Merits and Remission of Sins, and on the Baptism of Infants'.[58] He is quite clear that death follows upon sin and he uses 1 Corinthians 15:22 to make the point that the contrast being made is between death and resurrection and hence it must mean literal, physical death.[59]

Augustine develops his argument by saying that original sin (which his opponents deny) exists in all human beings at their birth and he insists that this is by 'natural descent' rather than by 'imitation' (as the Pelagians argued). Later he contrasts 'imitation' with 'propagation', which perhaps makes his meaning clearer.[60] He also argues that by baptism this original sin is remitted. It is, however, this notion of 'natural descent' or 'propagation' which makes Augustine's use of the Adam–Christ parallel important. He writes,

> Then mark well, brethren, the two birth-stocks, Adam and Christ: two men are; but one of them, a man that is man; the other, a Man that is God. By the man that is man we are sinners; by the Man that is God we are justified. That birth hath cast down unto death; this birth hath raised up unto life: that birth brings with it sin; this birth setteth free from sin. For to this end came Christ as Man, to undo the sins of men.[61]

---

58. Augustine, 'On the Merits and Remission of Sins, and on the Baptism of Infants: Book One', in *Nicene and Post Nicene Fathers 1st Series*, vol. 5: *Augustin: Anti-Pelagian Writings*, ed. P. Schaff (Peabody, MA: Hendrickson, 1994), pp. 15–43.
59. Augustine, 'On the Merits and Remission of Sins', Book 1, ch. 8.
60. Augustine, 'On the Merits and Remission of Sins', Book 1, ch. 15.
61. Augustine, '4th Homily on the First Epistle of St John', in *Nicene and Post Nicene Fathers 1st Series*, vol. 7: *Augustin: Homilies on the Gospel of John, Homilies on the First Epistle of John, Soliloquies*, ed. P. Schaff (Peabody, MA: Hendrickson, 1994), p. 486.

He stresses that only 'original sin' is propagated to the human race from Adam. Augustine also dealt with this subject in his *City of God*.[62] The question, of course, is precisely how this happens. How is it that all human beings are born with original sin because of Adam? The answer is that human beings 'participated' in the sin of our 'representative' and so are born with original sin. As to the subsequent question as to the means of transmission of this sin, it is by natural means, from parent to child. Adam's sin has caused 'a certain disease' or 'pestilential corruption' to enter into the human race, which affects everyone born into the race.[63] This is different from the 'federal' view which we shall consider shortly.[64]

The problem with Augustine's view is that his notion of the propagation of original sin through the propagation of the human race does not seem fully to capture the notion that it was the sin of the 'one man' which brought death. He seems rather to argue that the sin of the one man brought original sin to each of us but that it is our own sins thereafter which bring death upon us. In addition, the notion of original sin being remitted by baptism is problematic.

Over against these earlier views, the covenant theology which we have been exploring in this book is closest to accounting for the exegetical material discussed above. In developing their system, however, the covenant theologians supplement the Adam–Christ parallel by introducing a series of covenants. These serve to explain how it is that human beings are related to Adam and to Christ. At face value this provides the best and clearest account of why it is that human beings are 'in Adam' and 'in Christ' – it is because they are related to the respective 'heads' through the mechanism of covenants.

The problem with this view is that none of the three covenants is named thus in Scripture and so a complex structure is created which does not arise naturally from the text. There are also more complex problems such as the relationship between law and gospel, the meaning of the 'old covenant' in the New Testament (Sinai and not Gen. 2), the relationship between the covenant of works and Sinai and so on. We recognize, of course, that covenant theology

---

62. Augustine, 'The City of God', in *Nicene and Post Nicene Fathers 1st Series*, vol. 2: *Augustin: City of God, Christian Doctrine*, ed. P. Schaff (Peabody, MA: Hendrickson, 1994), Books 13–14, pp. 245–283.
63. Augustine, 'On the Merits and Remission of Sins', Book 1, ch. 23.
64. For a comparison of the two views see G. P. Fisher, 'The Augustinian and the Federal Theories of Original Sin Compared', *The New Englander*, July 1868, pp. 468–516.

is not a unified system, there being a range of positions taken within the broad schema, hence these criticisms do not apply to every expression of covenant theology.

Headship theology

The view being taken in this chapter is that, of the various attempts within the Reformed tradition to understand the Adam–Christ parallel, the scheme offered by covenant theology is the most persuasive. At the same time, however, it is burdened with many difficulties because of the way it has been constructed. As we have argued elsewhere,[65] our suggestion is that we develop a 'headship theology' which does not focus on two (or three) covenants but which focuses on two 'heads' and is drawn directly from 1 Corinthians 15 and Romans 5.

The way to do this, we believe, is to build on the theology of John Murray, who set a high store on the theological significance of the Adam–Christ parallel. He goes so far as to say this:

> These two heads of humanity and the two parallel yet opposing complexes bound up with them are the pivots on which the history of humanity turns. God's government of the race can be interpreted only in terms of these two headships and of the respective complexes which the heads set in operation. These are the pivots of redemptive revelation, the first as making redemption necessary, the second as accomplishing and securing redemption.[66]

Our argument is that Murray's position can be made even stronger by using the concept of 'headship' instead of 'covenant' as the organizing principle. Having rejected the term 'covenant of works' in favour of 'Adamic administration', Murray had already moved some distance in this direction. Headship theology maintains all of the main themes of the older covenant theology (the fall of humanity in Adam, imputation of sin, Christ as the second Adam, the imputation of righteousness and so on) while avoiding many of its fundamental problems.

It is interesting to note that at no point in his exposition of Romans 5:12–21 does Murray use the word 'covenant'. He merely insists that Adam and Christ

---

65. A. T. B. McGowan, 'In Defence of Headship Theology', in J. A. Grant and A. I. Wilson (eds.), *The God of the Covenant: Biblical, Theological and Contemporary Perspectives* (Leicester: Apollos, 2005).
66. Murray, *Romans*, p. 207.

must be viewed in terms of representative solidarity. In other words, he found it possible to exegete the passage without importing the language of covenant theology. Similarly, in his commentary on Romans, William Hendriksen makes no mention of covenant in his exposition of 5:12–21.[67] The same is true of Simon Kistemaker in his commentary on 1 Corinthians 15. Charles Hodge, in his commentary on Romans, does use the word 'covenant' but only in passing and without seeking to build a covenant theology into his exegesis of 5:12–21. In other words, four commentators whom we might have expected to interpret the text in the light of their covenant theology do not do so. This being the case, it surely means that it is possible to develop a headship theology directly from the text of Scripture, without the need to import the term 'covenant'. These passages do not require a covenantal underpinning to make their points. The great advantage of this is that we can take people to the Scriptures and show the relevance of the headship of Adam and the headship of Christ in a relatively straightforward way.

A headship theology might look something like this: God entered into a relationship with Adam in Genesis 2. In this relationship, Adam is viewed as the representative head of the human race such that his obedience or disobedience would affect all those whom he represented, namely, all humanity yet unborn. Following Murray, we might call this the 'Adamic administration'. Through his act of disobedience, judgment came upon the whole human race. The focus then turns to Christ. Out of his great love, God sent his Son to be a 'second Adam'. The second Adam represented all those who will ultimately be saved. We might call this the 'messianic administration'. Where Adam failed, Christ succeeded; where Adam disobeyed, Christ obeyed. Finally Christ offered himself up on the cross as an atoning sacrifice for sins, this to be understood in terms of penal substitution. By his one act of righteousness, Christ obtained salvation for all who are 'in him'.

Thus far from 1 Corinthians 15 and Romans 5. The question remaining concerns how we come to be 'in Christ'. The answer to that question is that all those whom God has chosen will, in the fullness of time, be effectually called by the Holy Spirit of God. In this effectual calling is given the gift of faith, by which we are united to Christ. This faith is the instrumental cause of our justification which leads inexorably to sanctification. Just as believers were once united to Adam, so they are now united to Christ. Union with Adam is important to this argument regarding his headship. Some, such as Oliver Crisp, have argued for an ontological union between Adam and his

---

67. W. Hendriksen, *Romans* (Edinburgh: Banner of Truth, 1980), vol. 1.

posterity[68] but this is not critical so long as we maintain that Adam was a 'public person' designated by God as a representative 'head'.

One other significant advantage of headship theology is that it helps us to deal with some of the difficulties between Presbyterians and Reformed Baptists. In this regard, Henri Blocher's article in which he seeks to find a new way forward to avoid the 'dissent that separates Baptists and paedobaptists within the theologically Reformed family' is most significant.[69] In our view, the development of headship theology may aid this rapprochement.

Conclusion

In short, then, everything which is achieved by covenant theology can be achieved by 'headship theology'. The word 'covenant' can then be liberated from the strictures of non-biblical terminology to be interpreted in its context, when dealing with the various covenants mentioned in Scripture. In other words, 'covenant' remains a vital word and concept in Reformed theology as a useful descriptor of God's relationship with his people but it need not be invested with a significance which is not claimed by the Scripture itself, or made to bear a weight it was never intended to bear. The union between Adam and all who are in him and the union between Christ and all who are in him stands by itself, on the basis of Romans 5 and 1 Corinthians 15, and does not require the use of covenant terminology to make it effective for purpose.

This allows us to read the covenants in Scripture as the means by which God relates to his people, Israel and the church. In the next chapter we shall spell out what that looks like.

---

68. O. D. Crisp, *Jonathan Edwards and the Metaphysics of Sin* (Aldershot: Ashgate, 2005), p. 106.
69. H. Blocher, 'Old Covenant, New Covenant', in A. T. B. McGowan (ed.), *Always Reforming: Explorations in Systematic Theology* (Leicester: Apollos, 2006), pp. 240–270.

7. HEADSHIP THEOLOGY: THE COVENANTS OF PROMISE

Introduction

In the last chapter we argued that the Adam–Christ parallel does not require a covenantal underpinning. In other words, although the representative headship of Adam and the representative headship of Christ are vital for our understanding of sin and salvation, we do not need to create a 'covenant of works' and a 'covenant of grace' to make sense of this headship. Clearly, all who are united to Adam will die and all who are united to Christ will be made alive. Without this representative headship we cannot understand why we are born as sinners, nor how we can become the righteousness of God.

Having said that, the relevant biblical passages on which we construct our 'headship theology' (Gen. 2; 1 Cor. 15; Rom. 5) do not use the word 'covenant' nor is a covenantal structure implied by those texts. Also, the terms 'covenant of works', 'covenant of redemption' and 'covenant of grace' are not found in Scripture. Having adopted a 'headship theology' liberated from a covenantal structure, we are now able to read and understand the covenants that *do* appear in Scripture and to try to understand their relationship to one another. That is to say, we can understand the biblical covenants on their own terms, rather than forcing them into a structure which does not arise naturally from the text of Scripture.

A simple reading of the Bible makes it clear that the first covenant God made was with Noah. He then went on to make covenants with Abraham and his heirs, with Moses and with David. Finally, he made a new covenant with his people in and through Christ. When we liberate these covenants from the structures created by seventeenth-century covenant theology, we are able to see these covenants in their own right and in their own context. By doing so, we shall see that there is a natural progression and development of these covenants. Above all, we shall see something of God's sovereign and gracious dealings with humanity, culminating in the incarnation of Jesus Christ, the Son of God. In this chapter, then, we shall offer an account of the biblical covenants which flows out of the 'headship theology' proposal.

The covenant with Noah

We begin with the covenant God made with Noah. In studying this covenant we will look at Genesis 9:1–17, where the covenant is established. We shall then examine the theological and practical significance of this covenant for human beings and for our planet.

Genesis 9:1–17

In Genesis 6 – 9 we have the story of Noah and the flood. In Genesis 6:17–18 God promised Noah that he would establish his covenant with him. When the flood was over and the waters receded, God duly established this promised covenant with Noah and his sons and made certain promises. We see this in 9:1–17. In verses 1–7 God tells Noah that mankind is once again to take up the responsibilities (sometimes called 'the cultural mandate') which God gave when he created human beings. We find that original mandate in Genesis 1:26–28:

> Then God said, 'Let us make man in our image, in our likeness, and let them rule over the fish of the sea and the birds of the air, over the livestock, over all the earth, and over all the creatures that move along the ground.'
>
> So God created man
>   in his own image,
> in the image of God
>   he created him;
> male and female
>   he created them.

> God blessed them and said to them, 'Be fruitful and increase in number; fill the earth and subdue it. Rule over the fish of the sea and the birds of the air and over every living creature that moves on the ground.'

Now that the flood is over and God is effectively beginning the human race again, through Noah and his family, this cultural mandate is repeated. They are to be fruitful and multiply; they are to rule over the created order. There is even a reminder of the sanctity of human life because human beings are made in the image of God. In wiping out the human race and beginning again, God reminds human beings of their status and their responsibilities.

That re-establishment of the cultural mandate provides the background for understanding 9:8–17. Having told them what they are to do, God makes a covenant. Most of the covenants that God established have to do with God's relationship with his chosen people: the Jews and later the church. This covenant is different. This covenant is made with every living creature and not just with God's elect, as we see from verses 9–11:

> I now establish my covenant with you and with your descendants after you and with every living creature that was with you – the birds, the livestock and all the wild animals, all those that came out of the ark with you – every living creature on earth. I establish my covenant with you: Never again will all life be cut off by the waters of a flood; never again will there be a flood to destroy the earth.

There are five things we can say about this covenant. First, it is a universal covenant, made with all human beings, with all creatures and even with the creation itself. Second, it is a unilateral covenant, having been sovereignly established by God. In other words, it is not a contract between two parties; it was a sovereign act of God which instituted the covenant. Third, it is an unconditional covenant, there being no conditions attached to it. Fourth, it is a covenant of promise. Fifth, it is an everlasting covenant, as we see from verse 16, which means that this covenant is still in operation today. These points will all be important as we go on to consider the other biblical covenants.

The content of the covenant is very straightforward. It involves a promise that there will never again be such a flood and never again will all life be destroyed. The rainbow is given as a sign of the covenant. As John Calvin pointed out, this does not mean that there were no rainbows before the flood but only that after the flood the rainbow had a new significance. God is saying: when you see a rainbow you will remember my covenant and be assured that I will never again wipe all human beings off the face of the earth. God also says that when he sees the rainbow, he will remember. He is speaking in very anthropomorphic terms but making an important point.

Theological significance
The main theological significance of this covenant with Noah is that it provides a basis for understanding God's gracious relationship with his whole creation. It provides a foundation for understanding life on the planet, as well as the promise of seasonal continuance. As we have seen, God's concern here is not just with his chosen people but with all humanity, with all the creatures and with the planet itself.

This covenant provides a basis for human society and human government, such that we can work together with other human beings who are not Christians in order to establish government and the rule of law. Society can only function because God has established some common ground between human beings. This covenant with Noah establishes that common ground. It also provides the basis for understanding what theologians call God's 'common grace'. Reformed theologians developed the concept of common grace to answer the following questions: Why are human beings not as bad as they could be? How can bad people do good things? Why do sinners experience so many blessings at the hand of a holy God?

There are various passages in the Bible which affirm God's care for the unrighteous as well as for the righteous. The key text is from Matthew's account of the Sermon on the Mount, Matthew 5:43–46:

> You have heard that it was said, 'Love your neighbour and hate your enemy.' But I tell you: Love your enemies and pray for those who persecute you, that you may be sons of your Father in heaven. He causes his sun to rise on the evil and the good, and sends rain on the righteous and the unrighteous. If you love those who love you, what reward will you get? Are not even the tax collectors doing that?

The strength of this passage is that God has a general love and concern for all humanity, righteous and unrighteous, this being the foundation of the command to human beings to love their enemies.

John Calvin developed this theme, which only much later came to be known as common grace. Given his teaching on total depravity, Calvin had a problem. How is it that fallen, depraved human beings are able to do good things? How can a fallen sinner produce works of art which are of the highest calibre and how can fallen sinners be good parents, good citizens and make valuable contributions to society? Calvin's answer was to develop two important themes. First, fallen human beings are enabled to create and preserve society and to engage in the arts and sciences because of the work of the Spirit of God. Second, fallen human beings are not as bad as they could be because God, by his grace, restrains and curtails their sin and depravity. Taken together, these two themes represent what became the Reformed doctrine of common grace. On the negative side, God restrains sin and, on the positive side, God enables human society and grants ability in the arts and sciences.

This means that fallen human beings can achieve great things and contribute significantly to our understanding, even if they themselves do not fully integrate their knowledge with what we know about God. It also means that we can celebrate music, poetry, theatre, cinema, literature and so on as good gifts of a gracious God, who blesses the lives of human beings – even those who are not believers. Common grace provides a way of understanding culture and provides a 'shared ground' between believer and unbeliever. It can also contribute to a more productive relationship between theologians and scientists. Above all, it affirms that human beings are made in the image of God and so their lives have dignity. Those lives are to be protected and valued. This is hugely important in the various discussions ongoing about abortion, genetic engineering, assisted suicide and so on.

Many Christians believe that God blesses only believers and that God is 'ours'. The doctrine of common grace, as expressed in the Noahic covenant, teaches us that the whole earth is the Lord's and that he is doing and can do surprising things. The covenant with Noah, then, speaks to us about the love of God and the providence of God. It explains his establishment of a world for which human beings have responsibility and it provides us with a common humanitarian interest in looking after the world and other human beings.

The covenant with Abraham

We now turn to consider the covenant with Abraham as we find it established in Genesis 15 and ratified in Genesis 17. We have seen that the covenant with Noah was founded upon God's 'common grace' to all creatures but this covenant involves 'special grace' and is made with God's chosen people. Once again, we see that it is sovereignly established by God and contains a promise from God. In Ephesians 2:12 Paul describes the covenants God made with Abraham and those who followed him as 'covenants of the promise'. So what we read of in Genesis 15 and 17 is a covenant of promise and most of what God does through succeeding generations involves the fulfilment of the promises made to Abraham. We will also see that, although the covenant relationship is unilateral (sovereignly established by God), it requires a response. Abraham and those who followed as God's covenant people were to respond to God's grace with faith and obedience.

The promise

To understand the covenant with Abraham, we have to begin with Genesis 12, where God came to Abram and called him to leave his home and his father's house and to set out on a journey. Listen to Genesis 12:1–3:

> The LORD had said to Abram, 'Leave your country, your people and your father's household and go to the land I will show you.
>
> 'I will make you into a great nation
>   and I will bless you;
> I will make your name great,
>   and you will be a blessing.
> I will bless those who bless you,
>   and whoever curses you I will curse;
> and all peoples on earth
>   will be blessed through you.'

God said that he would be with Abram and guide him and also made three promises: first, that he was going to make of Abram a great nation with many descendants; second, that he would give that great nation a land in which to live; and third, that Abram's descendants would be a blessing to all nations. That call to Abram in Genesis 12 to set out on this journey is really the beginning of the story of the nation of Israel, the chosen people of God. In chapter 15, as we shall see, God confirms the promises which he made in chapter 12 and does so by entering into a covenant with Abram.

This encounter between God and Abram in Genesis 12 is very important. Here, God binds himself to a particular man and his family, which would later grow into a nation. Out of all the people living at that time, God chose Abram. We are not told why God made this choice but it was truly momentous. The entire history of the world can only be understood properly if we set it in the context of this act of God. God chooses a man and makes promises to him. These promises are expanded and given more detail as the story moves on but the very fact that God makes these promises is the remarkable thing. No human being, not even Abram, deserved God's favour. This was an act of God's grace, to take one sinner out of many and to promise that he and his descendants would be God's special people and would know God's special blessing. Later, we shall see that the covenant with Abram was expanded into a new covenant

Headship theology: the covenants of promise

with Christ, when Gentiles as well as Jews would share in the blessings of the covenant. The church of Jesus Christ becomes part of the covenant people. The love and mercy of God are demonstrated in this call of Abram.

Although Abram and his descendants were to be God's chosen people, there was to be a wider blessing which would come to the whole world. As we read in Genesis 12:3, God said, 'all peoples on earth will be blessed through you'. The chosen people themselves were to be blessed but everyone else was to be blessed through them. Among other things, the blessing would include God's law. God said through the prophet in Isaiah 51:4, 'Listen to me, my people; hear me, my nation: The law will go out from me; my justice will become a light to the nations.'

The covenant

Genesis 15 is one of the most significant passages in the whole of the Old Testament because it helps us to understand how a sinner can be in a right relationship with God. It does so by dealing with the key themes of faith and covenant. These two themes of faith and covenant are intertwined in Scripture and it is useful to deal with them together. The key passage is Genesis 15:1–6:

> After this, the word of the LORD came to Abram in a vision:
>
> 'Do not be afraid, Abram.
> I am your shield,
> your very great reward.'
>
> But Abram said, 'O Sovereign LORD, what can you give me since I remain childless and the one who will inherit my estate is Eliezer of Damascus?' And Abram said, 'You have given me no children; so a servant in my household will be my heir.'
> Then the word of the LORD came to him: 'This man will not be your heir, but a son coming from your own body will be your heir.' He took him outside and said, 'Look up at the heavens and count the stars – if indeed you can count them.' Then he said to him, 'So shall your offspring be.'
> Abram believed the LORD, and he credited it to him as righteousness.

God comes to Abram in a dream and declares himself to be Abram's shield and reward but Abram is full of doubt and responds by asking God what good this is when he has no heir to succeed him. In other words, Abram is asking how God can possibly fulfil the promise given to him in chapter 12, that he will be the father of a great nation, if he has no children. God then takes Abram outside, points up to the sky and tells him that his descendants will be as numerous as the stars. Abram then moves from a position of doubt to a position of faith and we have the important conclusion in verse 6: 'Abram believed the Lord, and he credited it to him as righteousness.' This is a very important expression which is the key to understanding not only Abram's relationship with God but also our relationship with God. God declares us to be righteous (which means 'in a right relationship with God') through faith. In the New Testament the word 'justified', which means 'pardoned and accepted', is used to explain this.

Having confirmed the first of his promises, God then goes on in verses 7–8 to confirm the second one: 'He also said to him, "I am the Lord, who brought you out of Ur of the Chaldeans to give you this land to take possession of it." But Abram said, "O Sovereign Lord, how can I know that I shall gain possession of it?"' Once again, Abram was doubtful. How can I be sure? At this point God enters into a covenant with Abram, as we see in verses 9–21:

> So the Lord said to him, 'Bring me a heifer, a goat and a ram, each three years old, along with a dove and a young pigeon.'
>
> Abram brought all these to him, cut them in two and arranged the halves opposite each other; the birds, however, he did not cut in half. Then birds of prey came down on the carcasses, but Abram drove them away.
>
> As the sun was setting, Abram fell into a deep sleep, and a thick and dreadful darkness came over him. Then the Lord said to him, 'Know for certain that your descendants will be strangers in a country not their own, and they will be enslaved and ill-treated four hundred years. But I will punish the nation they serve as slaves, and afterwards they will come out with great possessions. You, however, will go to your fathers in peace and be buried at a good old age. In the fourth generation your descendants will come back here, for the sin of the Amorites has not yet reached its full measure.'
>
> When the sun had set and darkness had fallen, a smoking brazier with a blazing torch appeared and passed between the pieces. On that day the Lord made a covenant with Abram and said, 'To your descendants I give this land, from the river of Egypt to the great river, the Euphrates – the land of the Kenites, Kenizzites, Kadmonites, Hittites, Perizzites, Rephaites, Amorites, Canaanites, Girgashites and Jebusites.'

The covenant has been made and now Abram stands in a particular relation to God. His descendants would be God's people. This did not mean that the Jews would never suffer or go through difficult and testing times. In verses 13–16 of this passage God tells Abram that his people would be exiled in Egypt and that they would be 'enslaved and ill-treated' for four hundred years. They would endure much suffering before finally entering the Promised Land. In fact, to read the book of Exodus is to read in detail what is prophesied in these verses. Being the people of God did not mean that Abram's descendants would live a trouble-free life, living on the spiritual mountain top. It is the same with new-covenant believers, as Jesus warned his disciples in Matthew 10:18–22:

> On my account you will be brought before governors and kings as witnesses to them and to the Gentiles. But when they arrest you, do not worry about what to say or how to say it. At that time you will be given what to say, for it will not be you speaking, but the Spirit of your Father speaking through you.
>
> Brother will betray brother to death, and a father his child; children will rebel against their parents and have them put to death. All men will hate you because of me, but he who stands firm to the end will be saved.

The ratification

When we turn to Genesis 17, we find the covenant ratified and confirmed. Here we see that the covenant consisted of three promises. First, Abram would be the father of many nations. As a sign of this promise, his name was changed from Abram to Abraham. Second, he was going to have a son who would be his heir. As a sign of this promise, his wife's name was changed from Sarai to Sarah. Third, God promised to be his God and the God of his descendants. As a sign of this promise, the covenant of circumcision was given.

We must not forget, however, that faith was the key to the covenant. We must constantly remind ourselves of Genesis 15:6, which makes it clear that Abraham's relationship to God was not simply based on the covenant: it was based on faith. By the time of Jesus, many of the Jews had forgotten that faith was the key and were trusting in the covenant sign of circumcision or in keeping God's law. As long as someone is circumcised, they said, he is a true Jew and is in a right relationship with God. This was not true, as Paul pointed out in Romans 2:25–29:

> Circumcision has value if you observe the law, but if you break the law, you have become as though you had not been circumcised. If those who are not circumcised keep the law's requirements, will they not be regarded as though they were circumcised? The one who is not circumcised physically and yet obeys the law will condemn you who, even though you have the written code and circumcision, are a law-breaker.
>
> A man is not a Jew if he is only one outwardly, nor is circumcision merely outward and physical. No, a man is a Jew if he is one inwardly; and circumcision is circumcision of the heart, by the Spirit, not by the written code. Such a man's praise is not from men, but from God.

He makes the same point a little later in Romans 4:9–12:

> Is this blessedness only for the circumcised, or also for the uncircumcised? We have been saying that Abraham's faith was credited to him as righteousness. Under what circumstances was it credited? Was it after he was circumcised, or before? It was not after, but before! And he received the sign of circumcision, a seal of the righteousness that he had by faith while he was still uncircumcised. So then, he is the father of all who believe but have not been circumcised, in order that righteousness might be credited to them. And he is also the father of the circumcised who not only are circumcised but who also walk in the footsteps of the faith that our father Abraham had before he was circumcised.

The implications

This covenant in Genesis 15 and 17, between God and Abraham (and his descendants), involves what John Murray has called 'a sovereign administration' of grace. By this covenant God entered into a relationship with his chosen people such that he would be their God and they would be his people. Every descendant of Abraham was included and, from this time on, would be related to God by covenant. The blessings and benefits of the covenant, however, required faith and obedience. Simply to be a blood descendant of Abraham was not enough; there had also to be a personal relationship with God through faith and that faith was to be demonstrated by obedience to God. It was possible to break the covenant and to become separated from God.

So too in our day. It is possible to be part of the visible community of the church, which we can call 'God's covenant people', but to be a stranger to grace and mercy. Baptism is a sign that someone belongs to the covenant people (just as circumcision was for Abraham) and the Lord's Supper is the covenant meal (just as the Passover meal was for the Jews). These signs are important and all believers and their children ought to be baptized. Similarly, everyone who believes in Jesus ought to be at the Communion table. These signs of the covenant are what mark us out as the people of God. Having said that, it is possible to be baptized and to take Communion without having faith in Christ. Just as the sign of circumcision had to be accompanied by faith and obedience, so we too are called to faith and obedience.

The covenant with Moses

We have noted that, whereas the covenant with Noah was founded upon God's 'common grace' to all creatures, the covenant with Abraham involves 'special grace' and is made with God's chosen people. Once again, we see that it is sovereignly established by God and contains promises from God. Most of what God does through succeeding generations involves the fulfilment of those promises made to Abraham. We also saw that, although the covenant relationship was entirely gracious and God-given, Abraham and those who followed as God's covenant people were to respond to God's grace with faith and obedience.

We now turn to the covenant God established with his people through Moses after the exodus from Egypt. We will begin by looking at various passages of Scripture which describe this covenant, in order to answer some questions about its nature and purpose. We will then see that the giving of the law, especially the Ten Commandments, was at the heart of this covenant.

The exodus and the covenant

The exodus from Egypt was the most significant event in the history of God's chosen people. After four hundred years of slavery they were liberated, under the leadership of Moses. When Abraham's grandson Jacob (named Israel) and his children settled in Egypt they were just one large family but, by the time of the exodus, the twelve sons of Jacob had become twelve tribes and the family had become a nation. The Hebrews, as they were called, or the children of Israel, were now a significant small nation. When God entered into the covenant with Abraham, the covenant people were Abraham's family but the promise was that he would have many descendants and that they would become a great nation. That promise has been fulfilled by the time of the exodus and so it is no wonder that God would choose to re-establish his covenant with his people at this point in their history.

There is also the further point that, since the Israelites were now a nation and would (after forty years in the wilderness) enter the land God had promised them, there was a need to structure the life and worship of the nation. In this covenant with Moses, God tells them how and where to worship and he gives them his law. This included not only laws governing ethics and morality but also instructions governing the worship, priesthood and sacrificial system. It also provided structures of authority, leadership and governance for the nation of Israel.

There is a clear connection between the covenant God made with Abraham and the re-establishment of the covenant through Moses. Indeed, the exodus itself was a direct result of the covenant which God had made with Abraham. In Exodus 2:23–25, during their time of slavery in Egypt, we read this: 'The Israelites groaned in their slavery and cried out, and their cry for help because of their slavery went up to God. God heard their groaning and he remembered his covenant with Abraham, with Isaac and with Jacob. So God looked on the Israelites and was concerned about them.' Notice that 'God ... remembered his covenant'. As we saw in Genesis 15, when God made the covenant with Abraham he told him that his descendants would be slaves for four hundred years but would then be liberated and given their own land. Now, under Moses, that covenant promise has been fulfilled.

We find much the same in Exodus 6:1–5, when God speaks to Moses:

> Then the LORD said to Moses, 'Now you will see what I will do to Pharaoh: Because of my mighty hand he will let them go; because of my mighty hand he will drive them out of his country.'
>
> God also said to Moses, 'I am the LORD. I appeared to Abraham, to Isaac and to Jacob as God Almighty, but by my name the LORD I did not make myself known to them. I also established my covenant with them to give them the land of Canaan, where they lived as aliens. Moreover, I have heard the groaning of the Israelites, whom the Egyptians are enslaving, and I have remembered my covenant.'

We can sum it up like this: when God's people are suffering in slavery in Egypt, God remembers his covenant with Abraham and brings them out of Egypt. The exodus from Egypt having taken place, God now re-establishes his covenant with his chosen people, through Moses.

This covenant which God made with the people through Moses required holiness and obedience. That comes out clearly in Exodus 19:3–6:

> Then Moses went up to God, and the LORD called to him from the mountain and said, 'This is what you are to say to the house of Jacob and what you are to tell the people of Israel: "You yourselves have seen what I did to Egypt, and how I carried you on eagles' wings and brought you to myself. Now if you obey me fully and keep my covenant, then out of all nations you will be my treasured possession. Although the whole earth is mine, you will be for me a kingdom of priests and a holy nation."'

Holiness and obedience, however, must be seen as a response to God's love, grace and faithfulness. The Israelites are in a special relationship to God: they are God's 'treasured possession'. The whole earth belongs to God but out of all the nations he has chosen the descendants of Abraham to be his own people. Having received this great privilege, the people are to be holy and obedient.

In Exodus 24:4 we are told that Moses had written down everything God had said to him, including all the laws and statutes by which the people were governed. This becomes known as the Book of the Covenant and Moses reads it to all the people. When they promise to obey these laws and statutes, he sprinkles them with blood and the covenant is duly established. We read of this in Exodus 24:7–8: 'Then he took the Book of the Covenant and read it to the people. They responded, "We will do everything the LORD has said; we will obey." Moses then took the blood, sprinkled it on the people and said, "This is the blood of the covenant that the LORD has made with you in accordance with all these words."'

We must pay particular attention to the words Moses uses when speaking about the blood: he calls it the 'blood of the covenant'. That language is familiar to us because Jesus spoke those words about his own blood, at the Last Supper. We find this in Matthew 26:26–28: 'While they were eating, Jesus took bread, gave thanks and broke it, and gave it to his disciples, saying, "Take and eat; this is my body." Then he took the cup, gave thanks and offered it to them, saying, "Drink from it, all of you. This is my blood of the covenant, which is poured out for many for the forgiveness of sins."' We shall return to this theme later in the chapter.

We shall soon come to consider what the writer to the Hebrews calls 'the new covenant' but already we should be noticing points of progression and development from one covenant to another.

The law and the covenant

What marks out the covenant with Moses from the covenant with Abraham is the giving of the law to Moses on Mount Sinai. We will consider a useful delineation of the different types or aspects of the law but, before doing so, it is important to say that God's law was not given simply as a set of rules and regulations. Torah in its most complete sense is a worldview, with God at the centre. Its purpose is to act as a guide for the life of the covenant community. That is to say, the law represents a way of looking at everything from a God-centred perspective. It is an all-encompassing approach to God, self and the world, in which everything is viewed through the lens of the glory and sovereignty of God and his mission in the world.[1]

That said, Reformed theologians have traditionally identified three aspects of the law of God: the moral law, the civil law and the ceremonial law.

The moral law is centred on the Ten Commandments but includes the detailed spelling out of the law in Leviticus and Numbers. The moral law is seen as an expression of the holiness, justice and righteousness of God. God's people are to reflect that holiness, justice and righteousness as they obey the moral law.

---

1. For a definition of the meaning and semantic range of the word 'Torah', see C. J. H. Wright, *Old Testament Ethics for the People of God* (Nottingham: IVP, 2004), pp. 281–326.

The civil law is the law which was given to govern the life of Israel as a theocracy, a nation under God's rule. Israel in its earliest days was a theocracy. God was the one who told the leaders of the nation what to do. He guided them, sent prophets to them and established his authority over them. The Israelites were one nation under God and that nation needed laws to govern its affairs. The people of God today are scattered through many nations and we are told to be subject to the rulers of the nation of which we are citizens. Many aspects of the civil law, as we find it in the Old Testament, no longer apply to the new situation of the Christian church, although the underlying principles do.

The ceremonial law describes the system of worship and sacrifice which God established for his people. There was to be a priesthood, including a high priest. This worship was authorized to take place at the tabernacle, which was designed to move with the people wherever they went. The Tent of Meeting was built to contain the ark of the covenant and other items used in worship. Much later in the history of Israel, the temple was built in Jerusalem and that became the place of worship and of sacrifice. The ceremonial law was very detailed, even including the robes to be worn by the priests and later by the choirs. Sacrifices were established for different purposes, requiring different offerings. The principal sacrificial offering took place once each year, on the Day of Atonement, when the high priest went into the 'Most Holy Place' and offered a sacrifice for his own sins and then for the sins of the people.

The ceremonial law, with all its accompanying sacrifices, came to an end when Christ made one final sacrifice on the cross at Calvary. The writer to the Hebrews makes it clear that Jesus is our great high priest and he did, once for all, what the old high priests had to do each year. This aspect of the law, part of the covenant with Moses, was fulfilled by Christ. We might put it like this: when God came to earth in the person of his Son, all the 'temporary measures' which God had put in place through Moses were brought to completion.

Having said that we are no longer required to obey the civil law given for the governance of Israel as a nation under God and we are no longer required to make the sacrifices demanded by the ceremonial law, there are nevertheless lessons to be learned from the law. The WCF, speaking of the law God gave to Israel, says this in chapter 19 section 4: 'To them also, as a body politic, He gave sundry judicial laws, which expired together with the state of that people, not obliging any other now, further than the general equity thereof may require.' The key expression here is 'the general equity'. For example, in the civil law the Jews were told to put a fence round their roofs. That is because they spent time on the flat roofs of their houses. We in the West do not tend to spend time on the roof! The principle lying behind the law, however, was to protect family and friends from the danger of falling off the roof. So 'the general equity' means to take reasonable measures to ensure the safety of anyone on our property.

So God made a covenant with Moses and this covenant included the giving of the law of God. It was not enough that God had given his law, however; the covenant demanded a response from the people. To put it another way, when God made a covenant with Israel, he demanded covenant obedience.

We see this demand for obedience most clearly in Deuteronomy 28, where we have 'the blessings and the curses'. In verses 1–2 we read this: 'If you fully obey the LORD your God and carefully follow all his commands that I give you today, the LORD your God will set you high above all the nations on earth. All these blessings will come upon you and accompany you if you obey the LORD your God' and Moses goes on to list the blessings which will follow from obedience. Then in verse 15 we read this: 'However, if you do not obey the LORD your God and do not carefully follow all his commands and decrees I am giving you today, all these curses will come upon you and overtake you' and Moses then lists the curses that will follow disobedience.

The key to obedience was maintaining the fear of the LORD. In Exodus 20:18–20, the chapter in which the Ten Commandments are given, we read this:

> When the people saw the thunder and lightning and heard the trumpet and saw the mountain in smoke, they trembled with fear. They stayed at a distance and said to Moses, 'Speak to us yourself and we will listen. But do not have God speak to us or we will die.' Moses said to the people, 'Do not be afraid. God has come to test you, so that the fear of God will be with you to keep you from sinning.'

It was the fear of God which was to keep the people from sinning. They had been given the law but obedience to the law followed upon the fear of God.

When the exodus had taken place, God re-established his covenant. In doing so he gave the law. The law regulated the day-to-day life of the nation, its worship and its morality. This leaves one unanswered question, namely, the relationship between the covenant with Abraham and the covenant with Moses; or, to put it another way, the relationship between grace and law, between faith and works. It is to that question we now turn.

The Abrahamic and Mosaic covenants compared

We have seen that, in the covenant God made with Abraham, faith was the key to the relationship between God and Abraham. As we read in Genesis 15:6,

'Abram believed the LORD, and he credited it to him as righteousness.' This is confirmed by Paul, who says in Romans 4 that Abraham was saved by faith. So faith was at the heart of the covenant with Abraham. We have just examined the covenant that God made with Moses and we have seen that law was at the heart of the covenant. God gave his law through Moses: the moral law that applied to all human beings whom God had made, laws for the nation-state of Israel, and laws directing their worship, especially concerning the priests and the sacrificial system.

We must now address an apparent problem. If faith was at the heart of the covenant with Abraham and law was at the heart of the covenant with Moses, what is the relation between faith and law in God's dealings with his people?

As we have seen in earlier chapters, this is a subject over which there has been great disagreement, even among those who share a common commitment to Reformed theology as expressed in the WCF. We noted earlier the disagreement on this matter between James Hadow and Thomas Boston (and the Marrowmen) in the eighteenth century. We have also seen the disagreement between John Murray and Meredith Kline, the key to which was a disagreement over law and grace. We must now see what all of this has to do with understanding the relationship between the covenant made with Abraham and the covenant made with Moses.

For Murray, the covenant made with Moses was a continuation and development of God's gracious covenant promises to Abraham. For Kline, the covenant with Moses was a legal 'republication' of a 'covenant of works' originally made with Adam. Whereas for Murray there is continuity between the covenant made with Abraham and the covenant made with Moses, for Kline there is a radical discontinuity. Kline insists that the contrast between a covenant of works and a covenant of grace, undergirded by the contrast between law and grace, is vital for our Reformed theology.

So, is the covenant with Moses a continuation of the gracious, faith-centred covenant with Abraham, or is it a legal covenant, a republication of a covenant of works with Adam? How are we to judge between these two views? In order to resolve this dispute we turn to Galatians 3, because that passage deals with this very point. If we want to know the relationship between faith and law, this is where we must begin.

Galatians 3

Paul wrote his letter to the Galatians to deal with this problem of the relationship between faith and law. The Galatians, who had discovered the grace of God in Christ Jesus and had begun to live the Christian life, were in danger of going back to their Jewish ways. Some people had been telling the Galatians that obedience to the law was a condition of salvation. Paul was very disturbed by this. In Galatians 3:1–5 he writes,

> You foolish Galatians! Who has bewitched you? Before your very eyes Jesus Christ was clearly portrayed as crucified. I would like to learn just one thing from you: Did you receive the Spirit by observing the law, or by believing what you heard? Are you so foolish? After beginning with the Spirit, are you now trying to attain your goal by human effort? Have you suffered so much for nothing – if it really was for nothing? Does God give you his Spirit and work miracles among you because you observe the law, or because you believe what you heard?

It is, however, in the second half of Galatians 3 that Paul turns specifically to address the question of the relationship between God's covenant with Abraham and the giving of the law through Moses. Paul understands the problem. If God made a covenant with Abraham and that covenant was the basis for the relationship between God and his people, then what happened when the law was given through Moses? When God gave the law, did that cancel the Abrahamic covenant? Is there now a new situation, so that salvation is not by faith but by law? It could easily seem that way. After all, God promised Abraham descendants, land and blessing. This promise was regularly repeated through his family line. When God gave his law, centuries later, what was he doing? When the law came, did it overturn the promise made to Abraham? Is it possible that Abraham was told that salvation is by faith but, from the time of Moses onwards, salvation is through keeping the commandments?

The key verses are found in Galatians 3:17–18, where Paul writes, 'The law, introduced 430 years later, does not set aside the covenant previously established by God and thus do away with the promise. For if the inheritance depends on the law, then it no longer depends on a promise; but God in his grace gave it to Abraham through a promise.' There we have it: the covenant with Moses does not overturn the gracious promise-covenant previously made with Abraham and law does not take priority over grace. Salvation is still by faith and not by keeping the law. We might put it like this: the covenant God made with Abraham speaks of God's grace and the covenant God made with Moses reminds God's people of their duties and responsibilities.

To express this differently, the law given through Moses did not cancel the covenant made with Abraham; rather it was a continuation of it, a spelling out of the relationship between God and his people and of the obligations that came with this relationship. In other words, the proper way to interpret Galatians 3 is to view the covenant at Sinai as a spelling out of the obligations of the covenant with Abraham rather than as a republication of a covenant of works. We might put it like this: God says to Abraham, 'I will be your God and you will be my people', then through Moses he says, 'Since you are my people, this is how you should live.'

Faith and obedience

Taking the view that the covenant with Moses at Sinai represents a spelling out of the obligations of the covenant with Abraham has two advantages. The first advantage comes in understanding what Paul was saying to the Jews of his day. Many of the Jews in Paul's day viewed the Mosaic law as an entity in itself, instead of viewing it as a spelling out of the obligations of the Abrahamic covenant. Many of them believed that salvation was to be obtained by obeying the law. So a good thing, the law, became a snare. Paul did not want them to abandon the law or obedience to God but rather to see these in the context of the covenant with Abraham and thus in the context of faith.

The second advantage is that it enables us to deal with faith and works in the present. We can take seriously what the book of James has to say about the relationship between faith and works. In other words, we can understand the importance of obedience in the Christian life without thinking that we're trying to be saved by works. Faith is the means by which we are put in a right relationship with God and obedience must be understood in the context of faith but it remains, nevertheless, a vital component of the Christian life. We shall say more of this in chapter 8.

The covenant with David

We come now to consider the covenant which God established with King David. As we shall see, the covenant with David includes the promise that one day another king would come, in David's line, and his throne would be established for ever. In this way, all the covenant promises would be fulfilled. This covenant with David, then, is an important stepping stone towards an understanding of the new covenant in Christ.

A new stage

When God entered into the covenant with Abraham, the covenant people were Abraham's family but the promise was that he would have many descendants and that they would become a great nation. That promise was fulfilled and those who entered Egypt as a family left 430 years later as a nation. So God made a covenant with this new nation of Israel, to structure their life and worship and to give them his law. When God establishes this covenant with David, the people are at another new stage in the life of the nation. The kingship has been established and so God makes a covenant with King David.

The story leading up to the establishment of the kingship is not a happy one. Samuel was the last and most famous of the judges and he was the voice of God to the nation but, in 1 Samuel 8:1–9, the elders of Israel come to Samuel and ask for a king. This was a momentous occasion. There were two reasons for this request. The first reason was a real dissatisfaction with Samuel's sons, Joel and Abijah. Samuel was quite old by this time and so he had appointed his sons as judges but they were not like their father. They were dishonest men who took bribes and perverted justice. The elders of Israel had had enough of these wicked men and demanded that Samuel appoint a king. The second reason why the elders of Israel wanted a king is found in their request to Samuel in verse 5: 'appoint a king to lead us, such as all the other nations have.' Their first reason for wanting a king, the wickedness of Samuel's sons, was perhaps a good reason. They wanted the leadership of the nation to be placed in better hands. This second reason, however, was much more serious. They wanted to be like the other nations.

The problem was that they were not like the other nations: they were God's chosen people and they were not led in the way that those other nations were. Israel was a nation under God, a nation set apart from the other nations. It was governed by different principles, by the law of God and not by the decisions of a king. The elders and people of Israel did not want to be different; they wanted to be like all the other nations. Samuel was very displeased by the request for a king – indeed he was angry with the people – but, in 1 Samuel 8:7, God says to Samuel, 'it is not you they have rejected, but they have rejected me as their king.' The request for a king was really a rejection of God's kingship.

As a result of this, Saul is appointed as the first king of Israel. Israel is no longer the theocracy it was before; now it has a monarchy and it has become like the other nations. It would not be long before the behaviour of King Saul made the people realize that they had made a mistake in rejecting God's kingship for Saul's. God had given them what they wanted and had warned them what it would be like but they pressed on regardless.

A new king
Saul was soon rejected by God and a new king was needed. Saul had started reasonably well and appeared to be a spiritual man but was eventually rejected by God for his sin and disobedience. It is no surprise that God waited for the second king, King David, before he entered into a covenant with him.

When God rejected Saul as king, he sent Samuel to the house of Jesse, David's father, to anoint a new king. This is described in 1 Samuel 16, while Saul was still on the throne. Jesse brought each of his older sons before Samuel but all seven were rejected. Then Samuel asked if there was no other son and David was brought forward. God made it clear to Samuel that David was the one and so he was anointed as king. In 1 Samuel 17 we have David's defeat of Goliath. From then on he is in the king's court and becomes a close friend of Jonathan, the king's son. Later he becomes a soldier and leads the army. All the while, Saul becomes more and more jealous and on several occasions tries to kill David. Finally, David has to flee from the palace to escape Saul and he becomes an outlaw, gathering several hundred men to his cause. Although Saul tries to kill him, David has a deep respect for Saul as the Lord's anointed king and he refuses to kill him, even when he has the opportunity. When Saul and Jonathan die, David is full of grief.

Only after all of this does David finally become king, first in the southern kingdom of Judah and then over all Israel. A new king has come to the throne and he will be the greatest of all Israel's kings. Like every human being he had feet of clay and was guilty of sin, including adultery and murder, but when his sin was pointed out by the prophet Nathan he made no excuses, repented before God and found forgiveness.

A new covenant

Israel is at a new stage in its history, the period of the kings. Israel has a new king in David. Now God makes a covenant with the king. The establishment of God's covenant with David is found in 2 Samuel 7:12–16, where God says to David:

> When your days are over and you rest with your fathers, I will raise up your offspring to succeed you, who will come from your own body, and I will establish his kingdom. He is the one who will build a house for my Name, and I will establish the throne of his kingdom for ever. I will be his father, and he shall be my son. When he does wrong, I will punish him with the rod of men, with floggings inflicted by men. But my love will never be taken away from him, as I took it away from Saul, whom I removed from before you. Your house and your kingdom shall endure for ever before me; your throne shall be established for ever.

We have said that this was the point at which God made a covenant with David but the word 'covenant' does not appear in these verses. The reason we know that this was a covenant is because we are told it, in Psalm 89:1–4:

Headship theology: the covenants of promise

> I will sing of the LORD's great love for ever;
>   with my mouth I will make your faithfulness known through all generations.
> I will declare that your love stands firm for ever,
>   that you established your faithfulness in heaven itself.
> You said, 'I have made a covenant with my chosen one,
>   I have sworn to David my servant,
> I will establish your line for ever
>   and make your throne firm through all generations.'

We find the same thing towards the end of that same psalm, in verses 20–29:

> I have found David my servant;
>   with my sacred oil I have anointed him.
> My hand will sustain him;
>   surely my arm will strengthen him.
> No enemy will subject him to tribute;
>   no wicked man will oppress him.
> I will crush his foes before him
>   and strike down his adversaries.
> My faithful love will be with him,
>   and through my name his horn will be exalted.
> I will set his hand over the sea,
>   his right hand over the rivers.
> He will call out to me, 'You are my Father,
>   my God, the Rock my Saviour.'
> I will also appoint him my firstborn,
>   the most exalted of the kings of the earth.
> I will maintain my love to him for ever,
>   and my covenant with him will never fail.
> I will establish his line for ever,
>   his throne as long as the heavens endure.

If there is any doubt concerning this covenant with David, we can go to 2 Samuel 23:5, where David, speaking towards the end of his life, says: 'Is not my house right with God? Has he not made with me an everlasting covenant, arranged and secured in every part? Will he not bring to fruition my salvation and grant me my every desire?'

God kept his covenant promise to David and his direct descendants reigned on the throne in Jerusalem, in the southern kingdom of Judah, right up until they were taken away into exile. This was not the case in the northern kingdom of Israel, after the division of the kingdom. There the succession was often determined by violence and intrigue. In Jerusalem, however, the Davidic kingship remained secure until the exile.

There is a problem, however, in understanding this covenant with David. We are told that this covenant with David is to be an 'everlasting' covenant. How can this be? There is no descendant of David on the throne of Israel in Jerusalem today. So has this covenant promise been broken? The answer is that the covenant with David was fulfilled in the coming of Christ as the Son of David and as the King. We see this in the great messianic prophecy in Isaiah 55:1–4:

> Come, all you who are thirsty,
>   come to the waters;
> and you who have no money,
>   come, buy and eat!
> Come, buy wine and milk
>   without money and without cost.
> Why spend money on what is not bread,
>   and your labour on what does not satisfy?
> Listen, listen to me, and eat what is good,
>   and your soul will delight in the richest of fare.
> Give ear and come to me;
>   hear me, that your soul may live.
> I will make an everlasting covenant with you,
>   my faithful love promised to David.
> See, I have made him a witness to the peoples,
>   a leader and commander of the peoples.

One of the recurring themes of the Old Testament is that Messiah would be a king and would reign on David's throne. Particularly in the Psalms we have the teaching that the Messiah would win the victory, subdue his enemies and sit on his glorious throne. Many would regard Psalm 2 in this way, where God says, 'I have installed my King on Zion, my holy hill' (v. 6). A similar theme is found in Psalm 24:7–10:

> Lift up your heads, O you gates;
>   be lifted up, you ancient doors,
>   that the King of glory may come in.
> Who is this King of glory?
>   The Lord strong and mighty,
>   the Lord mighty in battle.

> Lift up your heads, O you gates;
>> lift them up, you ancient doors,
>> that the King of glory may come in.
> Who is he, this King of glory?
>> The Lord Almighty –
>> he is the King of glory.

In the New Testament there are also references to Jesus as King, not least the words of Nathanael in John 1:49 where he says, 'Rabbi, you are the Son of God; you are the King of Israel.'

The clearest connection between the covenant with David and the coming of Christ is found in Luke 1:30–33, where the angel told his mother Mary that her son would be a king:

> But the angel said to her, 'Do not be afraid, Mary, you have found favour with God. You will be with child and give birth to a son, and you are to give him the name Jesus. He will be great and will be called the Son of the Most High. The Lord God will give him the throne of his father David, and he will reign over the house of Jacob for ever; his kingdom will never end.'

As we move on next to the new covenant in Christ, described particularly in Hebrews, we shall see all these threads coming together.

The new covenant with Christ

So far in this chapter we have looked at the covenant with Noah, the covenant with Abraham, the covenant with Moses and the covenant with David. As we have worked our way through these covenants we have seen that each covenant was sovereignly established by God, each covenant contained promises and each covenant called for the response of faith and obedience. Now we come to the climax of all these covenants, namely, the new covenant God made through Jesus Christ.

The prophecy
To understand this covenant we need first to go back to the Old Testament. The prophet Jeremiah was born 650 years before Jesus, just a few miles north of Jerusalem. For forty years he passed God's message on to the people of Judah but they didn't want to hear it. This prophetic ministry of Jeremiah came at a critical point in the history of Judah. The Assyrians had been the most

powerful empire on earth but that was changing. Now the Babylonians and the Egyptians were the main powers. Eventually the Babylonians triumphed and Nebuchadnezzar became the most powerful ruler on earth. In 598 BC he captured Jerusalem and put Zedekiah, a puppet king, on the throne. Jeremiah advised Zedekiah to accept the situation but instead Zedekiah rebelled against Babylon. As a result, in 587 BC, the southern kingdom of Judah was attacked, the city of Jerusalem and its temple were destroyed and many of the people were taken away as slaves into exile in Babylon.

During most of his ministry Jeremiah had warned the people of the danger they were in by failing to do what God had commanded. He pointed out their sins and called them to repentance. He warned them that, unless they did so, God would use their enemies to bring judgment upon them. This prophecy came true but Jeremiah was able to look beyond the immediate crushing defeat by the Babylonians. He also said that, although Judah would be destroyed by the Babylonians, the exile in Babylon would not last for ever. We see this in Jeremiah 25:11: 'This whole country will become a desolate wasteland, and these nations will serve the king of Babylon for seventy years.' After a period of exile the nation of Judah would return to their land and would once again know the blessing of God. God's judgment would have passed. We see this in Jeremiah 29:10–14:

> This is what the LORD says: 'When seventy years are completed for Babylon, I will come to you and fulfil my gracious promise to bring you back to this place. For I know the plans I have for you,' declares the LORD, 'plans to prosper you and not to harm you, plans to give you hope and a future. Then you will call upon me and come and pray to me, and I will listen to you. You will seek me and find me when you seek me with all your heart. I will be found by you,' declares the LORD, 'and will bring you back from captivity. I will gather you from all the nations and places where I have banished you,' declares the LORD, 'and will bring you back to the place from which I carried you into exile.'

This prophecy came true with the return to Judah and the rebuilding of Jerusalem under the leadership of Zerubbabel and Nehemiah. The significant point for our present study, however, is that the prophet Jeremiah did not only look forward seventy years until the end of the exile: he looked much further forward. Indeed, he looked forward to the coming of Jesus and he gave us one of the most important prophecies in the Bible, which we find in Jeremiah 31:31–34:

> 'The time is coming,' declares the LORD,
>   'when I will make a new covenant
> with the house of Israel
>   and with the house of Judah.

Headship theology: the covenants of promise

> It will not be like the covenant
>   I made with their forefathers
> when I took them by the hand
>   to lead them out of Egypt,
> because they broke my covenant,
>   though I was a husband to them,'
>   declares the LORD.
> 'This is the covenant that I will make with the house of Israel
>   after that time,' declares the LORD.
> 'I will put my law in their minds
>   and write it on their hearts.
> I will be their God,
>   and they will be my people.
> No longer will a man teach his neighbour,
>   or a man his brother, saying, "Know the LORD,"
> because they will all know me,
>   from the least of them to the greatest,' declares the LORD.
> 'For I will forgive their wickedness
>   and will remember their sins no more.'

This is the first reference in the Bible to a 'new covenant' that God was going to make with his people and, as we can see, it is somewhat different from the covenants which have gone before. Jeremiah writes that this new covenant will not be like the covenant God made with Moses and the people after he brought them out of Egypt. He even tells us the ways in which this covenant will be different:

1. I will put my law in their minds and write it on their hearts.
2. I will be their God, and they will be my people.
3. I will forgive their wickedness and will remember their sins no more.[2]

The fulfilment

If we now move forward into the New Testament, to Hebrews 8:6–13, we can see the fulfilment of this prophecy. In this passage the writer to the Hebrews is comparing the ministry of the priests in the temple (and especially of the high priest) with the ministry of Jesus. In this comparison he quotes from Jeremiah.

---

2. A similar prophecy is found in Ezek. 36:24–28, which also mentions the work of the Holy Spirit.

But the ministry Jesus has received is as superior to theirs as the covenant of which he is mediator is superior to the old one, and it is founded on better promises.

For if there had been nothing wrong with that first covenant, no place would have been sought for another. But God found fault with the people and said:

'The time is coming, declares the Lord,
    when I will make a new covenant
with the house of Israel
    and with the house of Judah.
It will not be like the covenant
    I made with their forefathers
when I took them by the hand
    to lead them out of Egypt,
because they did not remain faithful to my covenant,
    and I turned away from them,
        declares the Lord.
This is the covenant I will make with the house of Israel
    after that time, declares the Lord.
I will put my laws in their minds
    and write them on their hearts.
I will be their God,
    and they will be my people.
No longer will a man teach his neighbour,
    or a man his brother, saying, "Know the Lord,"
because they will all know me,
    from the least of them to the greatest.
For I will forgive their wickedness
    and will remember their sins no more.'

By calling this covenant 'new', he has made the first one obsolete; and what is obsolete and ageing will soon disappear.

Do you see the point of this? Not only is Jesus our great high priest, having made one final sacrifice on the cross which renders the old temple priesthood redundant, but also he is the one who instigates a new covenant. In the next chapter, in Hebrews 9:15, the writer to the Hebrews puts it like this: 'For this reason Christ is the mediator of a new covenant, that those who are called may receive the promised eternal inheritance – now that he has died as a ransom to set them free from the sins committed under the first covenant.'

All of the priests and sacrifices of the old covenant looked forward to the day when, with one sacrifice, Jesus would pay the penalty for sins. Before that, the priests and sacrifices were merely 'covering over' sin until it would all be taken away. The high priest offered sacrifices for his own sins and for the sins of the people but only when Jesus our great high priest came (the one who had no sins of his own) would that whole system be brought to an end. Everything comes to its climax in the coming of Jesus. Everything that went before was looking forward, awaiting fulfilment.

The salvation
If we now go back to the three ways in which Jeremiah said that the new covenant would be different from the old covenant, we can understand what they mean:

I will put my law in their minds and write it on their hearts
This speaks of the work of the Holy Spirit. When Christ had finished the work he came to do, God sent his Holy Spirit to apply all of Christ's work to the hearts and lives of those who, by faith, trusted in him and were placed in a right relationship with God. The Holy Spirit applies God's truth to the minds of believers and writes it on their hearts.

I will be their God, and they will be my people
This speaks of the new relationship in which Christians stand with God, through Jesus Christ. We are still related to God by faith, as were Abraham and Moses, but now by faith we are united spiritually with Christ. We are new creatures, in a new covenant, having experienced a new birth, and nothing can remove us from our relationship with God.

I will forgive their wickedness and will remember their sins no more
This speaks of full and free salvation and eternal life. Our sins are not just covered over, they have been dealt with once and for all. The sins of Abraham and our sins were dealt with at the same time, on the cross at Calvary. We are now free from sin, free from death and free from the clutches of the evil one. We have salvation and the promise of eternal life.

We might sum the whole thing up in this way: the new covenant is not 'new' in the sense of being in opposition to the 'old' covenant but 'new' in the sense of being the final and complete fulfilment of all the promises made by God in previous covenants. Everything comes together in Jesus Christ, the second person of the Trinity, the eternal Son of God. It is also important to notice that, although this is a 'new' covenant as opposed to the 'old' covenant, nevertheless it is a covenant. In other words, God has not changed his way of dealing with human beings: he still works through covenants.

The blood of the covenant

One important aspect of the new covenant concerns the blood of Christ. In particular, we must consider the words of Jesus quoted in Matthew 26:28: 'This is my blood of the covenant, which is poured out for many for the forgiveness of sins.' There are actually three themes here: the covenant and the blood; the high priest and the blood; and the Passover and the blood.

The covenant and the blood
When we read the New Testament it is important to remember that much of its teaching can only be understood in the light of the Old Testament. That is certainly the case here as Jesus met with his disciples for the Passover meal. The disciples were Jews and they were steeped in the Scriptures of what we now call the Old Testament. When Jesus spoke about his blood and about the covenant, three aspects of Jewish religion would have been in their minds. When the disciples heard the words 'the blood of the covenant', the first thing that would have come into their minds was the story of Moses in the book of Exodus because that is the origin of the expression 'the blood of the covenant'. As we saw when looking at the Mosaic covenant, after the people had affirmed their promise to obey God, Moses sprinkled them with blood and said, 'This is the blood of the covenant that the LORD has made with you in accordance with all these words.' By the symbolism of the sprinkled blood God established a covenant between himself and the people. When Jesus said, 'This cup is the new covenant in my blood, which is poured out for you' (Luke 22:20) the disciples would immediately have seen the connection, because Moses and the covenant God used him to establish were at the very heart of their religion. They were God's covenant people. Now Jesus was talking about a 'new covenant'. This must have been startling for these disciples, if a little confusing.

Jesus was telling his disciples that the old covenant, made with Moses, was coming to an end. Now there was to be a new covenant and it too would be ratified with blood. The difference was that the blood to be used to ratify the new covenant would be the blood of Christ and not the blood of an animal sacrifice.

The high priest and the blood
When they heard the words 'the blood of the covenant', the second thing that would have come into the minds of the disciples was the Old Testament sac-

rificial system. The Old Testament is full of blood sacrifices. The best way to see the connection between the Old Testament sacrifices and what Jesus did is to ask the question: what did the death of Christ achieve? In Matthew's version of the story of the Last Supper, in Matthew 26:28, Jesus himself provides the answer. He says, 'This is my blood of the covenant, which is poured out for many for the forgiveness of sins.' This is the key to the whole subject, the forgiveness of sins; but that immediately raises another question: how can Jesus' death bring forgiveness of sins? There are many ways of answering that question but the most basic answer is brutally simple: Jesus took our place and God punished him instead of punishing us.

In the Old Testament the priests, especially the high priest, offered sacrifices yet these sacrifices were a temporary arrangement. The time would come when one final sacrifice would put an end to all of those Old Testament sacrifices. This one, final sacrifice was the sacrifice of Jesus Christ on the cross. Much of the letter to the Hebrews is written to explain that. The writer to the Hebrews compares Christ to the high priest in the Old Testament. In Leviticus 16 the office of the high priest was established with Aaron, Moses' brother, the first to hold it. It was then passed down to the oldest son in each generation. The high priest shared the duties of the other priests but there was one duty, his most important duty, which he alone performed. Once each year, on the Day of Atonement, the high priest would go into the innermost sanctuary of the Tent of Meeting (and later the temple), called 'the Most Holy Place', and there he would offer sacrifices. He began with a sacrifice for his own sins and then made a sacrifice for the sins of the people. He did this every year without fail.

The writer to the Hebrews tells us that Christ is our great high priest. The difference is that he offered only one sacrifice, on the cross at Calvary, and that brought an end to all sacrifices. The sacrifice he offered was himself because a blood sacrifice was necessary for the forgiveness of sins. As the writer to the Hebrews says in Hebrews 9:22: 'the law requires that nearly everything be cleansed with blood, and without the shedding of blood there is no forgiveness.' Here is the point: the shedding of blood brings forgiveness.

When most people think about the cross, all they see is a good man wrongly put to death by wicked religious leaders in partnership with a corrupt regime. As Christians we must look deeper. A great transaction was taking place on that cross. Something was happening which has soul-saving and life-changing potential. Our sins were laid upon Jesus and God punished those sins in the person of his beloved Son. There are various passages of Scripture which confirm this; for example, Isaiah 53:5–7:

> But he was pierced for our transgressions,
>   he was crushed for our iniquities;
> the punishment that brought us peace was upon him,
>   and by his wounds we are healed.
> We all, like sheep, have gone astray,
>   each of us has turned to his own way;
> and the LORD has laid on him
>   the iniquity of us all.
> He was oppressed and afflicted,
>   yet he did not open his mouth;
> he was led like a lamb to the slaughter,
>   and as a sheep before her shearers is silent,
>   so he did not open his mouth.

There are other New Testament passages which confirm this interpretation. Paul writes in 2 Corinthians 5:21 that 'God made him who had no sin to be sin for us, so that in him we might become the righteousness of God'. This idea that Christ becomes sin and in exchange we become the righteousness of God is central to the doctrine of justification, which we shall come to in chapter 9. Then in Galatians 3:13 Paul writes, 'Christ redeemed us from the curse of the law by becoming a curse for us, for it is written: "Cursed is everyone who is hung on a tree."' Here again is the central theme of our benefiting from what Christ has done on our behalf. The same theme can be found in Hebrews 9:28: 'Christ was sacrificed once to take away the sins of many people; and he will appear a second time, not to bear sin, but to bring salvation to those who are waiting for him.' Christ bore our sins and so brings salvation to us. Finally, in 1 Peter 2:24: 'He himself bore our sins in his body on the tree, so that we might die to sins and live for righteousness; by his wounds you have been healed.' He died for believers and healed them by his death, so in response believers must live for righteousness.

The Passover and the blood
When they heard the words 'the blood of the covenant', the third thing that would have come into the minds of the disciples was the Passover itself. The one point in all of this which we must remember is that when Jesus spoke about his 'blood of the covenant' he was speaking during a Passover meal. That context helps us to see another dimension of the significance of the blood of Christ. We must return in our minds to Exodus 12:1–13, the night when God took his people out of Egypt:

Headship theology: the covenants of promise

> The LORD said to Moses and Aaron in Egypt, 'This month is to be for you the first month, the first month of your year. Tell the whole community of Israel that on the tenth day of this month each man is to take a lamb for his family, one for each household. If any household is too small for a whole lamb, they must share one with their nearest neighbour, having taken into account the number of people there are. You are to determine the amount of lamb needed in accordance with what each person will eat. The animals you choose must be year-old males without defect, and you may take them from the sheep or the goats. Take care of them until the fourteenth day of the month, when all the people of the community of Israel must slaughter them at twilight. Then they are to take some of the blood and put it on the sides and tops of the door-frames of the houses where they eat the lambs. That same night they are to eat the meat roasted over the fire, along with bitter herbs, and bread made without yeast. Do not eat the meat raw or cooked in water, but roast it over the fire – head, legs and inner parts. Do not leave any of it till morning; if some is left till morning, you must burn it. This is how you are to eat it: with your cloak tucked into your belt, your sandals on your feet and your staff in your hand. Eat it in haste; it is the LORD's Passover.
>
> 'On that same night I will pass through Egypt and strike down every firstborn – both men and animals – and I will bring judgment on all the gods of Egypt. I am the LORD. The blood will be a sign for you on the houses where you are; and when I see the blood, I will pass over you. No destructive plague will touch you when I strike Egypt.'

In the New Testament we see this passage picked up in the words of John the Baptist in John 1:29: 'The next day John saw Jesus coming towards him and said, "Look, the Lamb of God, who takes away the sin of the world!"'

These words of the Baptist are a summary of his message and they take us to the very heart of the matters before us. As a good Jew he was using language which would immediately have been understood by those who were listening to him. He was making reference to the Passover lamb. Just as the Israelites in Egypt took shelter under the blood of the lamb and so escaped when the angel of death passed over, so we are to take shelter under the blood of Jesus Christ to escape from God's wrath and judgment today.

This interpretation of the words of John the Baptist is supported elsewhere in the Bible. Paul in 1 Corinthians 5:7 writes, 'Christ, our Passover Lamb, has been sacrificed.' And there are other passages we could also consider, such as Isaiah 53:7, where the Messiah is described as being 'led like a lamb to the slaughter'. In Revelation 5:6–9 Jesus is described as the Lamb who was slain and it is said that with his blood he purchased men for God.

If we now draw the threads of all this together we can go some way towards understanding the words of John the Baptist and tying them into our understanding of what Christ achieved in the new covenant. All human beings are sinners in need of salvation and God has provided this salvation. Just as he provided a way in Egypt for the Israelites to escape from death on that terrible night, so he has provided a way for us to escape the judgment of God on that terrible day when he will judge the world. Just as the people sheltered under the blood of a lamb sprinkled on the doorposts and lintels of their houses, so today we are to shelter under the blood of Christ. When Jesus died on the cross at Calvary he did so as a sacrificial offering for sin and God chose to accept the death of Christ in our place.

Conclusion

The new covenant refers to the relationship which we have with God as a direct result of what Christ has done in shedding his blood for us. In his farewell to the Ephesian elders, in Acts 20:28, Paul said this: 'Keep watch over yourselves and all the flock of which the Holy Spirit has made you overseers. Be shepherds of the church of God, which he bought with his own blood.' There it is in summary form: Jesus bought our salvation with his own blood. The death of Jesus Christ on the cross at Calvary and his subsequent resurrection are the most important events in the entire history of the world. As Christians we are among those for whom the blood of Christ was shed. The blood of the covenant cleanses us from all sin.

The new covenant requires faith, like the covenant with Abraham. In the new covenant Christ fulfils the law, given in the covenant with Moses. Above all, Christ is the fulfilment of the prophecies concerning the Davidic king who will reign for ever and ever. This should not surprise us because it is an axiom of Christian theology that all of God's revelation and all of God's dealings with human beings come to a climax in the incarnation. Indeed, we might say that everything finds its completion and fulfilment in Christ. Jesus Christ is the incarnate Son of God and comes to bring to completion God's plans for his creation. There is a cosmic and all-encompassing dimension to what Christ has done. Literally everything is affected by the person and work of Christ and nothing will ever be the same again. We cannot understand our universe or even our own lives if we do not understand who Jesus Christ is and what he has done. God's Son has become a man and, in doing so, has ushered in a completely new era in which we shall see new heavens and a new earth and the throne of God established for ever.

As we have considered the various covenants which God established, five points have emerged. First, each covenant was sovereignly established by God. They were not bargains or contracts between God and human beings. Second,

Headship theology: the covenants of promise

each covenant contains promises. Third, there is a connection between the covenants, as they all build up towards the new covenant in Christ. Fourth, we must note the responsibilities of God's people in the covenant relationship. Fifth, we must properly understand the relationship between grace and law in the covenants.

PART 3:

THE IMPLICATIONS

In this final section of the book we shall demonstrate that our 'headship theology' proposal has certain implications.

First, it offers some help in understanding vexed questions regarding God's law. We shall demonstrate that our understanding of the relationship between the covenants helps us to see the law in the context of grace. God says to Abraham, 'I will be your God and you will be my people' and then, through Moses, he says, 'Since you are my people, this is how you should live', thus placing the Mosaic law in its context as a continuation of the Abrahamic covenant. This has implications for understanding Adam and the law. It also helps us to see the connection between grace and law, faith and obedience.

Second, we shall demonstrate that our 'headship theology' proposal maintains the key themes of the older covenant theology while being much easier to explain and expound, since it lies on the face of Scripture rather than using the covenantal language and concepts of seventeenth-century theology. In particular, we shall demonstrate that core themes of union with Christ, justification and imputation remain at the heart of 'headship theology' while at the same time emphasizing union with Christ, imputation and the value of ontological language in terms of our incorporation into Christ.

8. THE LAW OF GOD

Introduction

We have argued that the relationship God established with Adam in Genesis 2 does not require an undergirding covenantal structure and that the Adam–Christ parallel as we find it in 1 Corinthians 15 and Romans 5 does not require an undergirding covenantal structure. We have further argued that grace comes before law and hence it was an act of God's grace to offer Adam, on condition of obedience, the promise of eternal life for himself and all his posterity. We have also argued that the Abrahamic covenant was unilaterally established by God in his grace and that the giving of the law in the Mosaic covenant was not a 'republication' of some primal 'covenant of works' with Adam but was rather the spelling out of the obligations of the gracious covenant made with Abraham and his descendants. On the basis of this proposal, which we have called 'headship theology', we are able to draw certain conclusions concerning the law of God.

First, we shall argue that our proposal helps to offer a way of solving the difficult question regarding Paul and the law. Second, we shall explore the question of Adam and the law. Third, we shall demonstrate that our proposal helps us to offer a more biblical understanding of the relationship between grace and law and therefore between faith and works. So, then, in this chapter we shall consider Paul and the law, Adam and the law and grace and law.

Paul and the law

One of the most difficult and controversial issues in biblical studies concerns Paul and the law. On some occasions Paul speaks very highly of the law. For example, in Romans 7 he makes several positive statements concerning the law: 'Is the law sin? Certainly not!' (v. 7); 'the law is holy, and the commandment is holy, righteous and good' (v. 12); and 'the law is spiritual' (v. 14). In Romans 9:4 Paul speaks of the law as one of the blessings which the Jews had received from God: 'Theirs is the adoption as sons; theirs the divine glory, the covenants, the receiving of the law, the temple worship and the promises.' Compare also Paul's comments in 1 Timothy 1:8–9: 'We know that the law is good if one uses it properly.'

At the same time, however, Paul argues that while the law in and of itself is good, sin used the law and 'produced death in me through what was good, so that through the commandment sin might become utterly sinful' (Rom. 7:13). Paul also teaches that the law served a purpose for a time but that, with the coming of Christ, the law no longer held sway. He puts it like this in Galatians 3:23–25: 'Before this faith came, we were held prisoners by the law, locked up until faith should be revealed. So the law was put in charge to lead us to Christ that we might be justified by faith. Now that faith has come, we are no longer under the supervision of the law.' In Galatians 4:4–5 he teaches that those who were 'under law' have been redeemed from that position of slavery by Christ who himself was 'under law'.

In his letter to the Galatians Paul goes even further, speaking of the law in very negative terms and contrasting the way of law with the way of faith (2:16, 21; 3:10–13; 5:4). The writer to the Hebrews speaks in similar vein (8:6–13).

Scholars have struggled to reconcile these apparently contradictory statements. A number of different proposals have been offered to resolve this tension. Perhaps the most recent is the proposal offered by Brian Rosner.[1] Recognizing the varying ways in which Paul speaks of the nature and use of the law, Rosner seeks to bring all of the relevant passages into consideration and not simply the usual Galatians and Romans texts. This more comprehensive look at the evidence is helpful, even to those who are not persuaded by his conclusions. Rosner argues that Paul deals with the law in three ways, which he calls repudiation, replacement and reappropriation.

Thus he argues that Paul repudiates the law, in the sense of repudiating the law as law-covenant. Paul also replaces the law, in the sense of recognizing that

---

1. B. S. Rosner, *Paul and the Law: Keeping the Commandments of God* (Nottingham: Apollos, 2013).

believers are not under law but under grace and therefore the important thing is not law but faith expressing itself through love. Finally, Paul reappropriates the law, both as wisdom and prophecy, making it fit for purpose in a new-covenant, Christian context.

The most significant debate on this subject, however, has been between those who take the 'traditional' view of Paul and the law and those who take the 'New Perspective on Paul' (NPP) view. Let's reflect on this debate before suggesting how a headship theology proposal might contribute to the discussion.

Traditional view

The traditional view was that the Jews of Paul's day were trying to be saved by works and not by grace, by keeping the law (doing the 'works of the law') and not by faith. This view has held sway for a very long time in the church and those who hold to this position point to Paul's letter to the Galatians, arguing that Paul's critique of the Galatians for trying to be saved by 'works of the law' was the primary message of the letter.

It is certainly true that the letter to the Galatians can be used to support this interpretation. Having been saved by faith in Jesus Christ, these Christians were in danger from some false teaching which said that it was not enough to believe in Christ; they must also be circumcised and keep the Mosaic law, with all its rules and regulations. In the first half of Galatians 2 Paul describes his experience of the great Council at Jerusalem, when it was decided that Peter should continue with his work among the Jews and Paul was given the blessing of the Jerusalem church for his work among the Gentiles. This was a happy, friendly conclusion and they parted having given one another 'the right hand of fellowship'. Yet in the second half of the chapter we find division, hypocrisy, separation and 'factions'. The picture we have of Peter in this chapter does him little credit. This is what Paul says in 2:11–13:

> When Peter came to Antioch, I opposed him to his face, because he was clearly in the wrong. Before certain men came from James, he used to eat with the Gentiles. But when they arrived, he began to draw back and separate himself from the Gentiles because he was afraid of those who belonged to the circumcision group. The other Jews joined him in his hypocrisy, so that by their hypocrisy even Barnabas was led astray.

Peter was weak, afraid and hypocritical, being more concerned with what other people thought than with what was right, and Paul would have none of it. Once again the issue was the one about Jews and Gentiles. Paul had really grasped the significance of the gospel for the solution of the Jew/Gentile problem, as we read in Galatians 3:26–29: 'You are all sons of God through faith in Christ Jesus, for all of you who were baptised into Christ have clothed yourselves with Christ. There is neither Jew nor Greek, slave nor free, male nor female, for you are all one in Christ Jesus. If you belong to Christ, then you are Abraham's seed, and heirs according to the promise.' Similarly, in Colossians 3:11: 'Here there is no Greek or Jew, circumcised or uncircumcised, barbarian, Scythian, slave or free, but Christ is all, and is in all.' Paul could see that the argument regarding whether or not Christians (especially Gentile Christians) should be obliged to be circumcised and keep the tenets of the Mosaic law was actually a deeply theological issue, rather than simply an issue of agreed practice.

Those who hold to the traditional view of Paul and the law would argue that this confrontation between Paul and Peter was really the confrontation between justification by faith and justification by works of the law. This is what Paul says in Galatians 2:15–16:

> We who are Jews by birth and not 'Gentile sinners' know that a man is not justified by observing the law, but by faith in Jesus Christ. So we, too, have put our faith in Christ Jesus that we may be justified by faith in Christ and not by observing the law, because by observing the law no-one will be justified.

Those who hold to this interpretation believe that justification is by faith alone and that one cannot be saved by 'works of the law'. Going further, Protestant theologians have been at pains to stress that 'works of the law' do not contribute in any sense to a believer's justification. Rather, justification is an act of God in which he declares to be righteous those who have received the righteousness of Christ as a free gift of God's grace. They are thereby pardoned and accepted.

The Protestant emphasis on this doctrine was constructed in response to medieval Catholic theology and can be traced to Martin Luther and the Reformation. The Counter-Reformation Council of Trent anathematized this doctrine of justification in canon xi:

> If any one saith, that men are justified, either by the sole imputation of the justice of Christ, or by the sole remission of sins, to the exclusion of the grace and the charity which is poured forth in their hearts by the Holy Ghost, and is inherent in them; or even that the grace, whereby we are justified, is only the favour of God; let him be anathema.[2]

---

2. J. Waterworth (ed.), *Canons and Decrees of the Council of Trent* (London: C. Dolman, 1848), p. 46.

The nineteenth-century Scottish theologian James Buchanan, commenting on the canons of the Council of Trent, summed up the Catholic position in this way:

> they denied that His righteousness is imputed to us, so as to become the immediate ground of our acceptance with God, or the sole reason on account of which He pardons our sins, and accepts us as righteous in His sight. The merits of Christ were rather, according to their doctrine, the procuring cause of that regenerating grace by which we are made righteous; while the inherent personal righteousness which is thus produced, is the real proximate ground of our justification.[3]

From the time of the Reformation the position expounded by Luther in respect of justification became the standard position of Protestant theology, as expressed in the various confessional and catechetical documents of the sixteenth and seventeenth centuries. For example, the WCF stated the doctrine of justification in this way:

> Those whom God effectually calleth he also freely justifieth; not by infusing righteousness into them, but by pardoning their sins, and by accounting and accepting their persons as righteous; not for anything wrought in them, or done by them, but for Christ's sake alone; not by imputing faith itself, the act of believing, or any other evangelical obedience, to them as their righteousness; but by imputing the obedience and satisfaction of Christ unto them, they receiving and resting on him and his righteousness by faith: which faith they have not of themselves; it is the gift of God.[4]

Those who have held to this traditional view have, almost unanimously, made the connection between Paul's critique of the Galatians for seeking to be justified by the 'works of the law' and human beings trying to get themselves into a right relationship with God by obedience, law-keeping or 'doing their best'. They see Paul's rebuke to the Galatians as a rebuke which can legitimately be used against anyone who seeks justification by any means other than through faith in Christ. That is to say, they believe that the argument in Galatians has to do with individual salvation, answering the question, 'How can I be saved?'

---

3. J. Buchanan, *The Doctrine of Justification* (Edinburgh: Banner of Truth, 1984), pp. 116–117.
4. *Westminster Confession of Faith* (Edinburgh: Free Presbyterian Church of Scotland, 1981), 11.1.

New Perspective view

In 1961 the Lutheran scholar Krister Stendahl published a paper entitled 'The Apostle Paul and the Introspective Conscience of the West'.[5] In that paper he argued that Luther read his own struggle with sin and guilt back into Paul and read parts of Romans and Galatians accordingly. He argued that this was an inappropriate reading of Paul who, he said, had a robust conscience. Indeed, Paul had no problem in affirming his righteousness in terms of the law (Phil. 3:4–6). For Stendahl, Luther failed to understand the difference between East and West, between the first century and the sixteenth century, and so misunderstood what Paul was saying. Paul was not dealing with individuals at all but with communities. Kim Riddlebarger sums up Stendahl's position:

> The Western mind errs, as did Luther, by reading transgression language individually and therefore psychologically, rather than corporately as Paul intended. This means that Paul's point is not about an individual finding peace with a gracious God and relief from personal guilt, but about how Jew and Gentile, as distinct ethnic groups, fit into salvation-history respectively.[6]

Stendahl's article was followed by the publication of E. P. Sanders' important book, *Paul and Palestinian Judaism*.[7] Stendahl having argued that our interpretation of Paul is based on a misunderstanding begun by Luther, Sanders argued that the real problem is a fundamental misunderstanding of the nature of Palestinian Judaism. He argued that Paul was not dealing with a Judaism which was legalistic and teaching 'works righteousness' but with a Judaism which can be described in terms of 'covenantal nomism'. He means by this that for the Judaism of the period, salvation was not based on the law or 'works righteousness' but upon membership of the covenant. Obedience to the law maintains one's position in the covenant but does not earn God's mercy or grace. He argued that Judaism of that period was in fact a religion of grace. Sanders

---

5. K. Stendahl, 'The Apostle Paul and the Introspective Conscience of the West', in *Paul among Jews and Gentiles* (Philadelphia, PA: Fortress Press, 1976), pp. 78–86.
6. K. Riddlebarger, 'Reformed Confessionalism and the "New Perspective" on Paul' (1996), p. 9: available as download at 'The Development of the New Perspective on Paul – Stendahl, Sanders, and Dunn', The Riddleblog (4 January 2007), http://kimriddlebarger.squarespace.com
7. E. P. Sanders, *Paul and Palestinian Judaism* (London: SCM Press, 1977).

followed up this ground-breaking work with another volume, entitled *Paul, the Law and the Jewish People*,[8] in which he expanded upon his earlier argument.

J. D. G. Dunn then set out to clarify, and to some extent correct, Sanders' argument. He did this in an article entitled 'The New Perspective on Paul',[9] which gave the title to this new school of thought (henceforth NPP), and then developed his argument further in his book *Jesus, Paul and the Law*.[10] Dunn's main contribution to the debate at this stage was to deal with the thorny issue of the 'works of the law'. Since Luther, this expression had generally been interpreted as meaning those legalistic works whereby someone earns God's favour. Dunn argued that 'works of the law' referred to circumcision or the food laws or similar aspects of the law. These works of the law were therefore to be seen as badges of covenant membership rather than as a means of securing a right relationship with God. What Paul is saying, then, when he argues that a man is not justified by works of the law, is that salvation is not obtained through membership of the covenant community with its 'works of the law' as badges of 'covenantal nomism'. Rather, salvation is by faith.

N. T. Wright has developed this thesis and has become its most significant exponent.[11] He has also become its great popularizer, particularly in the evangelical community. On the disputed question of the 'works of the law', Wright takes a rather different view of Galatians 2:16 from the more common position. In a book written in response to an attack on his theology by John Piper,[12] Wright says that we must read Galatians 2:16 in its immediate context, such that

---

8. E. P. Sanders, *Paul, the Law and the Jewish People* (London: SCM Press, 1983).
9. J. D. G. Dunn, 'The New Perspective on Paul', *The Bulletin of the John Rylands Library* 65 (1983), pp. 95–122.
10. J. D. G. Dunn, *Jesus, Paul and the Law* (London: SPCK, 1990).
11. N. T. Wright's earlier writings in which he espoused these NPP views include 'The Paul of History and the Apostle of Faith', *Tyndale Bulletin* 29 (1978), pp. 61–68; and *The Climax of the Covenant* (Edinburgh: T & T Clark, 1991). His development of these ideas comes in his series 'Christian Origins and the Question of God', comprising four volumes: *The New Testament and the People of God* (London: SPCK, 1992); *Jesus and the Victory of God* (London: SPCK, 1996); *The Resurrection of the Son of God* (London: SPCK, 2003); and the massive *Paul and the Faithfulness of God* (London: SPCK, 2013). He has also published numerous books presenting his views at a more popular level.
12. N. T. Wright, *Justification: God's Plan and Paul's Vision* (London: SPCK, 2009). This in response to J. Piper, *The Future of Justification: A Response to N. T. Wright* (Wheaton, IL: Crossway, 2007).

'works of the law' refers to those matters which separated Jews from Gentiles (including refusal of table fellowship).[13]

Whereas Piper believes that Paul's critique of the Jews was that they were trying to earn their salvation by works, Wright believes that Paul's critique of the Jews was that they had failed to understand God's 'single-plan-through-Israel-for-the-world' and so were continuing to use the law as a 'boundary marker' separating them from the Gentiles. This involves a certain understanding of the word 'covenant'. He writes, 'Here we have it: *God's single plan, through Abraham and his family, to bless the whole world.* That is what I have meant by the word "covenant" when I have used it as a shorthand in writing about Paul.'[14] He concludes that '*the point of the covenant always was that God would bless the whole world through Abraham's family*'.[15]

Baptism is the means whereby we enter this family, the means of our incorporation into Christ. Wright quotes Galatians 3:27 which says that we are baptized 'into Christ'. This has implications for the whole argument:

> *There is a single family*, because this is the whole point: the one God, the creator, always intended to call into being a single family for Abraham. The single plan through Israel for the world has turned out to be the single plan through *Israel's representative, the Messiah*, for the world *including Israel*, and all those who belong to the Messiah now form the one promised family.[16]

If this is the case, how should we understand the nature and purpose of the law? Wright answers in this way:

> God's purpose in calling Abraham was to bless the whole world, to call out a people from gentiles as well as Jews. This purpose has now been accomplished through the faithfulness of the Messiah, and all who believe in him constitute this fulfilled-family-of-Abraham. The law was given to keep ethnic Israel, so to speak, on track. But it could never be the means by which the ultimate promised family was demarcated, partly because it kept the two intended parts of the family separate, and partly because it merely served to demonstrate, by the fact that it was impossible to keep it perfectly, that Jews, like the rest of the human race, were sinful. The Messiah's death deals with (what seems to us) this double problem.[17]

---

13. Wright, *Justification*, p. 96.
14. Wright, *Justification*, p. 48. Italics are the author's.
15. Wright, *Justification*, p. 49. Italics are the author's.
16. Wright, *Justification*, p. 109. Italics are the author's.
17. Wright, *Justification*, p. 98.

This is not a book on the doctrine of justification and so we do not have space to enter into all of the issues which have opened up in the debate between the traditional view and the NPP view. Even in this quotation from Wright we see some of the hinterland of the dispute, such as whether imputation or incorporation is the means to becoming the righteousness of God and whether we should focus on faith *in* Christ or on the faithfulness *of* Christ.

Many writers have already responded to the 'New Perspective' school and the whole debate has spawned a huge literature. Some scholars have questioned the validity of the interpretation of the Judaism of the period.[18] Others have concentrated on the exegetical questions and have sought to demonstrate that sections of Paul's writings simply do not fit into this 'New Perspective'.[19] A word of caution, however, may be in order. Those who have read Piper's critique of Wright's position and Wright's response (as cited above) might be led to the conclusion that this is a battlefield with no demilitarized zone and that one must simply choose one position or the other. This is very far from being the case. One of the sad aspects of the whole debate on the NPP is the way in which N. T. Wright has been demonized by certain sections of the evangelical community, for some of whom there are only 'good guys' and 'bad guys' with nothing in between. Others have suggested that there are lessons to be learned from both sides.[20] Careful biblical and theological study, carried out with gentleness and respect, is the method to which we are called by the apostle Peter (1 Pet. 3:15).

Headship theology view

On the basis of our headship theology proposal, how can we contribute to an interpretation of Paul's view of the law? Obviously there is much common ground with the various other views mentioned above but perhaps we can bring one distinctive feature to the debate, based on what we have said about the close connection between the Abrahamic covenant and the Mosaic covenant.

---

18. D. A. Carson, P. T. O'Brien and M. Seifrid (eds.), *Justification and Variegated Nomism*, vols. 1 and 2 (Tübingen: Mohr Siebeck, 2001 and 2004).
19. See S. Gathercole's review of Wright's *Paul and the Faithfulness of God*: 'Paul and the Faithfulness of God: A Review', Reformation21 (July 2014), http://www.reformation21.org, accessed September 2015.
20. M. F. Bird, *The Saving Righteousness of God: Studies on Paul, Justification and the New Perspective* (Eugene, OR: Wipf & Stock, 2007); M. F. Bird, 'What Is There between Minneapolis and St Andrews? A Third Way in the Piper–Wright Debate', *JETS* 54, no. 2 (June 2011), pp. 299–309.

Our argument is that Paul's complaint against the Galatians and others was that they had failed to understand the connection between the Abrahamic covenant (grace) and the Mosaic covenant (law). The Jews had taken the Mosaic covenant to be a stand-alone law-covenant, which required obedience to law as a way of achieving a right relationship with God. Having failed to see the Mosaic covenant in its proper context, as a spelling out of the obligations of the Abrahamic covenant, they failed to see that law can only properly be understood in the context of grace.

It is no coincidence that, when Paul is writing to those who believed that obedience to the law was the way to a right relationship with God, he brings them back to Abraham. We see that in Romans 4 and also in Galatians 3. He was arguing that Moses must be read in the context of Abraham and so law must be read in the context of grace.

This enables us to say that Paul was neither confused nor contradictory. He spoke highly of the law when understood in its proper context, as a spelling out of the obligations of grace, always recognizing that the law was a temporary provision until Messiah came. At the same time, Paul criticized the idea that the law could be taken on its own (forgetting the Abrahamic covenant) and used as a means of obtaining a right relationship with God.

Another advantage of this proposal is that it occupies territory on which the traditional and NPP views have some shared interest. Wright already makes it clear that the two views have a certain common ground. He writes, 'For John Calvin, the Mosaic law was given as the way of life for a people already redeemed'[21] and in support of this view quotes Ed Clowney, a traditionalist.[22] He then provocatively goes on to say, 'That is "covenantal nomism": now that you're in the covenant, here is the law to keep.'[23] He later says:

> God gave Israel the Torah as the way of life for the people with whom he had already entered into covenant, and whom he had now rescued from slavery. The Torah was itself the covenant charter, setting Israel apart from all the other nations: Which other country, Israel was to ask itself, has laws like these? All the 'obedience' that the law then required would fall under the rubric of 'response to God's saving grace', even when this was not explicitly mentioned.[24]

---

21. Wright, *Justification*, p. 53.
22. D. A. Carson (ed.), *Right with God: Justification in the Bible and the World* (Carlisle: Paternoster, 1992), p. 25.
23. Wright, *Justification*, p. 53.
24. Wright, *Justification*, pp. 53–54.

Our headship theology proposal in relation to Paul and the law offers a way forward which tries to take account of the various statements Paul makes about the law and perhaps helps to bring together the various strands of thought on this subject.

Adam and the law

Given our argument that the central axis around which the Scriptures revolve is the headship of Adam and the headship of Christ, it is interesting to consider Adam's relationship to the law in his pre-fall condition.

The traditional way to address this issue is to say that Adam had the law 'written on his heart'. In other words, he knew by nature what the law required, as a creature made in the image of God. This is usually related to the prophecy of Jeremiah that the day would come when believers would have the law written on their hearts, a prophecy fulfilled at the coming of Christ, as taught in Romans 2:15. It is, however, important to be clear about what we mean when we read this back into Adam's situation, since the Scriptures do not actually say that Adam had the law written on his heart.

We can certainly affirm that Adam knew the will of God and understood the righteous requirements of a holy God. At the same time, however, we must recognize that this innate knowledge of God's law was not, in and of itself, sufficient. God also gave him certain commands to supplement what he already knew. For example, he was told that he must not eat from the tree of the knowledge of good and evil. Speaking of the 'creation ordinances', John Murray said:

> These original mandates are germane to our present inquiry precisely because they are so closely related to the powers and instincts with which man is naturally endowed, and they show unmistakeably that native endowment or instinct is not sufficient for man's direction even in the state of original integrity. The exercise of native instincts, the institutions within which they are to be exercised, and the ends to be promoted by their exercise are prescribed by specially revealed commandments.[25]

The best place to begin when seeking to understand Adam's knowledge of the law is Genesis 3. By noting what he lost at the fall we can understand better what Adam possessed before this calamitous event. The chapter describes how

---

25. J. Murray, *Principles of Conduct* (London: Tyndale Press, 1957), p. 26.

mankind's first parents, when tempted by the serpent, disobeyed God's express command by eating the fruit of the tree of the knowledge of good and evil. The human race fell into sin, they were banished from the Garden and every human being since then (except Christ) has been affected.

There are three related issues which will help us to understand the fall and to open up this theme. First, the problem of self-centredness; second, the problem of the human mind; and third, the knowledge of good and evil. No-one has expressed these problems better than a colleague of John Murray's, another professor from Westminster Theological Seminary, Cornelius Van Til.

The problem of self-centredness

Cornelius Van Til argued that, in a certain sense, the fall took place before Adam and Eve took the forbidden fruit. It took place when our first parents decided that they would listen to Satan, listen to God and then make a decision. In other words, the basis of their sin was to put themselves rather than God at the centre of the universe, believing that they had the capacity to decide who was speaking the truth. Van Til put it like this:

> The result was that man tried to interpret everything with which he came into contact without reference to God. The assumption of all his future interpretation was the self-sufficiency of intra-cosmical relationships. This does not signify that man would immediately and openly deny that there is a God. Nor does it mean that man would always and everywhere deny that God is in some sense transcendent. What he would always deny, by implication at least, would be that God is self-sufficient or self-complete.[26]

John Murray expressed a similar thought: 'The fall of our first parents did not begin with the overt act of disobedience; it was preceded by a process of defection that culminated in it.'[27]

It is vital that we see the point at issue in this matter. Prior to the fall, Adam lived a life that was God-centred. What God said, Adam believed; what God commanded, Adam obeyed. He viewed everything out of a centre in God and so looked at everything from God's perspective. At the fall, Adam made the choice to become self-centred rather than God-centred. He decided that he was capable of making decisions and that he himself could decide what was good

---

26. C. Van Til, *The Defense of the Faith* (Philadelphia, PA: Presbyterian & Reformed, 1976), p. 47.
27. Murray, *Principles*, p. 40.

or bad, true or false. The essence of sin is to be self-centred rather than God-centred. Human beings were created and designed to live in a God-centred relationship with their Creator and, outwith that relationship, human beings are not what they should be.

This affects our knowledge too. No true knowledge can be had of anything unless that knowledge is understood in relation to the Creator, with him at the centre. It is possible to possess a number of facts which in themselves are true but if these facts are not seen in relation to God and the system of thought which constitutes the rational structure of the universe, then they do not constitute real knowledge. Cornelius Van Til provides us with a fine explanation of the noetic effects of sin.[28] Fallen man is unable to understand anything fully and properly because, without a God-centred worldview, nothing makes sense. Man may think that he possesses 'facts' and that one day he will be able to piece them all together and make sense of everything but in fact there are no such things as 'brute facts', only 'God-interpreted facts'. That is to say, only when we think in a God-centred way can we understand how the various facets of our knowledge fit together. We must think 'out of a centre in God'.

The problem of the human mind
The second consequence of the fall, and one which follows naturally from what we have just seen, is the problem of the fallen human mind.

When we think about the effects of the fall we tend to think of sin's effects on the human will and on the moral choices that people make; but sin also affects the human mind, so that people are not able to see clearly or to think clearly. In Romans 8:5–8 we see the mindset of the believer as opposed to the mindset of the unbeliever:

> Those who live according to the sinful nature have their minds set on what that nature desires; but those who live in accordance with the Spirit have their minds set on what the Spirit desires. The mind of sinful man is death, but the mind controlled by the Spirit is life and peace; the sinful mind is hostile to God. It does not submit to God's law, nor can it do so. Those controlled by the sinful nature cannot please God.

Paul explains very clearly that this is the result of Satan's work. As we read in 2 Corinthians 4:4: 'The god of this age has blinded the minds of unbelievers, so that they cannot see the light of the gospel of the glory of Christ, who is the image of God.' There is, then, a difference between the mind of the believer

---

28. Van Til, *Defense of the Faith*.

and the mind of the unbeliever. This is well expressed in 1 Corinthians 2:14: 'The man without the Spirit does not accept the things that come from the Spirit of God, for they are foolishness to him, and he cannot understand them, because they are spiritually discerned.'

When we become Christians our minds, as well as our wills, are renewed and reoriented. We are then called to rethink everything in a God-centred way. This is the meaning of Romans 12:2: 'Do not conform any longer to the pattern of this world, but be transformed by the renewing of your mind.' When we become Christians we must think in a new way, see the world in a new way. We must rethink everything out of a centre in God. This notion of a God-centred worldview and thinking everything out of a centre in God has been much more pronounced in Dutch Reformed theology (Van Til, of course, was Dutch), not least through the work of Abraham Kuyper and Herman Bavinck, but it has often been neglected in British and American Reformed theology. It is an emphasis we must recover.

The point being made here is that the human mind has been damaged by sin and only when the Holy Spirit acts to renew the mind, to give us real understanding and to open us up to recognize the truth of God, will we truly be Christians. In other words, our fallen human minds need to be renewed by the Holy Spirit. Today we live in a disordered world because men and women live self-centred rather than God-centred lives. These men and women fail to see their true condition and do not understand how disordered the world is, because their minds have been blinded by Satan. If we put our faith in Christ, we begin to see things clearly. We then recognize that our world is not normal but distorted and disordered. We then see that the only solution to the problems of our world is for men and women to turn to Christ, that their lives and their minds might be renewed. Then they can join with other believers to rethink everything out of a centre in God, with a view to the re-formation, renewal and reconstruction of our world.

The knowledge of good and evil

One key to understanding the place of law prior to the fall is to ask what is meant by the biblical teaching that, post-fall, human beings became like God, knowing good and evil. Part of the serpent's temptation of Eve was to suggest that by eating of the forbidden tree she would become like God in this way (Gen. 3:5). After the fall, in Genesis 3:22, God says, 'The man has now become like one of us, knowing good and evil.' In one sense, then, what the serpent said has come true – but what does it mean? What is this knowledge of good and evil? How can our first parents have been more like God after the fall than they were before?

There are several things that it cannot mean. It cannot mean that our first parents were morally or spiritually more like God after the fall, since they were now sinners. It cannot mean that they were more like God through an experimental knowledge of sin, because God does not know sin in that way. It cannot be that they had more real, God-given knowledge than they had before, because the knowledge of good and evil led to judgment and banishment.

One way of understanding Genesis 3:22 is to think about the sinful human desire for autonomy, which we have just discussed. With this focus, it could mean that our first parents became like God in the sense of making decisions about good and evil, in other words, deciding for themselves what was good and evil. This is the sin of fallen human beings because only God can establish what is good and evil. When human beings try to do this they are trying to take the place of God. When governments do this they have abandoned God's Word.

Fallen human beings, in their desire for autonomy, deliberately suppress the knowledge of God, which is the possession of every human being (Rom. 1). In this self-centred autonomous, knowledge-suppressing condition, human beings believe themselves able to weigh up alternatives and make moral choices. In fact, this is impossible. Human beings can never be the arbiters of truth and hence the moral and ethical decisions they make are simply a sinful human substitute for the will of God. This means that even the 'best' decisions human beings make and even their 'best' actions are as 'filthy rags' before God – not because they are inadequate or sinful per se but because they are the result of fallen humankind using their 'knowledge of good and evil' as a criterion for decision-making rather than the will of God.

Adam before the fall had true freedom. He did not, however, possess 'by nature' the law, the knowledge of good and evil. What Adam possessed 'by nature' was a knowledge of God and of the will of God. Consequently, the choice he made in relation to the forbidden fruit was not a choice between a good act and an evil act but the choice between obedience to the will of God and disobedience to that will. The root of the sin was a belief that human beings were capable of standing apart from God as autonomous beings able to decide what was good and what was evil.

Grace and law

Our headship theology proposal also helps us in the matter of grace and law. Given our view of the relationship between the Abrahamic covenant and the Mosaic covenant, we can say that there is no contradiction between grace and law. Similarly, there is no contradiction between faith and works (or faith and obedience).

As the letter of James makes clear, faith that does not lead to works is not true faith (Jas 2:17, 26). Also, as the letter to the Hebrews makes clear, works that do not proceed from faith are not acceptable before God because without faith it is impossible to please God (Heb. 11:6). Only when faith and works are viewed as inseparable can we make sense of all of Scripture. Unfortunately, for five hundred years there has been a tendency to emphasize the discontinuity between faith and works, rather than their integral connection.

At the Reformation in the sixteenth century, Protestant theologians stressed that salvation was by faith alone, in contrast to their understanding of Roman Catholic theology which, they believed, taught that we are saved by faith and also by works (meaning sacramental and moral obedience). This emphasis on faith as the sole instrument of justification and a somewhat negative view of works of obedience were carried through into the confessions and catechisms of the seventeenth century and became standard orthodoxy in the eighteenth century. This determination to stand against Catholic theology and to affirm salvation by faith alone led to an undermining of the significance of works and obedience.

In the nineteenth and twentieth centuries, in reaction to classical liberal theology, evangelical theology again took up a strong position against the liberal emphasis on works. This led to a serious division within Christianity. On an anecdotal note, I recall that the university I was at during the 1970s had two Christian organizations. The Student Christian Movement focused its attention on practical Christian action, not least in relation to issues of justice and care of the poor. The SCM members often engaged in political protest, on the basis of a Christian socialism. The other organization was the Christian Union, then part of the Inter-Varsity Fellowship (now the Universities and Colleges Christian Fellowship). The CU focused on Bible teaching and evangelism, accused the members of the SCM of holding to a 'social gospel' (although most had never heard of Rauschenbusch) rather than the 'real gospel' and were not entirely sure that members of the SCM were Christians at all! It was only with the advent of John Stott's work, both in his writing[29] and through his work in the Lausanne Movement,[30] that this failure

---

29. J. R. W. Stott, *Issues Facing Christians Today* (Basingstoke: Marshall, Morgan & Scott, 1984). The later 'companion volume' was J. R. W. Stott, *The Contemporary Christian* (Leicester: IVP, 1992).
30. Stott was the principal author of the Lausanne Covenant: 'Lausanne Occasional Paper 3 – The Lausanne Covenant: An Exposition and Commentary', Lausanne Committee for World Evangelization, Lausanne Movement (1975), https://www.lausanne.org/, accessed October 2015.

to address social, economic and political issues from a Christian perspective began to be addressed by evangelicals.[31]

In the late twentieth century until the present time, due to an overreaction against the NPP and the FV, a good deal of conservative Presbyterian theology in the USA has been so keen to emphasize faith (particularly as the instrument of justification) that it has tended to undermine the significance of works, perhaps even to the point where some important scriptural teaching has been neglected.

Our headship theology proposal can make a contribution to this debate. If we reject the view that the Mosaic covenant was a 'republication' of a covenant of works made with Adam, this enables us to look at the law of God in a different way. As we have seen, the headship theology view is that the Mosaic covenant is a spelling out of the obligations of the Abrahamic covenant. To Abraham God says, 'I will be your God and you will be my people.' Through Moses he says, 'Since you are my people, this is how you should live.' The law, then, is given to the people of God, who are under grace, as a guide for the life of the covenant community.

This interpretation of the relationship between grace and law enables us to offer a biblical understanding of faith and works. In other words, God brought the descendants of Israel into covenant with himself and then gave them the law. The law was not some throwback to a primitive Adamic covenant of works but, as Paul spells out in Galatians, a continuation and spelling out of the obligations of the promise-covenant made with Abraham. There is, therefore, no incompatibility between grace and law and therefore no incompatibility between faith and obedience.

All of this provides us with a way of taking law, works and obedience seriously and affirming unhesitatingly the importance of works and obedience as vital components of the Christian life. Reformed theologians have typically avoided speaking about the importance of 'works' because they believed that Paul saw works and faith as two entirely contrasting ways of obtaining salvation. In the 'faith versus works' debate, some have even set Paul against James; others have adopted what they believe to be Paul's view of 'salvation by faith alone' and struggled with the book of James.

This interpretation also enables us to take seriously the whole question of the relationship between faith and obedience. We noted in chapter 5 that Guy

---

31. See also the 2010 Cape Town Commitment from the Third Lausanne Convention: Lausanne Movement, 'The Cape Town Commitment' (2011), https://www.lausanne.org/, accessed October 2015.

Waters, in his critique of the FV, did not consider those passages of Scripture which argue for the significance of works in relation to justification (Jas 2:24), nor did he consider those passages which say that final judgment is on the basis of works (Matt. 16:27; 25:31–46; Rom. 2:6; 1 Cor. 3:12–15; 2 Cor. 5:10; Rev. 20:12; 22:12). The view being presented here allows us to take those passages seriously. Faith and works are never separated in the life of the believer and the works we do will be judged.

Brad Green has recently published a fine book on the whole question of the law of God and Christian obedience.[32] In this book he offers us a way through these difficulties which is in fundamental harmony with the key elements of our headship theology proposal. I believe that his exegesis and theological reflection are fundamentally sound and I support both his approach to the subject and the conclusions reached.

In all of this, it is important to say again unequivocally that justification is by faith alone. Having said that, we must not undermine all that Scripture has to say about obedience and good works. We are saved by faith in Jesus Christ but this faith is always accompanied by works, or it is not real faith. Faith working by love ensures an obedient response to the grace of God, made known to us in Christ Jesus. Thus law, understood properly, is for our good. Law on its own is one thing; law in the context of grace and love is something else altogether. We might go further and say that law, without love and grace, is deeply damaging. Even from a strictly human perspective we can perhaps think of people whose upbringing was entirely governed by law and regulation and where there was no love. Many of these people are deeply damaged. On the other hand, law applied in the context of a loving family is understood and can be seen to be for our benefit.

Conclusion

In this chapter we have seen the significance of our headship theology proposal for an understanding of the law of God. It helps us to place a new construction on Paul's critique of the Jews, particularly in Galatians; it enables us to re-examine Adam's situation in relation to law; and, finally, it helps us to see the connection between faith and obedience.

---

32. B. G. Green, *Covenant and Commandment: Works, Obedience and Faithfulness in the Christian Life* (Nottingham: Apollos, 2014).

9. UNION WITH CHRIST

Introduction

Given that headship theology requires a strong doctrine of union with Christ, it is important to explain exactly what we mean by this.[1] This will involve demonstrating our agreement (or otherwise) with the way others in the Reformed tradition have used the doctrine of union with Christ in their systems. It will also enable us to demonstrate the significance of this for justification and imputation. We shall demonstrate that headship theology is able to do everything the old covenant theology was intended to do, in terms of justification and imputation, without creating a complexity of covenants.

In all of the discussions between the various strands of covenant theology, the issues of justification and imputation are to the fore. The proponents of John Murray's position hold to a high doctrine of union with Christ. The proponents of Meredith Kline's position argue that without a sharp law/grace contrast, justification is lost. Those who hold to Barth's position, as well as some of the FV proponents, argue that union with (or incorporation into) Christ, in an ontological sense, is the key to justification. One key issue concerns the place of 'imputation'

---

1. For a short study of the biblical teaching on union with Christ see A. T. B. McGowan, *The Person and Work of Christ: Understanding Jesus* (Milton Keynes: Paternoster, 2012), pp. 157–168.

in the system. On the one hand, it can be argued that, with a strong view of union with Christ, imputation is not required. On the other hand, without some 'reckoning' of Adam's sin and of Christ's righteousness, where does that leave the doctrine of justification? These are the issues we shall explore in this final chapter.

Anyone who stands within the Reformed theological tradition and who has an interest in the history of that tradition will have been fascinated to observe a changing approach to this subject. For most of its history Reformed theologians have generally sought to understand and explain the application of redemption by means of an '*ordo salutis*' method, namely, by demonstrating the relationship between the various doctrines in terms of the order in which they impact on the human condition. So, for example, some have argued that the *ordo salutis* begins with effectual calling, which leads to regeneration, which in turn produces faith, which leads to justification and so on. There is nothing wrong in principle with such a method. It might even be argued that Paul has an *ordo salutis* in Romans 8:28–30. The problem arises when the various doctrines are conceived of in terms of a 'domino' effect, such that, the process having begun, one follows from the other automatically.

In more recent Reformed theology, theologians have chosen to approach the application of redemption by focusing on union with Christ, instead of following an *ordo salutis* method. Paradoxically, this 'union with Christ' method has been adopted by two schools of thought within Reformed theology which, in most other respects, are normally opposed to one another, namely, neo-orthodoxy on the one hand and the theologians associated with Westminster Theological Seminary in Philadelphia on the other. Not surprisingly, there is a marked contrast in the way in which these two schools use the 'union with Christ' method, leading to quite different conclusions.

In order to open up the discussion, this chapter is divided into four sections: first, a brief general introduction to the concept of the *ordo salutis*; second, an identification of some of the important theological issues raised in seeking to discern the place of justification within the *ordo salutis* in Reformed theology; third, a discussion of the 'union with Christ' method as developed within neo-orthodox theology and as developed by scholars associated with Westminster Theological Seminary; and fourth, an attempt to draw some conclusions and to suggest possible ways forward for Reformed theology.

The *ordo salutis*

Louis Berkhof defines the *ordo salutis* in this way: 'The *ordo salutis* describes the process by which the work of salvation, wrought in Christ, is subjectively realized in the hearts and lives of sinners. It aims at describing in their logical order, and also in their interrelations, the various movements of the Holy Spirit in the application of the work of redemption.'[2]

The origins of the term have been traced to two Lutheran scholars, Frank Buddeus and Jakobus Karpov, writing between 1724 and 1739.[3] As Sinclair Ferguson notes, however, the concept 'has an older pedigree, stretching back into pre-Reformation theology's attempts to relate the various experiential and sacramental steps to salvation. In this context Luther's personal struggle may be viewed as a search for a truly evangelical *ordo salutis*.'[4]

The difficulty experienced in developing an *ordo salutis* is that the biblical evidence for the creation of an *ordo salutis* does not lie on the surface of the text but has to be deduced and inferred from various places.[5] This problem, however, did not deter many of those within the Reformed tradition from developing an *ordo salutis*, drawing their structure from Romans 8:28–30 and elsewhere.

Within Reformed theology the development of an *ordo salutis* involved three main considerations. First, it was recognized that God takes the initiative in salvation and that he does so through his Word and by his Spirit. Second, the *ordo salutis* was developed in such a way as to give proper expression to the Calvinistic theology and its understanding of the application of salvation. Third, it was clearly understood that the *ordo salutis* must account for the two problems which fallen human beings face, namely, their broken relationship to God and their polluted, sinful condition. Thus in the *ordo salutis* the various doctrines were divided into two groups: those which described the change in the sinner's relationship to God and those which described the renovation and renewal of the human condition.

The construction of an *ordo salutis* in order to describe the work of the Holy Spirit in the application of redemption was essentially a Reformation and post-Reformation development. As Berkhof writes,

> The doctrine of the order of salvation is a fruit of the Reformation. Hardly any semblance of it is found in the works of the Scholastics. In pre-Reformation theology

---

2. L. Berkhof, *Systematic Theology* (Grand Rapids, MI: Eerdmans, 1996), pp. 415–416.
3. S. B. Ferguson, 'Ordo Salutis', in S. B. Ferguson and D. F. Wright (eds.), *New Dictionary of Theology* (Leicester: IVP, 1988).
4. Ferguson, 'Ordo Salutis'.
5. See G. C. Berkouwer, *Faith and Justification* (Grand Rapids, MI: Eerdmans, 1954), pp. 31–32.

scant justice is done to soteriology in general. It does not constitute a separate locus, and its constituent parts are discussed under other rubrics, more or less as *disjecta membra*. Even the greatest of the Schoolmen, such as Peter the Lombard and Thomas Aquinas, pass on at once from the discussion of the incarnation to that of the Church and the sacraments.[6]

Berkhof goes on to say that 'Calvin was the first to group the various parts of the order of salvation in a systematic way',[7] while recognizing that this was a very preliminary attempt at such a process. Indeed, we might say that Calvin's *ordo salutis* was very simple, consisting of faith, justification and sanctification.[8] As Ronald Wallace has written, 'Calvin defines what we receive from Jesus Christ by faith as a "double grace", or a twofold benefit, the whole of which can be summed up for the purpose of theological discussion under two headings: Justification and Sanctification.'[9] Geoffrey Bromiley argues that the way in which Calvin dealt with the relationship between justification and sanctification was itself highly significant:

> Perhaps Calvin's most important contribution to the understanding of justification is his reuniting of two things which for purposes of clarity had in a sense been divided, namely, justification and sanctification. Now obviously neither Luther nor Cranmer nor others meant to keep the two apart. Their anxiety to relate faith to works bears ample testimony to this. On the other hand, the Reformers in general can hardly be said to have presented a comprehensive view of Christian salvation and the Christian life in a way which brings out the full relationship of justification and sanctification. This was to be the great achievement of Calvin.[10]

Berkouwer puts it slightly differently, arguing that, in discussions about the *ordo salutis*, the emphasis should be on salvation in Christ and this he sees in Calvin:

---

6. Berkhof, *Systematic Theology*, p. 417.
7. Berkhof, *Systematic Theology*, p. 417.
8. J. Calvin, *The Institutes of the Christian Religion*, tr. F. L. Battles, ed. J. T. McNeill, Library of Christian Classics, vols. 20 and 21 (Philadelphia, PA: Westminster Press, 1977), 3/11–17.
9. R. S. Wallace, *Calvin's Doctrine of the Christian Life* (Edinburgh: Oliver & Boyd, 1959), p. 23.
10. G. W. Bromiley, *Historical Theology: An Introduction* (Grand Rapids, MI: Eerdmans, 1978), p. 237.

Though one does not find an *ordo salutis* in Calvin, in the sense of its later development, there is nonetheless an order, perhaps better called an orderliness, which is determined by salvation in Christ. Salvation in Christ – this is the center from which the lines are drawn to every point of the *way of salvation*. The lines themselves may be called faith.[11]

Those who followed Calvin, however, developed the *ordo salutis* considerably. This was particularly true of Theodore Beza on the continent and William Perkins in England, both of whom developed charts (or *Tabulae*) in which the various doctrines were located in a logical (although not necessarily chronological) order. Perkins' 'golden chain' was particularly decisive for Puritan theology. The *ordo salutis* developed by Perkins involved, first, effectual calling, which produced faith; second, justification, involving the remission of sin and the imputation of righteousness; third, sanctification, which involved mortification, vivification and repentance; finally, glorification and life eternal.[12]

It is important to point out, however, that the *ordo salutis* as developed by Beza and Perkins was not driven and controlled by a predestinarian or deterministic worldview, as some have argued.[13] Richard Muller, in a profound and scholarly analysis of the relationship between Christology and predestination in early Reformed theology, says this:

> It would be a mistake to say that there were no deterministic tendencies in Beza's thought, but these tendencies existed in tension with a christocentric piety and a very real sense of the danger of determinism. Beza did not produce a predestinarian or necessitarian system nor did he ineluctably draw Reformed theology toward formulation of a causal metaphysic. Nor did he develop one *locus* to the neglect, exclusion, or deemphasis of others. Beza's role in the development of Reformed system may better be described as a generally successful attempt to clarify and to render more precise the doctrinal definitions he had inherited from Calvin and the other Reformers of the first era of theological codification.[14]

---

11. Berkouwer, *Faith and Justification*, p. 29.
12. See W. Perkins, *A Golden Chaine*, in I. Breward (ed.), *Works of William Perkins* (London: Sutton Courteney Press, 1970), vol. 3 and accompanying diagram.
13. J. B. Torrance, 'Strengths and Weaknesses of the Westminster Theology', in A. I. Heron (ed.), *The Westminster Confession in the Church Today* (Edinburgh: St Andrew Press, 1982), pp. 40–53.
14. R. A. Muller, *Christ and the Decree: Christology and Predestination in Reformed Theology from Calvin to Perkins* (Durham, NC: The Labyrinth Press, 1986), p. 96.

Rather than predestination, the key to the *ordo salutis* in early Reformed theology was effectual calling. This was defined as that work of God the Holy Spirit whereby the outward call of the gospel was combined with the effectual call of the Spirit. In the first half of the seventeenth century theologians tended to define the term 'effectual calling' in such a way as to include regeneration. This is reflected in the WCF, which has a chapter on effectual calling but no chapter on regeneration.[15] In the later seventeenth century, for example in John Owen, a clearer distinction was made between effectual calling and regeneration, with much more stress being placed on the latter.[16] The general shape of the *ordo salutis* was thus clarified. It was argued that effectual calling produces regeneration. Faith being the first fruit of regeneration, the *ordo salutis* then divided into two streams. On the one hand, faith led to justification and adoption, thus dealing with the sinner's relationship to God; on the other hand, faith led to repentance and sanctification, thus dealing with the sinner's inner condition.

Some of the discussions about the *ordo salutis* in seventeenth-century Reformed theology were occasioned by internal debates. For example, Arminius and the Remonstrants wanted to put faith before regeneration, in order to emphasize the human decision, as over against the Reformed view that regeneration must precede faith, in order to emphasize *sola gratia*. It is in this context that Berkouwer refers to Arminianism as 'this particular over-estimation of faith as a spiritual achievement'.[17]

This is only one example of the many variations among Reformed scholars on the *ordo salutis*. A more recent example concerns the disagreement between the Dutch theologians Abraham Kuyper, Herman Bavinck and G. C. Berkouwer. Kuyper taught that justification was from eternity, in order to stress the priority of grace. Berkouwer sums up his position: 'If justification is a divine act of grace which no human merit can achieve, then it must also precede faith . . . as eternity "precedes" time.'[18] Kuyper's argument is that justification is from eternity by grace but is 'appropriated' in time through faith. Bavinck rejected this theory of eternal justification because, he argued, it is not taught in Scripture and could be used in respect of many other doctrines as well.[19] He did, however,

---

15. *Westminster Confession of Faith* (Edinburgh: Free Presbyterian Church of Scotland, 1981), ch. 10.
16. J. Owen, *The Works of John Owen*, vol. 3, ed. W. H. Goold (London: Banner of Truth, 1966), pp. 188–366.
17. Berkouwer, *Faith and Justification*, p. 87.
18. Berkouwer, *Faith and Justification*, p. 145.
19. Berkouwer, *Faith and Justification*, p. 147.

want to affirm with Kuyper that 'all the benefits of the covenant of grace are established in eternity'.[20] Berkouwer later comments, 'This concept of eternal justification reveals how a speculative logic can invade a scriptural proclamation of salvation and torture it beyond recognition. This is the danger of an apparently consistent logical process which at first imperceptibly and then quite finally estranges itself from scriptural reality.'[21] He concludes by agreeing with Bavinck in rejecting Kuyper's notion of eternal justification and does so in quite strong terms:

> He who allows justification and redemption to ascend out of time into eternity is never again able to avoid the fatal conclusion that everything occurring in time merely formalizes or illustrates what has been molded in eternal quietness. Even the terrible reality of the cross is swallowed in the deep, still waters of eternity.[22]

The concept of the *ordo salutis*, then, was developed in post-Reformation theology, although the precise 'order' of the doctrines varied considerably from scholar to scholar.

Justification in the *ordo salutis*

We must now turn more specifically to the place that has been given to justification in the *ordo salutis*. In general, we can say that justification has been regarded by most scholars as following upon faith, which in turn is brought about by effectual calling and/or regeneration. There are, however, at least three significant issues on which Reformed theologians have been divided in relation to justification, namely, imputation, the nature of saving faith and the place given to repentance.

Imputation
The word 'impute' is used in the Authorized Version of the Bible as a translation of the Greek word *logizomai*, meaning 'to reckon' or 'to count'. It has the sense of something being applied or counted to someone else. Thus Adam's sin is said to be 'imputed' to all his posterity, such that all human beings share

---

20. Berkouwer, *Faith and Justification*, p. 147.
21. Berkouwer, *Faith and Justification*, p. 150.
22. Berkouwer, *Faith and Justification*, p. 151.

in his guilt. Similarly, the righteousness of Christ is 'imputed' to those who believe in Christ, such that they are reckoned to be righteous in the sight of God.

Justification was defined in forensic terms as the remission of sin and the imputation of righteousness, all of which in later Reformed theology was set in the context of a federal structure involving a covenant of redemption, a covenant of works and a covenant of grace. Just as the sin of Adam was imputed to all those whom he represented in the covenant of works, on the basis that he was their federal head, so the righteousness of Christ is imputed to all those whom he represents as federal head in the covenant of grace.

This matter of imputation is vital to any proper understanding of the Reformed view of justification. Indeed, the very nature of the imputation became a significant issue. This is demonstrated by the way in which the doctrine of justification is presented in the confessional documents. More specifically, it is highlighted by the way in which the Savoy Declaration differs from the Westminster Confession of Faith on the issue of imputation. The Savoy Declaration is, on most matters, almost identical to the WCF, on which it was based. On justification, however, there is an interesting difference.

Note first of all the section from the WCF statement on justification:

> Those whom God effectually calleth, he also freely justifieth: not by infusing righteousness into them, but by pardoning their sins, and by accounting and accepting their persons as righteous; not for any thing wrought in them, or done by them, but for Christ's sake alone; not by imputing faith itself, the act of believing, or any other evangelical obedience to them, as their righteousness; but by imputing *the obedience and satisfaction of Christ unto them*, they receiving and resting on him and his righteousness by faith; which faith they have not of themselves, it is the gift of God.[23]

When we come to the statement on justification in the Savoy Declaration, however, one part has been changed and expanded. As Alan Clifford puts it, 'Through alterations proposed by John Owen, the teaching on imputation became even more explicit.'[24]

> Those whom God effectually calleth, he also freely justifieth; not by infusing righteousness into them, but by pardoning their sins, and by accounting and accepting their persons as righteous; not for anything wrought in them, or done by them, but

---

23. *Westminster Confession of Faith*, 11.1 (italics mine).
24. A. C. Clifford, *Calvinus* (Norwich: Charenton Reformed Publishing, 1996), p. 83.

for Christ's sake alone; nor by imputing faith itself, the act of believing, or any other evangelical obedience to them, as their righteousness; but by imputing *Christ's active obedience to the whole law, and passive obedience in his death for their whole and sole righteousness*, they receiving and resting on him and his righteousness by faith; which faith they have not of themselves, it is the gift of God.[25]

This was not an alteration which all Reformed scholars accepted. William Cunningham, for example, discussing this issue, pointed out that it was not to be found in the writings of Calvin:

> It is to be traced rather to the more minute and subtle speculations, to which the doctrine of justification was afterwards subjected; and though the distinction is quite in accordance with the analogy of faith, and may be of use in aiding the formation of distinct and definite conceptions, – it is not of any great practical importance and need not be much pressed or insisted on, if men heartily and intelligently ascribe their forgiveness and acceptance wholly to what Christ has done and suffered in their room and stead. There is no ground in anything Calvin has written for asserting, that he would have denied or rejected this distinction, if it had been presented to him. But it was perhaps more in accordance with the cautious and reverential spirit in which he usually conducted his investigations into divine things, to abstain from any minute and definite statements regarding it.[26]

No matter which position is taken on the issue of the imputation of the active and passive obedience of Christ, however, one thing is clear: the imputation of the righteousness of Christ is at the very heart and centre of the Reformed understanding of justification.[27]

Faith
Another issue which Reformed theologians have debated, in their thinking about justification, concerns the nature of saving faith and the location of faith in the

---

25. The Savoy Declaration (1658), 11:1 (italics mine).
26. W. Cunningham, *The Reformers and the Theology of the Reformation* (Edinburgh: Banner of Truth, 1967), p. 404.
27. J. Buchanan, *The Doctrine of Justification* (Edinburgh: Banner of Truth, 1984), pp. 278–338. See also S. Gathercole, 'The Doctrine of Justification in Paul and Beyond: Some Proposals', in B. L. McCormack (ed.), *Justification in Perspective: Historical Developments and Contemporary Challenges* (Grand Rapids, MI: Baker, 2006), pp. 219–241.

ordo salutis. In general, Reformed theologians have taught that faith is the formal or instrumental cause of justification and is not in itself meritorious. That is to say, faith is not something which sinners bring to God from out of themselves, in exchange for which God justifies them. Rather, faith is a free gift of God and is the 'instrument' (or means) by which justification is obtained.

Some Reformed theologians have also been concerned lest the significance of faith be lost by regarding it simply as another step in the *ordo salutis*. Berkouwer, for example, expresses the concern in this way:

> If the *ordo salutis* were really intended to be a straight line drawn through a sequence of causal factors it would be open to the same objections that we have against the Roman Catholic concept of the function of faith as a preparatory phase preceding justification or infused grace. Reformation theology has always protested that faith thus loses its cynical and total character and becomes a mere step on the way of salvation. In contrast to this devaluation of faith, the Reformation confessed *sola fide*, meaning thereby to emphasize the universal significance of faith. In this way faith possesses no unique functional value; it rests wholly in God's grace. Theological study of the *way of salvation*, or *ordo salutis*, must, then, always revolve about the correlation between faith and justification. It must simply cut away everything which blocks its perspective of this *sola fide*. Heresy always invades the *ordo salutis* at this point, and this is why it is so necessary to realize that the entire *way of salvation* is only meant to illuminate *sola fide* and *sola gratia*. For only thus can it be confessed that *Christ is the way*.[28]

He underlines this point and concludes by stressing that 'it is perpetually necessary for the Church to reflect on the *ordo salutis*, or, as we think better to say, on the *way of salvation*. The purpose of her reflection is not to refine and praise the logical systematization. It is to cut off every way in which Christ is not confessed exclusively as *the Way*.'[29]

We can now take the argument a step further and say that the righteousness of Christ is imputed through the instrumentality of faith, a faith which is not itself meritorious and which exists only because of God's grace.

Repentance

In formulating its understanding of the place of justification in the *ordo salutis*, Reformed theology has often been divided over the place of repentance.

---

28. Berkouwer, *Faith and Justification*, pp. 32–33.
29. Berkouwer, *Faith and Justification*, p. 36.

Some Scottish theologians, for example, argued that repentance was a condition of salvation and therefore must come before justification in the *ordo salutis*.[30]

There have, of course, been Reformed theologians who wanted to put repentance before justification in the *ordo salutis* but who would certainly not regard justification as conditional upon repentance. Robert Reymond, for example, argues on scriptural grounds that repentance comes before justification.[31] His *ordo* is: effectual calling, regeneration, repentance unto life, faith in Jesus Christ, justification, definitive sanctification, adoption (and the Spirit's sealing), progressive sanctification, perseverance in holiness and glorification.[32] Despite the fact that repentance comes before justification (and even faith) he is careful to insist that faith is the sole instrument of justification and that repentance is 'not to be rested in as if it were itself a satisfaction for sin or the cause of pardon, for repentance *per se* is and can be neither'.[33]

On the whole, however, Reformed theologians have viewed repentance as following upon justification as a result, rather than going before it as a cause. Irrespective of the view taken on the place of repentance in the *ordo salutis*, however, Reformed theologians are at least in agreement that neither justification nor the faith which is its instrumental cause is occasioned by repentance, which must rather be regarded as a non-meritorious but necessary accompaniment to faith.

Union with Christ

As we now turn to consider the two schools of thought which, in their teaching concerning the application of redemption, have followed the 'union with Christ' method as over against an '*ordo salutis*' method, it must not be imagined that the Reformed theologians of earlier centuries ignored this vital doctrine. We noted earlier the emphasis on effectual calling in early seventeenth-century theology. We should also note that it was characteristic of these theologians to see effectual

---

30. Principal James Hadow of St Andrews took this view during the Marrow controversy in the early 1800s. See discussion of this point in A. T. B. McGowan, *The Federal Theology of Thomas Boston* (Carlisle: Paternoster, 1997), pp. 168–184.
31. R. L. Reymond, *A New Systematic Theology of the Christian Faith* (2nd ed., Nashville, TN: Thomas Nelson, 1998), p. 706.
32. Reymond, *Systematic Theology*, p. 711.
33. Reymond, *Systematic Theology*, p. 722.

calling as that which unites believers to Christ. Heinrich Heppe writes, 'At the root of the whole doctrine of the appropriation of salvation lies the doctrine of *insitio* or *insitio in Christum*, through which we live in him and he in us.'[34] Heppe goes on to quote Witsius: 'The goal to which we are called is Christ and communion with himself . . . The result of this communion is communion in all the benefits of Christ, in grace as well as in glory, to both of which alike we are called.'[35]

Similarly, John Owen among the English Puritans and Thomas Boston among the Scottish covenant theologians are good examples of scholars who gave due emphasis to union with Christ. John Owen followed in the general line of those we have noted above. As Sinclair Ferguson notes, 'For Owen, then, such order as there is in the *ordo salutis* would seem to be: Effectual Calling; Regeneration; Faith; Repentance; Justification; Adoption; and Sanctification.'[36] Yet Owen could speak about union with Christ as 'the sole fountain of our blessedness'.[37] His understanding was that this union took place by the indwelling of the Holy Spirit through effectual calling.[38] This was a very significant element in his overall understanding of the *ordo salutis*. Ferguson sums up Owen's position in this way:

> Thus divine election, and the outworking of it through the *ordo salutis* find their meeting place in *union with Christ*. This union, and all aspects of the plan of salvation are, for Owen, the application and fruit of the covenant of grace. To become a Christian is therefore to be taken into covenant with God in Christ, by the Holy Spirit.[39]

Thomas Boston was an orthodox covenant theologian who developed the *ordo salutis* in line with Calvinist theology and who understood the place of justification accordingly. He argued that effectual calling leads to regeneration, which in turn produces faith by which we are justified. Nevertheless, he placed such emphasis upon union with Christ as to be able to say,

---

34. H. Heppe, *Reformed Dogmatics* (London: Harper Collins, 1950), p. 511.
35. Heppe, *Reformed Dogmatics*, p. 511.
36. S. B. Ferguson, *John Owen on the Christian Life* (Edinburgh: Banner of Truth, 1987), p. 35.
37. J. Owen, *The Works of John Owen*, vol. 11, ed. W. H. Goold (London: Banner of Truth, 1966), p. 336.
38. Owen, *Works*, vol. 11, pp. 337–341.
39. Ferguson, *John Owen*, p. 36.

> It is the leading, comprehensive, fundamental privilege of believers, 1 Cor. iii. 23. 'Ye are Christ's.' All their other privileges are derived from and grafted upon this, their justification, adoption, sanctification, and glorification. All these grow on this root; and where that is wanting, none of these can be. All acceptable obedience comes from the soul's union with Christ, John xv. 4. Hence faith is the principal grace, as uniting us to Christ.[40]

Clearly, Boston saw no incompatibility between emphasizing an *ordo salutis* and at the same time recognizing that union with Christ is vital for salvation. For example, in another place Boston insists that 'Union with Christ is the only way to sanctification'.[41] He was also very clear in his specifications as to the nature of this union with Christ. It was not an external union, such as might exist, for example, between a ruler and his subjects. Rather it was an internal and spiritual union. He did not regard the benefits which flow from union with Christ as being like benefits which might be passed on to us externally but rather as benefits which flow because of the nature of the union. In seeking to explain this union and the benefits which accrue from it, he uses an illustration: the benefits we receive by union with Christ are not like those of the beggar who is thrown some money by a rich man but rather like those of a poor, debt-ridden widow who, by marrying the rich man, has her situation transformed.[42]

This view is shared by Louis Berkhof, who writes, 'Since the believer is "a new creature" (II Cor. 5:17), or is "justified" (Acts 13:39) only in Christ, union with Him logically precedes both regeneration and justification by faith, while yet, chronologically, the moment when we are united with Christ is also the moment of our regeneration and justification.'[43]

We must recognize, however, that although these scholars gave a place (sometimes a significant place) to union with Christ, they did so without any intended critique of the *ordo salutis* method. Those scholars we are to consider now, in placing emphasis upon union with Christ, do so with the clear theological intention of raising questions about the usefulness of the *ordo salutis* method.

Union with Christ in neo-orthodoxy

Based upon his Christological approach to theology, Karl Barth views the

---

40. T. Boston, *The Complete Works of the Late Rev Thomas Boston*, ed. S. McMillan (London: William Tegg & Co., 1853), 1:549.
41. Boston, *Complete Works*, 2:9.
42. Boston, *Complete Works*, 1:545. See also M. Luther, *Three Treatises* (Philadelphia, PA: Fortress Press, 1966), pp. 286–287.
43. Berkhof, *Systematic Theology*, p. 450.

application of redemption from the perspective of Christ, rather than from the perspective of the individual human being. He does not regard justification, adoption, sanctification and so on as a series of separate but connected events or processes in the life of the believer. Instead he emphasizes that all of these blessings come to human beings as a direct result of their being united to Christ.[44] He was particularly concerned that the relation between justification and sanctification be properly understood.[45]

For Barth, questions such as whether regeneration precedes effectual calling, or whether justification has a logical priority over regeneration, are largely irrelevant. For him, all of these are embodied in Christ and we come to share in all of them as we are united with Christ. As we noted earlier, in his lectures on the Reformed confessions Barth touches upon the *ordo salutis* in the Westminster Confession of Faith. His objection is not the same as that of later Barthians, who have argued that the Confession puts predestination at the head of the *ordo* and works out everything logically from there.[46] Rather, Barth's objection is that, by placing such a heavy emphasis upon the application of redemption and upon the means by which the individual believer finds peace and assurance, it seeks 'to make Reformed theology into anthropology'.[47] He asks, 'Why could the successors of John Knox celebrate the Pyrrhic victory of Puritanism in the Westminster Confession so that they gave up their Scots Confession and exchanged the idea of the "holy city" for the deficient idea of the "order of salvation", the theology of the assurance of salvation?'[48]

T. F. Torrance followed the main tenets of Barth's theology in this matter of union with Christ, as in other areas, although preferring to call himself an Athanasian rather than a Barthian! As Duncan Rankin has demonstrated, however, there is a significant difference between Torrance and Barth in their developed positions.[49] Torrance built his theology around two separate notions of union with Christ: first, an incarnational (or carnal) union, which is with all

---

44. K. Barth, *Church Dogmatics*, ed. G. W. Bromiley and T. F. Torrance, vol. 4/3:2 (Edinburgh: T & T Clark, 1956), pp. 520–554.
45. Barth, *Church Dogmatics*, vol. 4/2, pp. 499–511.
46. For example, J. B. Torrance, as we have seen.
47. K. Barth, *The Theology of the Reformed Confessions*, tr. and annotated by D. L. Guder and J. J. Guder, Columbia Series in Reformed Theology (Louisville, KY/London: Westminster John Knox Press, 2002), p. 151.
48. Barth, *Theology of the Reformed Confessions*, pp. 151–152.
49. See W. D. Rankin, 'Carnal Union with Christ in the Theology of T. F. Torrance', PhD thesis, University of Edinburgh, 1997.

humanity by the very act of incarnation; and second, a spiritual union which is only between Christ and believers. It is not at all clear how one moves from the first union to the second, or indeed (given that Torrance is not a universalist) how unbelievers fall out of the first union. The key point here, however, is that the union itself is presented in such a way as to obviate the need for a forensic explanation of the atonement.

The position is outlined with considerable clarity by Trevor Hart, who argues that both traditional Protestant theology and traditional Catholic theology have made the mistake of understanding salvation as the application of 'benefits'.[50] In contrast to this, he argues, we must see salvation in terms of our union with Christ who has already, in the incarnation, taken up sinful human flesh, united it with the divine and purified it from all sin. When we are united to Christ, we share in that reconciled and purified humanity.[51]

In Barth, Torrance and Hart, then, justification is not conceived of in forensic terms, involving the imputation of the righteousness of Christ and the non-imputation of sin, but rather in terms of the participation in and the sharing of Christ's righteousness.

Union with Christ in Westminster Calvinism

We now turn to the second group of theologians who have focused attention on union with Christ rather than on the traditional *ordo salutis* method. We must ask whether, in taking this position, these Westminster theologians have somehow managed to maintain forensic justification involving the imputation of sin and the imputation of the righteousness of Christ.

From the influence of Geerhardus Vos and John Murray, there has gradually developed within Westminster Theological Seminary (henceforth WTS) an approach to the application of redemption which seeks to draw together strands of the two positions considered so far. There is indeed an emphasis upon the 'union with Christ' method but there is also a commitment to forensic justification involving the imputation of Christ's righteousness.

To understand how this position holds together, we must consider an important work by Richard Gaffin. Originally a doctoral dissertation submitted

---

50. T. A. Hart, 'Humankind in Christ and Christ in Humankind: Salvation as Participation in Our Substitute in the Theology of John Calvin', *SJT* 42, no. 1 (1989), pp. 67–84.
51. These themes are also explored in several of the essays contained in *Christ in Our Place: The Humanity of God in Christ for the Reconciliation of the World*, ed. T. A. Hart and D. P. Thimell (Exeter: Paternoster, 1989).

to WTS under the title 'Resurrection and Redemption: A Study in Pauline Soteriology' in 1969, it was published in 1978 as *The Centrality of the Resurrection: A Study in Paul's Soteriology*.[52] Gaffin argues that the key element in understanding Paul's soteriology is the resurrection of Christ and that a redemptive–historical outlook is 'decidedly dominant and determinative'.[53] He argues that it is not possible to understand either the accomplishment or the application of redemption without focusing on the union between Christ and believers in resurrection. The resurrection of believers is entirely dependent upon Christ's resurrection, both historically (already realized) and eschatologically (we will be raised).[54]

On the basis of this study, Gaffin argues that the traditional *ordo salutis* ought to be revisited. In particular he raises three problems with the traditional *ordo salutis*. First, he notes the failure to take seriously the eschatological perspective of the Pauline doctrine: 'The traditional *ordo salutis* lacks the exclusively eschatological air which pervades the entire Pauline soteriology.'[55] Second, he points out that, traditionally, the various elements in the *ordo salutis* are regarded as separate acts, which he regards as a serious mistake: 'Nothing distinguishes the traditional *ordo salutis* more than its insistence that the justification, adoption and sanctification which occur at the inception of the application of redemption are separate acts. If our interpretation is correct, Paul views them not as distinct acts but as distinct aspects of a single act.'[56]

Gaffin emphasizes this point by showing the difficulty the traditional method has in dealing with the relationship between the various doctrines in the *ordo salutis* and the doctrine of union with Christ. That is to say, if union with Christ comes before these various acts, why are they necessary? If, on the other hand, union with Christ follows these other acts, does that not devalue its meaning and significance?

Gaffin's third issue in relation to the traditional *ordo salutis* concerns the prominent place given to regeneration and whether or not this is compatible with Paul's soteriology. His concern is whether a 'distinct enlivening act (causally or temporally) prior to the initial act of faith' might actually involve a 'distortion of Paul's viewpoint'.[57] He does not elaborate on this point, however, saying

---

52. R. B. Gaffin Jr, *The Centrality of the Resurrection: A Study in Paul's Soteriology* (Grand Rapids, MI: Baker, 1978).
53. Gaffin, *The Centrality of the Resurrection*, p. 135.
54. Gaffin, *The Centrality of the Resurrection*, p. 60.
55. Gaffin, *The Centrality of the Resurrection*, p. 137.
56. Gaffin, *The Centrality of the Resurrection*, p. 140.
57. Gaffin, *The Centrality of the Resurrection*, p. 142.

that it 'brings us to the limits of this study',[58] although he clearly believes it to be an important question for further work.

Gaffin's view has been very influential at WTS and others have followed his line of reasoning, including Sinclair Ferguson, who writes, 'Union with Christ must therefore be the dominant motif in any formulation of the application of redemption and the dominant feature of any "order" of salvation.'[59]

There is, however, a marked difference between the understanding of union with Christ as developed by Gaffin, Ferguson and others and that as developed by the neo-orthodox theologians. As we saw in the previous section, particularly in Torrance and Hart, neo-orthodoxy views union with Christ as an alternative to a forensic understanding of atonement with its key component of imputation. In Gaffin, Ferguson and the WTS theologians, the forensic element is retained. The imputation of the righteousness of Christ to believers remains a key element in their theology; it is simply that the means by which this imputation is effected is located in the prior doctrine of union with Christ.

This position has not gone unchallenged, related as it is to the development of John Murray's modified covenant theology in which he argued against a legal 'covenant of works' in favour of a gracious 'Adamic administration'. Meredith Kline and others, particularly Mark Karlberg, have argued that this failure to pursue a clear law/grace antithesis is a departure from Reformed theology and endangers the doctrine of justification which they believe to be dependent upon this antithesis. Karlberg goes so far as to say that John Murray, Norman Shepherd, Richard Gaffin and Sinclair Ferguson all moved towards a 'Barthian' theology![60]

Summary and conclusions

We have seen, then, that Reformed theology has characteristically dealt with the application of redemption in terms of an *ordo salutis*. Within that *ordo salutis* justification has normally been placed after faith and before sanctification. Faith itself is seen as a gift of God, which is granted in effectual calling/regeneration. This is to ensure the priority of grace and to avoid any notion that justification could be earned or achieved by sinful human beings.

---

58. Gaffin, *The Centrality of the Resurrection*, p. 142.
59. Ferguson, 'Ordo Salutis'. See also S. B. Ferguson, *The Holy Spirit*, Contours of Christian Theology Series (Leicester: IVP, 1996), pp. 93–113.
60. M. W. Karlberg, *The Changing of the Guard: Westminster Theological Seminary in Philadelphia* (Unicoi, TN: The Trinity Foundation, 2001).

This schema, however, involves several difficulties. First, there is the difficulty of establishing the order in which the various doctrines are to be placed (based on very little direct scriptural evidence) and whether the sequence is logical or chronological. Second, there is the danger of viewing the various doctrines as mere steps in a sequence, which, having once begun, will continue until complete. Third, and most significantly, there is the problem of ascertaining the precise relationship between the steps in the *ordo salutis* and the act of God whereby he unites believers to Christ.

In order to avoid these difficulties, particularly the third, some modern Reformed theologians have largely abandoned the use of an *ordo salutis* method and opted instead to view the various doctrines in the *ordo salutis*, not as a series of connected acts and processes, but rather as aspects of union with Christ. We considered briefly two schools of thought within Reformed theology which have taken this approach and noted the differences between them. In particular, we noted the crucial difference, namely, that the neo-orthodox understanding of union with Christ obviated the need for a clear forensic doctrine of the imputation of the righteousness of Christ. The WTS theologians, on the other hand, maintained both the doctrine of union with Christ as the key to understanding the application of salvation and a clear forensic doctrine of imputation.

In our view, we have a great deal to learn from Gaffin, Ferguson and others in this regard. It is not necessary, of course, to abandon totally the concept of the *ordo salutis*. It may well be important to retain the concept in order to clarify the nature of the various doctrines and to guard against mistakes in the relationship posited between them. Two things, however, are certainly clear: first, the doctrine of justification by faith cannot be properly and fully understood unless it is seen in the context of union with Christ; second, any understanding of justification which fails to maintain a forensic notion of the imputation of the righteousness of Christ involves a departure from the earlier Reformed tradition.

CONCLUSION

The purpose of this book has been to explore the different ways in which theologians have used the ideas of 'covenant' and of the parallel between Adam and Christ. We have looked at the historical expression of covenant theology, as codified in the WCF and as represented by Thomas Boston, one of its most famous exponents. We have considered the attack on covenant theology and the alternative system offered by Karl Barth. Then we compared three views coming from within the school of covenant theology itself, those of John Murray, Meredith Kline and the Federal Vision.

Having 'set the scene' in this way, we offered another proposal, which we have called 'headship theology'. That is to say, instead of holding to a 'covenant theology' in which the whole schema of theology revolves around two (or three) covenants, we are suggesting a 'headship theology' in which everything revolves around two 'heads', namely, Adam and Christ. Our argument is that, by getting the 'headship' issue mixed up in the 'covenant' issue, we have weakened the impact of both. There is no mention of a covenant in Genesis 2 and in the passages where Scripture speaks about Adam and Christ (1 Cor. 15 and Rom. 5) there is no mention of a covenant. Thus our case is that the Adam–Christ parallel, which we hold to be the fundamental key to opening up our understanding of life, death and salvation, does not require a covenantal underpinning to make it work. By releasing the Adam–Christ parallel from the strictures of a two- (or three-) covenant system, we liberate it to be used as Paul intended.

The further advantage is that we can then expound the covenants in Scripture in a systematic and chronological manner, demonstrating continuity and development. This stands in opposition to the idea that the Mosaic covenant is a 'republication' of a primal 'covenant of works' made with Adam. This enables us to take seriously what Paul says in Galatians concerning the relationship between the Abrahamic covenant and the Mosaic covenant. In one sense this involves a return to Calvin, who sees covenant (one covenant) as describing God's relationship with his people. It also suggests that much of the seventeenth-century elaboration on the ideas of covenant, together with the incorporation into the scheme of the Adam–Christ parallel, complicated the matter unnecessarily.

By separating the covenants from the Adam–Christ parallel we solve various other problems. First, we recognize that the issues of life, death and salvation belong in the Adam–Christ parallel. In other words, those who are in Adam will die and those who are in Christ will be made alive. Whether we experience death or life, salvation or damnation, depends entirely upon whether we are in Adam or in Christ.

Second, we can then take seriously what the Scriptures say concerning being 'in the covenant' or 'out of the covenant' as well as 'breaking the covenant'. Since the covenants function as a description of God's relationship with his people, rather than as a description of those who are saved, we can see how some people might be in the covenant only temporarily and instead become 'covenant breakers'. This also allows us to take seriously the language of apostasy, particularly in the letter to the Hebrews. There are those who are part of the covenant people through baptism who will reject Christ and be lost. The reason many have struggled with this is because we have had such a 'low' view of the church. Those who have been baptized are incorporated into the church and are in covenant with God. They are then under obligation to 'keep the covenant'. Ultimately, however, only those who are spiritually united to Christ will be saved.

Third, by holding closely together the Abrahamic covenant and the Mosaic covenant, we are able to understand the place of law in God's dealings with his people. God says to Abraham, 'I will be your God and you will be my people' and through Moses he says, 'Since you are my people, this is how you should live.' Law, then, involves a spelling out of the covenant obligations, which remains in place until Christ comes. Even then, the general tenor of the law (the 'third use of the law' in traditional Reformed language) continues to be useful for believers in Christ, as they seek to live out the life of faith.

Fourth, given what we have just said, we are able to suggest that Paul's problem with the Galatians was not that they were trying to be saved by 'works of the law' as opposed to being saved by faith. Rather, they were trying to take the Mosaic covenant as a stand-alone covenant, obedience to which would place them in a right relationship with God. What they failed to see was that the Mosaic covenant only makes sense in the light of the Abrahamic covenant which preceded it. Thus, law must always be seen in the context of grace.

Fifth, this being the case, we are able to make sense of the many passages which speak about obedience, law-keeping and 'works'. Instead of avoiding these passages lest we fall into the categories of Roman Catholic theology, we must embrace them. By understanding law in the context of grace and obedience in the context of faith, we can give a good account of the need for Christians to live obedient lives and to recognize that the faith which justifies is a faith which is never alone. As Paul says in Galatians 5:6, 'For in Christ Jesus neither circumcision nor uncircumcision has any value. The only thing that counts is faith expressing itself through love.' We cannot ignore James when he says, 'You see that a person is justified by what he does and not by faith alone' (2:24). Nor can we ignore the many passages which speak about final judgment on the basis of works. There is no necessary contradiction between justification by faith and the importance of works, although we must express our views on this very carefully.

John Murray moved in the general direction we have outlined above by speaking of the 'Adamic administration' instead of the 'covenant of works'. Why, then, can we not go further and speak of a 'messianic administration'? By this means we can place the emphasis on headship solidarity. Either we are 'in Adam' as a result of that solidarity created by the establishment of the 'Adamic administration' in Genesis 2, or we are 'in Christ' as the result of a spiritual union with Christ.

Some aspects of what we have proposed will be accepted by some theologians from each of the strands of covenant theology which we have considered. Inevitably, none of them will be inclined to embrace it completely! At the very least it is my hope that this book will open up a debate which will help to clarify and renew a Reformed understanding of salvation and the Christian life.

BIBLIOGRAPHY

Augustine, '4th Homily on the First Epistle of St John', in *Nicene and Post-Nicene Fathers 1st Series*, vol. 7: *Augustin: Homilies on the Gospel of John, Homilies on the First Epistle of John, Soliloquies*, ed. P. Schaff (Peabody, MA: Hendrickson, 1994), pp. 481–487.
——, 'The City of God', in *Nicene and Post-Nicene Fathers 1st Series*, vol. 2: *Augustin: City of God, Christian Doctrine*, ed. P. Schaff (Peabody, MA: Hendrickson, 1994), Books 13–14, pp. 245–283.
——, 'On the Merits and Remission of Sins, and on the Baptism of Infants: Book One', in *Nicene and Post-Nicene Fathers 1st Series*, vol. 5: *Augustin: Anti-Pelagian Writings*, ed. P. Schaff (Peabody, MA: Hendrickson, 1994), pp. 15–43.
Barrett, C. K., *The First Epistle to the Corinthians*, Black's New Testament Commentaries (2nd ed., London: A & C Black, 1971).
Barth, K., *Christ and Adam: Man and Humanity in Romans 5* (New York: Collier Books, 1962).
——, *Church Dogmatics*, ed. G. W. Bromiley and T. F. Torrance (Edinburgh: T & T Clark, 1956–1977).
——, *The Theology of the Reformed Confessions*, tr. and annotated by D. L. Guder and J. J. Guder, Columbia Series in Reformed Theology (Louisville, KY/London: Westminster John Knox Press, 2002).
Beaton, D., 'The "Marrow of Modern Divinity" and the Marrow Controversy', *Records of the Scottish Church History Society* 1, part iii (c.1925), pp. 112–134.
Beisner, E. C., *The Auburn Avenue Theology Pros and Cons: Debating the Federal Vision* (Fort Lauderdale, FL: Knox Theological Seminary, 2004).

Bell, M. C., 'Calvin and the Extent of the Atonement', *EQ* 55 (1983), pp. 115–123.
——, *Calvin and Scottish Theology: The Doctrine of Assurance* (Edinburgh: Handsel Press, 1985).
Berkhof, L., *Systematic Theology* (Grand Rapids, MI: Eerdmans, 1996).
Berkouwer, G. C., *Faith and Justification* (Grand Rapids, MI: Eerdmans, 1954).
Bird, M. F., *The Saving Righteousness of God: Studies on Paul, Justification and the New Perspective* (Eugene, OR: Wipf & Stock, 2007).
——, 'What Is There between Minneapolis and St Andrews? A Third Way in the Piper–Wright Debate', *JETS* 54, no. 2 (June 2011), pp. 299–309.
Blocher, H., *In the Beginning: The Opening Chapters of Genesis* (Leicester: IVP, 1984).
——, 'Old Covenant, New Covenant', in A. T. B. McGowan (ed.), *Always Reforming: Explorations in Systematic Theology* (Leicester: Apollos, 2006), pp. 240–270.
Boersma, H., *Violence, Hospitality, and the Cross: Reappropriating the Atonement Tradition* (Grand Rapids, MI: Baker, 2004).
Boston, T., *The Complete Works of the Late Rev Thomas Boston*, ed. S. McMillan (London: William Tegg & Co., 1853).
Bromiley, G. W., *Historical Theology: An Introduction* (Grand Rapids, MI: Eerdmans, 1978).
——, *Introduction to the Theology of Karl Barth* (Edinburgh: T & T Clark, 1979).
Bruggink, D. J., 'The Theology of Thomas Boston 1676–1732', PhD thesis, University of Edinburgh, 1956.
Buchanan, J., *The Doctrine of Justification* (Edinburgh: Banner of Truth, 1984).
Calvin, J., *The First Epistle of Paul the Apostle to the Corinthians*, in *Calvin's Commentaries*, tr. J. W. Fraser, ed. D. W. Torrance and T. F. Torrance (Carlisle: Paternoster, 1996).
——, *The Institutes of the Christian Religion*, tr. F. L. Battles, ed. J. T. McNeill, Library of Christian Classics, vols. 20 and 21 (Philadelphia, PA: Westminster Press, 1977).
Campbell, J. M., *The Nature of the Atonement* (Carberry: Handsel Press, 1996).
Carson, D. A., (ed.), *Right with God: Justification in the Bible and the World* (Carlisle: Paternoster, 1992).
——, O'Brien, P. T., and Seifrid, M., (eds.), *Justification and Variegated Nomism*, vols. 1 and 2 (Tübingen: Mohr Siebeck, 2001 and 2004).
Clifford, A. C., *Calvinus* (Norwich: Charenton Reformed Publishing, 1996).
Conzelmann, H., *A Commentary on the First Epistle to the Corinthians*, tr. J. W. Leitch (Philadelphia, PA: Fortress Press, 1975).
Cranfield, C. E. B., *A Critical and Exegetical Commentary on the Epistle to the Romans*, International Critical Commentary (Edinburgh: T & T Clark, 1975).
Crisp, O. D., *Jonathan Edwards and the Metaphysics of Sin* (Aldershot: Ashgate, 2005).
Cunningham, W., *The Reformers and the Theology of the Reformation* (Edinburgh: Banner of Truth, 1967).
Duncan, J. L., 'The Covenant Idea in Ante-Nicene Theology', PhD thesis, University of Edinburgh, 1995.

Dunn, J. D. G., *Christology in the Making: A New Testament Inquiry into the Origins of the Doctrine of the Incarnation* (2nd ed., Grand Rapids, MI: Eerdmans, 1989).
——, *Jesus, Paul and the Law* (London: SPCK, 1990).
——, 'The New Perspective on Paul', *The Bulletin of the John Rylands Library* 65 (1983), pp. 95–122.
——, *Romans 1–8*, Word Biblical Commentary, vol. 38a (Dallas: Word, 1988).
——, *The Theology of Paul the Apostle* (Edinburgh: T & T Clark, 1998).
Enns, P., *The Evolution of Adam: What the Bible Does and Doesn't Say about Human Origins* (Grand Rapids, MI: Brazos Press, 2012).
Fee, G. D., *The First Epistle to the Corinthians*, New International Commentary on the New Testament (Grand Rapids, MI: Eerdmans, 1987).
Ferguson, S. B., *The Holy Spirit*, Contours of Christian Theology Series (Leicester: IVP, 1996).
——, *John Owen on the Christian Life* (Edinburgh: Banner of Truth, 1987).
——, 'The Marrow Controversy', three audio lectures (2–9 February 2004), SermonAudio. Com, http://www.sermonaudio.com/main.asp
——, 'Ordo Salutis', in S. B. Ferguson and D. F. Wright (eds.), *New Dictionary of Theology* (Leicester: IVP, 1988).
——, *The Whole Christ: Legalism, Antinomianism, and Gospel Assurance – Why the Marrow Controversy Still Matters* (Wheaton, IL: Crossway, 2016).
Fisher, G. P., 'The Augustinian and the Federal Theories of Original Sin Compared', *The New Englander*, July 1868, pp. 468–516.
Fitzmyer, J. A., *Romans*, The Anchor Bible (London: Chapman, 1992).
Frame, J., *Escondido Theology: A Reformed Response to Two Kingdom Theology* (Lakeland, FL: Whitefield Media, 2011).
Gaffin Jr, R. B., *The Centrality of the Resurrection: A Study in Paul's Soteriology* (Grand Rapids, MI: Baker, 1978).
Gathercole, S., 'The Doctrine of Justification in Paul and Beyond: Some Proposals', in B. L. McCormack (ed.), *Justification in Perspective: Historical Developments and Contemporary Challenges* (Grand Rapids, MI: Baker, 2006), pp. 219–241.
——, 'Paul and the Faithfulness of God: A Review', Reformation21 (July 2014), http://www.reformation21.org, accessed September 2015.
Green, B. G., *Covenant and Commandment: Works, Obedience and Faithfulness in the Christian Life* (Nottingham: Apollos, 2014).
Griffith, H., and Muether, J. R., (eds.), *Creator, Redeemer, Consummator: A Festschrift for Meredith G. Kline* (Eugene, OR: Wipf & Stock, 2000), pp. 235–252.
Hall, B., 'Calvin against the Calvinists', in G. E. Duffield (ed.), *John Calvin* (Grand Rapids, MI: Eerdmans, 1966).
Hart, T. A., 'Humankind in Christ and Christ in Humankind: Salvation as Participation in Our Substitute in the Theology of John Calvin', *SJT* 42, no. 1 (1989), pp. 67–74.

——, 'Irenaeus, Recapitulation and Physical Redemption', in T. A. Hart and D. P. Thimell (eds.), *Christ in Our Place: The Humanity of God in Christ for the Reconciliation of the World*, (Exeter: Paternoster, 1989), pp. 152–181.

——, and Thimell, D. P., (eds.), *Christ in Our Place: The Humanity of God in Christ for the Reconciliation of the World* (Exeter: Paternoster, 1989).

Helm, P., *Calvin and the Calvinists* (Edinburgh: Banner of Truth, 1982).

——, 'Calvin and the Covenant: Unity and Discontinuity', *EQ* 55 (1983), pp. 65–81.

Hendriksen, W., *Romans* (Edinburgh: Banner of Truth, 1980).

Heppe, H., *Reformed Dogmatics* (London: Harper Collins, 1950).

Hewitson, I. A., *Trust and Obey: Norman Shepherd and the Justification Controversy at Westminster Theological Seminary* (distributed by Minneapolis, MN: NextStep Resources, 2011).

Horton, M. S., *Covenant and Eschatology: The Divine Drama* (Louisville, KY: Westminster John Knox Press, 2002).

——, *Covenant and Salvation: Union with Christ* (Louisville, KY: Westminster John Knox Press, 2007).

——, *Introducing Covenant Theology* (Grand Rapids, MI: Baker, 2006).

——, *Lord and Servant: A Covenant Christology* (Louisville, KY: Westminster John Knox Press, 2005).

Irenaeus, 'Against Heresies', in *Ante-Nicene Fathers*, vol. 1: *The Apostolic Fathers, Justin Martyr, Irenaeus*, ed. A. Roberts and J. Donaldson (Peabody, MA: Hendrickson, 1994), pp. 309–567.

Jeon, J. K., *Covenant Theology: John Murray's and Meredith Kline's Response to the Historical Development of Federal Theology in Reformed Thought* (Lanham, MD: University Press of America, 1999).

Karlberg, M. W., *The Changing of the Guard: Westminster Theological Seminary in Philadelphia* (Unicoi, TN: The Trinity Foundation, 2001).

——, 'Reformed Theology as the Theology of the Covenants: The Contributions of Meredith G. Kline to Reformed Systematics', in H. Griffith and J. R. Muether (eds.), *Creator, Redeemer, Consummator: A Festschrift for Meredith G. Kline* (Eugene, OR: Wipf & Stock, 2000), pp. 235–252.

Kendall, R. T., *Calvin and English Calvinism to 1649* (Oxford: OUP, 1979).

Kistemaker, S. J., *Exposition of the First Epistle to the Corinthians*, New Testament Commentary (Grand Rapids, MI: Baker, 1993).

Kline, M. G., *By Oath Consigned: A Reinterpretation of the Covenant Signs of Circumcision and Baptism* (Grand Rapids, MI: Eerdmans, 1968).

——, 'Dynastic Covenant', *WTJ* 23 (1960), pp. 1–15.

——, *Kingdom Prologue: Genesis Foundations for a Covenantal Worldview* (Eugene, OR: Wipf & Stock, 2006).

——, 'Space and Time in the Genesis Cosmogony', *Perspectives on Science and the Christian Faith* 48, no. 1 (March 1996), pp. 2–15.

———, *The Structure of Biblical Authority* (Grand Rapids, MI: Eerdmans, 1972).
———, *The Treaty of the Great King* (Grand Rapids, MI: Eerdmans, 1963).
———, 'The Two Tables of the Covenant', *WTJ* 22 (1960), pp. 133–134.
Kruger, C. B., *Jesus Christ and the Undoing of Adam* (Jackson, MS: Perichoresis Press, 2001; available at http://www.perichoresis.org/downloads/jesusandundoingofadam.pdf).
Lachman, D., *The Marrow Controversy* (Edinburgh: Rutherford House, 1988).
Lane, A. N. S., 'The Quest for the Historical Calvin', *EQ* 55 (1983), pp. 95–113.
Lausanne Movement, 'The Cape Town Commitment' (2011), https://www.lausanne.org/, accessed October 2015.
Leithart, P. J., *The Baptized Body* (Moscow, ID: Canon Press, 2007).
———, *The Priesthood of the Plebs: A Theology of Baptism* (Eugene, OR: Wipf & Stock, 2003).
Lillback, P. A., *The Binding of God: Calvin's Role in the Development of Covenant Theology* (Grand Rapids, MI: Baker, 2001).
Lusk, R., 'Paedobaptism and Baptismal Efficacy: Historic Trends and Current Controversies', in S. Wilkins and D. Garner (eds.), *The Federal Vision* (Monroe, LA: Athanasius Press, 2004), pp. 76–83.
Luther, M., *Three Treatises* (Philadelphia: Fortress Press, 1966).
McComiskey, T. E., *The Covenants of Promise: A Theology of the Old Testament Covenants* (Nottingham: IVP, 1985).
McCoy, C. S., and Baker, J. W., *Fountainhead of Federalism: Heinrich Bullinger and the Covenantal Tradition* (Louisville, KY: Westminster John Knox Press, 1991).
McGowan, A. T. B., 'Crafting an Evangelical, Reformed and Missional Theology for the Twenty-First Century', in S. T. Logan (ed.), *Reformed Means Missional: Following Jesus into the World* (Greensboro, NC: New Growth Press, 2013), pp. 237–252.
———, *The Federal Theology of Thomas Boston* (Carlisle: Paternoster, 1997).
———, 'In Defence of Headship Theology', in J. A. Grant and A. I. Wilson (eds.), *The God of the Covenant: Biblical, Theological and Contemporary Perspectives* (Leicester: Apollos, 2005), pp. 178–199.
———, 'Justification and the *Ordo Salutis*', in B. L. McCormack (ed.), *Justification in Perspective: Historical Developments and Contemporary Challenges* (Grand Rapids, MI: Baker, 2006), pp. 147–163.
———, 'Karl Barth and Covenant Theology', in D. Gibson and D. Strange (eds.), *Engaging with Barth: Contemporary Evangelical Critiques* (Nottingham: Apollos, 2008), pp. 113–135.
———, *The Person and Work of Christ: Understanding Jesus* (Milton Keynes: Paternoster, 2012).
———, 'Scottish Covenant Theology', in J. A. Pipa and C. N. Willborn (eds.), *The Covenant: God's Voluntary Condescension* (Taylors, SC: Presbyterian Press, 2005), pp. 61–72.
———, 'Should We Leave Liberal Denominations?', *Reformation and Revival Journal* 13, no. 1 (Winter 2004), pp. 59–74.
———, 'Thomas Boston', in T. A. Hart (ed.), *The Dictionary of Historical Theology* (Carlisle: Paternoster, 2000).

——, 'The Unity of the Covenant', in J. A. Pipa and C. N. Willborn (eds.), *The Covenant: God's Voluntary Condescension* (Taylors, SC: Presbyterian Press, 2005), pp. 1–13.

——, (ed.), *Always Reforming: Explorations in Systematic Theology* (Leicester: Apollos, 2006).

McIlhenny, R. C., (ed.), *Kingdoms Apart: Engaging the Two Kingdoms Perspective* (Phillipsburg, NJ: P&R, 2012).

McWilliams, D. B., 'The Covenant Theology of the *Westminster Confession of Faith* and Recent Criticism', *WTJ* 53 (1991), pp. 109–124.

Mendenhall, G. E., 'Covenant Forms in Israelite Tradition', *The Biblical Archaeologist* 17 (1954), pp. 3, 50–76.

Moo, D., *The Epistle to the Romans*, New International Commentary on the New Testament (Grand Rapids, MI: Eerdmans, 1996).

Muller, R. A., 'Calvin and the "Calvinists": Assessing Continuities and Discontinuities between the Reformation and Orthodoxy', *Calvin Theological Journal* 30 (1995), pp. 345–375; 31 (1996), pp. 125–160.

——, *Christ and the Decree: Christology and Predestination in Reformed Theology from Calvin to Perkins* (Durham, NC: Labyrinth Press, 1986).

Murray, J., *Christian Baptism* (Nutley, NJ: Presbyterian & Reformed, 1977).

——, *Collected Writings of John Murray*, ed. I. Murray (Edinburgh: Banner of Truth, 1977).

——, *The Covenant of Grace* (London: Tyndale Press, 1954).

——, *The Epistle to the Romans: The English Text with Introduction, Exposition and Notes* (London: Marshall, Morgan & Scott, 1960).

——, *Principles of Conduct* (London: Tyndale Press, 1957).

Owen, J., *An Exposition of the Epistle to the Hebrews*, vol. 7, in *Works*, vol. 22 (Edinburgh: Banner of Truth, 1998).

——, *The Works of John Owen*, ed. W. H. Goold, vol. 3 (London: Banner of Truth, 1966).

——, *The Works of John Owen*, ed. W. H. Goold, vol. 11 (London: Banner of Truth, 1966).

Perkins, W., *A Golden Chaine*, in I. Breward (ed.), *Works of William Perkins*, vol. 3 (London: Sutton Courteney Press, 1970).

Piper, J., *The Future of Justification: A Response to N. T. Wright* (Wheaton, IL: Crossway, 2007).

Poole, D. N. J., *Stages of Religious Faith in the Classical Reformation Tradition: The Covenant Approach to the Ordo Salutis* (Lampeter: Edwin Mellen Press, 1995).

Rankin, W. D., 'Carnal Union with Christ in the Theology of T. F. Torrance', PhD thesis, University of Edinburgh, 1997.

Reymond, R. L., *A New Systematic Theology of the Christian Faith* (2nd ed., Nashville, TN: Thomas Nelson, 1998).

Ridderbos, H., *Paul: An Outline of His Theology* (London: SPCK, 1977).

Riddlebarger, K., 'Reformed Confessionalism and the "New Perspective" on Paul' (1996): available as download at 'The Development of the New Perspective on Paul – Stendahl, Sanders, and Dunn', The Riddleblog (4 Jan. 2007), http://kimriddlebarger.squarespace.com

Robertson, A., and Plummer, A., *A Critical and Exegetical Commentary on the First Epistle of St Paul to the Corinthians*, International Critical Commentary (2nd ed., Edinburgh: T & T Clark, 1963 [1911]).

Robertson, O. P., *The Christ of the Covenants* (Phillipsburg, NJ: Presbyterian & Reformed, 1980).

Rollock, R., *Tractatus De Vocatione Efficaci* (1597). For English translation see W. M. Gunn (ed.), *Select Works of Robert Rollock* (Edinburgh: Wodrow Society, 1849), pp. 1–288.

Rolston III, H., *John Calvin versus the Westminster Confession* (Richmond, VA: John Knox Press, 1972).

——, 'Responsible Man in Reformed Theology: Calvin versus the Westminster Confession', *SJT* 23 (1970), pp. 129–156.

Rosner, B. S., *Paul and the Law: Keeping the Commandments of God* (Nottingham: Apollos, 2013).

Sanders, E. P., *Paul and Palestinian Judaism* (London: SCM Press, 1977).

——, *Paul, the Law and the Jewish People* (London: SCM Press, 1983).

Scott, J. L., 'The Covenant in the Theology of Karl Barth', *SJT* 17, no. 2 (1964), pp. 182–198.

Shepherd, N., *The Call of Grace: How the Covenant Illuminates Salvation and Evangelism* (Phillipsburg, NJ: P&R, 2000).

Stendahl, K., 'The Apostle Paul and the Introspective Conscience of the West', in *Paul among Jews and Gentiles* (Philadelphia, PA: Fortress Press, 1976), pp. 78–86.

Stott, J. R. W., *The Contemporary Christian* (Leicester: IVP, 1992).

——, *Issues Facing Christians Today* (Basingstoke: Marshall, Morgan & Scott, 1984).

——, 'Lausanne Occasional Paper 3 – The Lausanne Covenant: An Exposition and Commentary', Lausanne Committee for World Evangelization, Lausanne Movement (1975), https://www.lausanne.org/, accessed October 2015.

Tertullian, 'On the Resurrection of the Flesh', in *Ante-Nicene Fathers*, vol. 3: *Latin Christianity: Its Founder, Tertullian*, ed. A. Roberts and J. Donaldson (Peabody, MA: Hendrickson, 1994).

Thiselton, A. C., *The First Epistle to the Corinthians: A Commentary on the Greek Text*, New International Greek Text Commentary (Grand Rapids, MI: Eerdmans, 2000).

Torrance, J. B., 'The Contribution of McLeod Campbell to Scottish Theology', *SJT* 26 (1973), pp. 295–311.

——, 'The Covenant Concept in Scottish Theology and Politics and Its Legacy', *SJT* 34 (1981), pp. 225–243.

——, 'Covenant or Contract?', *SJT* 23 (1970), pp. 51–76.

——, *A Critique of Federal Theology in the Light of the Gospel: Was John Calvin a 'Federal' Theologian?* (Victoria: Burning Bush Society of Victoria, 1997).

——, 'The Incarnation and Limited Atonement', *EQ* 55 (1983), pp. 83–94.

——, 'Strengths and Weaknesses of the Westminster Theology', in A. I. Heron (ed.), *The Westminster Confession in the Church Today* (Edinburgh: St Andrew Press, 1982), pp. 40–54.

Torrance, T. F., *God and Rationality* (Oxford: OUP, 1971).

——, *Scottish Theology: From John Knox to John McLeod Campbell* (Edinburgh: T & T Clark, 1996).

Trueman, C. R., and Clark, R. S., (eds.), *Protestant Scholasticism: Essays in Reassessment* (Carlisle: Paternoster, 1999).

Van Til, C., *The Defense of the Faith* (Philadelphia, PA: Presbyterian & Reformed, 1976).

VanDoodewaard, W., *The Marrow Controversy and Seceder Tradition: Atonement, Saving Faith, and the Gospel Offer in Scotland (1718–1799)* (Grand Rapids, MI: Reformation Heritage Books, 2011).

——, *The Quest for the Historical Adam: Genesis, Hermeneutics and Human Origins* (Grand Rapids, MI: Reformation Heritage Books, 2015).

VanDrunen, D., *Divine Covenants and Moral Order: A Biblical Theology of Natural Law*, Emory University Studies in Law and Religion (Grand Rapids, MI: Eerdmans, 2014).

——, *Living in God's Two Kingdoms: A Biblical Vision for Christianity and Culture* (Wheaton, IL: Crossway, 2010).

——, *Natural Law and the Two Kingdoms: A Study in the Development of Reformed Social Thought*, Emory University Studies in Law and Religion (Grand Rapids, MI: Eerdmans, 2010).

Vos, G., *The Pauline Eschatology* (Grand Rapids, MI: Eerdmans, 1972).

Wallace, R. S., *Calvin's Doctrine of the Christian Life* (Edinburgh: Oliver & Boyd, 1959).

Waters, G. P., *The Federal Vision and Covenant Theology: A Comparative Analysis* (Phillipsburg, NJ: P&R, 2006).

Waterworth, J., (ed.), *Canons and Decrees of the Council of Trent* (London: C. Dolman, 1848).

Webster, J., *Barth* (London: Continuum, 2000).

Weir, D. A., *The Origins of the Federal Theology in Sixteenth-Century Reformation Thought* (Oxford: Clarendon, 1990).

Westminster Confession of Faith (Edinburgh: Free Presbyterian Church of Scotland, 1981).

Wilkins, S., and Garner, D., (eds.), *The Federal Vision* (Monroe, LA: Athanasius Press, 2004).

Wilson, D., *Against the Church* (Moscow, ID: Canon Press, 2013).

——, *Reformed Is Not Enough: Recovering the Objectivity of the Covenant* (Moscow, ID: Canon Press, 2002).

Wiseman, D. J., *The Vassal-Treaties of Esarhaddon* (London: British School of Archaeology in Iraq, 1958).

Witsius, H., *The Economy of the Covenants between God and Man: Comprehending a Complete Body of Divinity*, vol. 2 (London: T. Tegg & Son, 1837).
Woolsey, A. A., *Unity and Continuity in Covenantal Thought* (Grand Rapids, MI: Reformation Heritage Books, 2012).
Wright, C. J. H., *Old Testament Ethics for the People of God* (Nottingham: IVP, 2004).
Wright, N. T., *The Climax of the Covenant* (Edinburgh: T & T Clark, 1991).
——, *Jesus and the Victory of God* (London: SPCK, 1996).
——, *Justification: God's Plan and Paul's Vision* (London: SPCK, 2009).
——, *The New Testament and the People of God* (London: SPCK, 1992).
——, *Paul and the Faithfulness of God* (London: SPCK, 2013).
——, 'The Paul of History and the Apostle of Faith', *Tyndale Bulletin* 29 (1978), pp. 61–68.
——, *The Resurrection of the Son of God* (London: SPCK, 2003).

INDEX OF AUTHORS

Ames, William 16
Augustine 124, 125

Bahnsen, Greg 92
Baker, J. W. 12
Barach, John 81, 89, 90, 93, 94
Barrett, C. K. 115, 116, 118
Barth, Karl 1, 3, 7, 22–45, 83, 183, 195 196, 197, 201
Bavinck, Herman 87, 178, 188, 189
Beisner, Calvin 80, 83, 90
Bell, M. C. 12, 42
Berkhof, Louis 184, 185, 186, 195
Berkouwer, G. C. 185, 186, 188, 189, 192
Beza, Theodore 4, 20, 187
Bird, Michael F. 173
Blocher, Henri 63, 117, 178
Boersma, Hans 123, 124
Boston, Thomas 2, 16, 17, 18, 19, 20, 21, 36, 41, 48, 49, 57, 58, 59, 86, 103, 144, 194, 195, 201
Bromiley, Geoffrey 24, 186
Bruggink, D. J. 42

Bucer, Martin 4
Buchanan, James 169, 191
Buddeus, Frank 185
Bullinger, Heinrich 4, 31
Bunyan, John 17

Calvin, John 1, 4, 12, 13, 20, 30, 33, 39, 42, 55, 71, 77, 83, 85, 88, 89, 90, 103, 104, 105, 119, 131, 132, 174, 186, 187, 191, 202
Carson, Donald A. 173, 174
Clark, R. Scott 13
Clifford, Alan 190
Clowney, E. 174
Cocceius, Johannes 14, 31, 37
Conzelmann, Hans 115
Cranfield, C. E. B. 120
Crisp, Oliver 127
Cunningham, William 191

Dickson, David 42
Duffield, G. E. 12
Duncan, J. Ligon 9

Dunn, J. D. G. 43, 44, 45, 112, 113, 118, 171
Durham, James 42

Ellul, Jacques 25
Enns, Peter 116, 117
Erskine, Ebenezer 21
Erskine, Ralph 21

Fee, Gordon D. 112, 120
Fenner, Dudley 13, 14
Ferguson, Sinclair B. 20, 185, 194, 199, 200
Fisher, Edward 20
Fisher, G. P. 125
Fitzmyer, J. A. 120
Frame, John 76

Gaffin, Richard 83, 106, 197, 198, 199, 200
Garner, D. 93
Gathercole, Simon 173, 191
Green, Bradley G. 182
Griffith, H. 76
Gunton, Colin 72

Hadow, James 20, 41, 144, 193
Hall, Basil 12
Hart, Trevor 16, 43, 44, 45, 197, 199
Helm, Paul 13
Hendriksen, William 127
Heppe, Heinrich 193, 194
Hewitson, I. A. 81
Hodge, Caspar Wistar 47
Hodge, Charles 127
Horton, Michael S. 2, 62, 72, 73, 74, 75, 76, 87
Hutchinson, Chris 81

Irenaeus 39, 43, 122, 123, 124

Jenkins, Steffen 95
Jeon, J. Koo 36
Jeremias, Joachim 115

Karlberg, Mark 76, 82, 199
Karpov, Jakobus 185
Kelsey, David 72
Kendall, R. T. 12
Kistemaker, Simon 113, 114, 115, 116, 127
Kline, Meredith G. 2, 3, 7, 21, 36, 46, 58, 62–78, 79, 86, 87, 117, 144, 183, 199, 201
Kline, Meredith M. 63
Knight, George W. 81
Knox, John 1, 42, 196
Kruger, Baxter 43, 44, 45,
Kuyper, Abraham 89, 178, 188, 189

Lachman, David 19
Lane, A. N. S. 13
Leithart, Peter 79, 81, 84, 95, 96, 97, 98, 99, 100, 106
Lillback, Peter A. 13
Lusk, Rich 81, 83, 87, 95, 101, 102, 103, 105
Luther, Martin 33, 83, 168, 169, 170, 171, 185, 186

McComiskey, Thomas E. 60
McCoy, S. S. 12
McGowan, A. T. B. 4, 16, 20, 21, 35, 36, 126, 183
Machen, J. Gresham 47
McIlhenny, R. C. 76
McLeod Campbell, John 41, 42
McWilliams, David B. 77
Mendenhall, G. E. 63, 65
Moo, Douglas 113, 116, 119, 121, 122

Index of authors

Muether, John R. 76
Muller, Richard A. 13, 187
Murray, John 1, 2, 3, 5, 7, 9, 16, 21, 36, 37, 38, 40, 46–61, 62, 63, 65, 66, 71, 73, 75, 76, 78, 79, 81, 86, 88, 105, 106, 109, 119, 120, 121, 126, 127, 138, 144, 175, 176, 183, 197, 199, 201, 203

O'Brien, P. T. 173
Olevianus, Caspar 4, 13
Owen, John 70, 188, 190, 194

Perkins, William 14, 16, 42, 187
Phillips, Richard D. 81, 85, 87, 88, 89
Pipa, Joseph 81, 83, 84, 86
Piper, John 87, 171, 172, 173
Plummer, Alfred 116
Poole, D. N. J. 12, 14

Rankin, Duncan 43, 196
Rauschenbusch, Walter 180
Reymond, Robert 193
Ridderbos, Herman 115
Riddlebarger, Kim 170
Robbins, Carl D. 81
Robertson, Archibald 116
Robertson, O. Palmer 2, 60
Rollock, Robert 15
Rolston, Holmes 12
Rosner, Brian 166
Rutherford, Samuel 20, 42

Sanders, E. P. 170, 171
Schlissel, Steve 81, 84
Scott, J. L. 37, 38
Shepherd, Norman 70, 80, 81, 82, 86, 102, 199
Sibbes, Richard 20
Smith, Morton 81, 86

Stendahl, Krister 170
Stott, John 180

Tertullian 122
Thimell, D. P. 43
Thiselton, Anthony 112, 113, 115
Thornwell, James Henley 90
Torrance J. B. 1, 3, 7, 22, 25, 35, 40, 41, 43, 51, 187, 196
Torrance, T. F. 1, 3, 7, 22, 40, 42, 196
Trouwborst, Tom 81, 90
Trueman, Carl R. 13

Ursinus, Zacharias 4, 13, 31

Van Til, Cornelius 71, 176, 177, 178
VanDoodewaard, William 19, 116, 117, 118
VanDrunen, D. 76
Vermigli, Peter Martyr 4
Vos, Geerhardus 63, 71, 114, 115, 197

Wallace, Ronald 186
Waters, Guy 88, 100, 101, 102, 103, 104, 181, 182
Webster, John 23, 72
Weir, D. A. 12, 13
White, R. Fowler 81, 85
Wilkins, Steve 85, 86, 93
Wilson, Douglas 79, 81, 83, 84, 85, 90, 91, 92, 94, 95, 96, 97, 100, 102
Wiseman, D. J. 64
Witsius, Herman 59, 194
Woolsey, A. A. 13
Wright, C. J. H. 141
Wright, N. T. 80, 83, 101, 121, 123, 171, 172, 173, 174

Zwingli, Ulrich 4, 31

INDEX OF SCRIPTURE REFERENCES

Genesis *116, 117, 118, 119*
1 *63, 68*
1 – 2 *117*
1:26–28 *130*
2 *17, 39, 48, 57, 58, 59, 125, 127, 129, 165, 201, 203*
2 – 3 *116*
2:7 *118*
2:15–17 *68*
2:16–17 *10, 17*
3 *114, 175*
3:5 *178*
3:15 *10, 36, 56, 68, 71, 123*
3:22 *114, 178, 179*
6:17–18 *130*
9:1–7 *130*
9:1–17 *130*
9:6–9 *130*
9:8–17 *131*
9:9–11 *131*
9:16 *131*
12 *10, 25, 134*
12:1–3 *134*
12:3 *135*
15 *10, 133, 134, 135, 138, 140*
15:1–6 *135*
15:6 *136, 137, 143*
15:7–8 *136*
15:9–21 *136*
15:13–16 *136*
17 *10, 89, 133, 137, 138*

Exodus
2:23–25 *139*
2:24 *52*
6:1–5 *140*
12:1–13 *158*
19:3–6 *140*
19:5–6 *52*
20:18–20 *143*
24:4 *140*
24:7–8 *52, 141*

Leviticus *141*
16 *157*

Numbers *141*

Deuteronomy *64*
28 *143*
28:1–2 *143*
28:15 *143*

1 Samuel
8:1–9 *147*
8:7 *147*
16 *148*
17 *148*

2 Samuel
7:12–16 *148*
7:12–17 *53*
23:5 *53, 149*

Psalms
2 *150*
2:6 *150*
24:7–10 *150*
89 *53*
89:1–4 *148*

Psalms (*cont.*)
89:20–29   *149*
132:11–12   *53*

Isaiah
51:4   *135*
53:5–7   *157*
53:7   *159*
54:9–10   *53*
55:1–4   *150*

Jeremiah   *153*
25:11   *152*
29:10–14   *152*
31   *27*
31, 32   *27*
31:31–34   *152*

Ezekiel
36:24–28   *153*

Hosea
6:7   *18, 59, 87*

Malachi
3:1   *53*

Matthew
5:43–46   *132*
10:18–22   *137*
16:27   *102, 182*
25:31–46   *102, 182*
26:26–28   *141*
26:28   *54, 156, 157*

Mark
14:24   *54*

Luke
1:30–33   *151*

1:72–73   *53*
22:20   *54, 156*

John
1:29   *159*
1:49   *151*
14:23–24   *93*
15   *94*
15:4   *195*
17:20–23   *93*

Acts
2:38   *91*
13:39   *195*
20:28   *160*
22:16   *91*

Romans   *113, 119, 127*
1   *179*
2:6   *102, 182*
2:15   *175*
2:25–29   *137*
3:21–26   *113*
4   *144, 174*
4:9–12   *138*
5   *1, 34, 58, 109, 111, 116, 126, 127, 128, 129, 165, 201*
5:12   *120, 121*
5:12–14   *100*
5:12–19   *57*
5:12–21   *11, 39, 86, 112, 113, 115, 116, 119, 126, 127*
5:18   *120, 121*
5:18–19   *120, 121*
5:19   *120*
6:1–3   *102*
7   *166*
7:7   *166*
7:12   *166*
7:13   *166*

7:14   *166*
8:3   *113*
8:5–8   *177*
8:28–30   *184*
9:4   *54, 166*
9:6–13   *85*
12:2   *178*

1 Corinthians   *115, 119*
2:14   *178*
3:12–15   *102, 182*
3:23   *195*
5:7   *159*
11:25   *54*
15   *1, 58, 109, 111, 119, 122, 124, 126, 127, 128, 129, 165, 201*
15:12–34   *39*
15:20–28   *112*
15:21–22   *11, 112, 113, 118*
15:22   *57, 113, 115, 119, 124*
15:44–49   *57*
15:45   *118*
15:45–46   *57*
15:45–49   *11, 112, 113, 118*

2 Corinthians
3:6   *54*
4:4   *177*
5:10   *102, 182*
5:17   *195*
5:21   *83, 158*
11:3   *119*

Galatians   *144*
2   *167*
2:11–13   *167*
2:15–16   *168*
2:16   *166, 171*
2:21   *166*

3 *60, 74, 75, 144, 145, 174*
3:1–5 *145*
3:10–13 *166*
3:13 *158*
3:15 *54*
3:15ff. *70*
3:15–18 *74*
3:17 *54*
3:17–18 *145*
3:23–25 *166*
3:26–29 *167*
3:27 *102, 172*
4 *60, 75*
4:4–5 *113, 166*
4:24 *59*
5:4 *166*
5:6 *82, 203*
8 *146*

Ephesians
2:12 *54, 133*

Philippians
2:6–8 *113*

3:4–6 *170*

Colossians
3:11 *168*

1 Timothy
1:8–9 *166*
2:14 *119*

Titus
3:5 *91*

Hebrews *141*
1:1–2 *37, 57*
2:5–9 *113*
2:10–18 *44*
8 *54*
8:6–13 *54, 153, 166*
8:10 *54*
8:11 *55*
8:12 *55*
9:15 *154*
9:22 *157*
9:28 *158*

10:19–22 *91*
10:29 *94*
11:6 *180*

James
2:17 *180*
2:24 *82, 102, 182, 203*
2:26 *180*

1 Peter
2:24 *158*
3:15 *173*
3:15–16 *5*
3:18–22 *96*
3:21 *91*

2 Peter
1:2–4 *93*
2:20 *99*

Revelation
5:6–9 *159*
20:12 *102, 182*
22:12 *102, 182*

www.ingramcontent.com/pod-product-compliance
Ingram Content Group UK Ltd.
Pitfield, Milton Keynes, MK11 3LW, UK
UKHW022241230426
12048UKWH00018BA/1401